CHILD PORNOGRAPHY AND SEXUAL GROOMING

Child pornography and sexual grooming provide case study exemplars of problems that society and law have sought to tackle to avoid both actual and potential harm to children. Yet despite the considerable legal, political and societal concern that these critical phenomena attract, they have not, thus far, been subjected to detailed socio-legal and theoretical scrutiny. How do society and law construct the harms of child pornography and grooming? What impact do constructions of the child have upon legal and societal responses to these phenomena? What has been the impetus behind the expanding criminalization of behaviour in these areas? Suzanne Ost addresses these and other important questions, exploring the critical tensions within legal and social discourses which must be tackled to discourage moral panic reactions towards child pornography and grooming, and advocating a new, more rational approach toward combating these forms of exploitation.

SUZANNE OST is a Senior Lecturer in Law at Lancaster University. She is also assistant editor for the *Medical Law Review* journal and a member of both the Society of Legal Scholars and the Socio-Legal Studies Association.

CAMBRIDGE STUDIES IN LAW AND SOCIETY

Cambridge Studies in Law and Society aims to publish the best scholarly work on legal discourse and practice in its social and institutional contexts, combining theoretical insights and empirical research.

The fields that it covers are: studies of law in action; the sociology of law; the anthropology of law; cultural studies of law, including the role of legal discourses in social formations; law and economics; law and politics; and studies of governance. The books consider all forms of legal discourse across societies, rather than being limited to lawyers' discourses alone.

The series editors come from a range of disciplines: academic law; socio-legal studies; sociology; and anthropology. All have been actively involved in teaching and writing about law in context.

Series Editors

Chris Arup *Monash University, Victoria*
Martin Chanock *La Trobe University, Melbourne*
Sally Engle Merry *New York University*
Pat O'Malley *University of Sydney*
Susan Silbey *Massachusetts Institute of Technology*

Books in the Series

The Politics of Truth and Reconciliation in South Africa
Legitimizing the Post-Apartheid State
Richard A. Wilson

Modernism and the Grounds of Law
Peter Fitzpatrick

Unemployment and Government
Genealogies of the Social
William Walters

Autonomy and Ethnicity
Negotiating Competing Claims in Multi-Ethnic States
Yash Ghai

Constituting Democracy
Law, Globalism and South Africa's Political Reconstruction
Heinz Klug

The Ritual of Rights in Japan
Law, Society, and Health Policy
Eric A. Feldman

The Invention of the Passport
Surveillance, Citizenship and the State
John Torpey

Governing Morals
A Social History of Moral Regulation
Alan Hunt

The Colonies of Law
Colonialism, Zionism and Law in Early Mandate Palestine
Ronen Shamir

Law and Nature
David Delaney

Social Citizenship and Workfare in the United States and Western Europe
The Paradox of Inclusion
Joel F. Handler

Law, Anthropology and the Constitution of the Social
Making Persons and Things
Edited by Alain Pottage and Martha Mundy

Judicial Review and Bureaucratic Impact
International and Interdisciplinary Perspectives
Edited by Marc Hertogh and Simon Halliday

Immigrants at the Margins
Law, Race, and Exclusion in Southern Europe
Kitty Calavita

Lawyers and Regulation
The Politics of the Administrative Process
Patrick Schmidt

Law and Globalization from Below
Toward a Cosmopolitan Legality
Edited by Boaventura de Sousa Santos and Cesar A. Rodriguez-Garavito

Public Accountability
Designs, Dilemmas and Experiences
Edited by Michael W. Dowdle

Law, Violence and Sovereignty Among West Bank Palestinians
Tobias Kelly

Legal Reform and Administrative Detention Powers in China
Sarah Biddulph

The Practice of Human Rights
Tracking Law Between the Global and the Local
Edited by Mark Goodale and Sally Engle Merry

Judges Beyond Politics in Democracy and Dictatorship
Lessons from Chile
Lisa Hilbink

Paths to International Justice
Social and Legal Perspectives
Edited by Marie-Bénédicte Dembour and Tobias Kelly

Law and Society in Vietnam
The Transition from Socialism in Comparative Perspective
Mark Sidel

Constitutionalizing Economic Globalization
Investment Rules and Democracy's Promise
David Schneiderman

The New World Trade Organization Agreements: 2nd Edition
Globalizing Law Through Intellectual Property and Services (2nd Edition)
Christopher Arup

Justice and Reconciliation in Post-Apartheid South Africa
Edited by François du Bois, Antje du Bois-Pedain

Militarization and Violence against Women in Conflict Zones in the Middle East
A Palestinian Case-Study
Nadera Shalhoub-Kevorkian

Child Pornography and Sexual Grooming
Legal and Societal Responses
Suzanne Ost

CHILD PORNOGRAPHY AND SEXUAL GROOMING

Legal and Societal Responses

Suzanne Ost

CAMBRIDGE
UNIVERSITY PRESS

CAMBRIDGE UNIVERSITY PRESS
Cambridge, New York, Melbourne, Madrid, Cape Town, Singapore, São Paulo, Delhi

Cambridge University Press
The Edinburgh Building, Cambridge CB2 8RU, UK

Published in the United States of America by Cambridge University Press, New York

www.cambridge.org
Information on this title: www.cambridge.org/9780521885829

First published 2009

Printed in the United Kingdom at the University Press, Cambridge

A catalogue record for this publication is available from the British Library

Library of Congress Cataloguing in Publication data
Ost, Suzanne.
Child pornography and sexual grooming : legal and societal responses / Suzanne Ost.
p. cm. – (Cambridge studies in law and society)
Includes bibliographical references and index.
ISBN 978-0-521-88582-9 (hardback) 1. Child pornography. 2. Child sexual abuse. 3. Child pornography–Law and legislation. I. Title. II. Series.
HQ471.O88 2009
363.4′7083–dc22 2009006854

ISBN 978-0-521-88582-9 hardback

CONTENTS

ACKNOWLEDGEMENTS

I am grateful to Wiley-Blackwell Publishing for allowing me to include work that has been developed from my article 'Children at Risk: Legal and Societal Perceptions of the Potential Threat that the Possession of Child Pornography Poses to Society' (2002) 29 *Journal of Law and Society* 436–60. I am also grateful to Taylor and Francis (www.informaworld.com) for granting permission for the same regarding my article 'Getting to Grips with Sexual Grooming? The New Offence Under the Sexual Offences Act 2003' (2004) 26 *Journal of Social Welfare and Family Law* 147–59.

The Faculty of Arts and Social Sciences at Lancaster University kindly funded my visit to consult the National Viewers' and Listeners' Association Archives, kept at the University of Essex's Albert Sloman Library, in April 2008. The School of Law at Lancaster University provided me with much appreciated support and financial assistance as I reached the final stages of the book's completion.

My sincere thanks go to friends and colleagues at Lancaster University, several of whom I sounded out some of my ideas to, and who provided valuable feedback when I presented an earlier version of part of this work at a staff seminar. I would especially like to thank Hazel Biggs and Sara Fovargue for reading a full draft of this work and providing constructive feedback. Thanks are also due to former colleagues from elsewhere. Neil Duxbury and Charles Erin both provided invaluable counsel when I initially formulated and put into writing my ideas for this book. Susan Fletcher offered me helpful advice regarding defamation, image and reputation. Much appreciated feedback upon the empirical aspects of my research was given by Angela Melville. I am grateful to Margot Brazier for her support throughout this and all other research projects.

Thanks are due to the police officers at Lancashire Constabulary who kindly gave up their time to allow me to interview them for the purposes of this study. I have the utmost respect for the crucial work that they do to combat child pornography and sexual grooming. I am also very grateful to Finola O'Sullivan, Tom O'Reilly and Richard Woodham at Cambridge

University Press for their patience, guidance and support. Thanks to my proofreader, Bridget Gevaux, for her efficient and thorough work.

Finally, this book would have remained an abstract idea without the unwavering support and encouragement of my husband. At times, I wondered whether I would ever complete it. Whilst Nick may have had the same thought, he only ever expressed complete confidence that an end product would materialize. Either he has a great deal of faith in me, or he is a very convincing liar. My greatest debt of gratitude is to him and also to my daughter, Lily Jorja, who provided a diversion during the writing of this book at times when I needed it most, in her own very special and indomitable way. This book is dedicated to them both and to Matthew Luke, whose imminent arrival made its completion all the more imperative.

The law as discussed within this work is up-to-date as of September 2008.

TABLE OF CASES

Below, in the first shadows, drooped hosts of little white flowers,
so silent and sad; it seemed like a holy communion of pure wild things,
numberless, frail, and folded meekly in the evening light …
We have lost their meaning. They do not belong to us,
who ravish them.

From *The White Peacock*, D. H. Lawrence (1911)

INTRODUCTION: CONSTRUCTIONS, THEMES AND CRITICAL TENSIONS

In writing this book, I have chosen to focus upon two highly sensitive and disturbing phenomena that tend to generate a commonly shared repugnance, matters which our contemporary society has chosen to target as one part of its attempts to protect children from sexual abuse and related acts. Social, medical and legal narratives upon the subject of child sexual abuse abound. However, despite the considerable political, legal and societal concern and media coverage that child pornography and sexual grooming attract, these critical phenomena have not, thus far, been subjected to detailed socio-legal and theoretical scrutiny. Moreover, legal research and literature on child pornography and grooming are, at this point, still fairly sparse. The time is thus ripe for us to engage in a critical analysis and evaluation of the way in which society and law are responding to these subjects. A close analysis of child pornography and grooming is particularly important, since they offer case study exemplars of problems that law and society have sought to tackle to avoid not only actual, but also potential and more remote, harms to children.

However, one of the consequences of the increased legal and societal attention paid to child sexual abuse and related acts over the last few decades is that anyone wishing to carry out critical socio-legal research does so only after much serious thought and with caution. There is an inevitable concern about the reception of a work that critically analyses society's attempts to address and eradicate what is considered to be an abhorrent evil in our society. Child sexual abuse, after all, is a subject that is capable of evoking strong and raw emotion. An author may be treading on dangerous ground if he or she tries to predict the way in which readers will respond to his or her work or the impact that it will have, but I can at least explain my rationale for writing this book. I intend to encourage a reassessment of the way in which we, as a society, endeavour to protect children from the threat of physical and psychological harm that child pornography and grooming represent. As a consequence, a central theme explored within this work is that of children's vulnerability to harm and their exploitation.

My main objective is to expose and analyse what are, in my view, the critical tensions that exist within current legal and social discourses surrounding child pornography and grooming. These critical tensions form the principal themes of the book. Throughout, my analysis revolves around the framing and constructions of children, child pornography and grooming in legal, social, political and cultural narratives. There is a pivotal argument that runs through this book. It may not come as a surprise that I will reason that child pornography and grooming are both stark examples of adults exploiting children. However, I will argue that, in certain important respects, society is not dealing with this exploitation in an appropriate way. It is vital that we reframe the way in which this exploitation is ideologically presented if we truly wish to offer children the best protection that we can and, at the same time, respect and value them for who they really are. I develop my argument through socio-legal analysis, and there is also an empirical dimension to my research. The remainder of this chapter will introduce the main theories that inform the analysis within this book and highlight significant themes and tensions that the work addresses.

SOCIAL CONSTRUCTION THEORY AND A DISCOURSE OF MORALITY

All of the themes that I identify and analyse in the next section involve tensions that society must deal with so that it can get to grips with what it really wants to protect children from. Moreover, these tensions must be tackled in order to discourage a reaction to child pornography and grooming that inadvertently places children at further risk of harm. These tensions have emerged because of the way in which children are constructed as social and legal beings. Just as crucially, they exist because of the manner in which society and law construe the harms of child pornography and grooming. As a consequence, social construction theory and the concept of a morality discourse underpin my central analysis and method and thus it is to these that I first turn.

Social construction theory gained prominence in the late 1960s following the publication of Berger and Luckmann's influential work,

The Social Construction of Reality.[1] Berger and Luckmann contended that the reality that exists around us is socially defined, the result of human activity, and their work provides an explanation of the processes by which 'knowledge' within a society becomes established as 'reality'.[2] According to Berger and Luckmann, 'all social phenomena are constructions produced historically through human activity'.[3] In any social world, meanings are attached to experiences, activities, institutional processes and social phenomena, and become embedded into the objective reality of that society. Berger and Luckmann introduced the idea of a symbolic universe within which all human experience takes place. Essentially, 'Symbolic universes … are bodies of theoretical tradition that integrate different provinces of meaning and encompass the institutional order in a symbolic totality.'[4] The symbolic universe ensures the continued existence and acceptance of the objective reality of the social world. This book is concerned with exploring a symbolic universe in which problematic constructions of children exist, and in which perceptions of the prevalence of, and harms engendered by, child pornography and grooming may be distorted.

The idea that 'the child' and childhood are constructions is, of course, not new. In 1989, James and Prout saw social construction as an essential tenet of what they described as the emergent paradigm for the sociological study of childhood.[5] Some eight years later, social construction discourse had become sufficiently prominent in this field for the same authors to comment that 'writers or researchers who do not acknowledge the constitution of childhood within socially and historically situated discourse or who fail to give weight to its variability and relativity are currently more or less guaranteed a much more critical reception than was previously the case'.[6] As a consequence of recognizing the role that constructions play in the definition of childhood, it becomes apparent that there is no universal child or childhood.[7] For particular reasons, however, certain constructions of childhood can gain special prominence and become defining, taken-for-granted characteristics of 'the child'. As will become apparent, it is the dominant, critical constructions of childhood innocence and vulnerability that I am concerned with in this book. These categorizations may seem

1 Berger and Luckmann 1967.
2 Berger and Luckmann 1967: 116. 3 Ibid.: 106. 4 Ibid.: 95.
5 James and Prout 1990: 3. See also James *et al.* 1998: 26–8. 6 James and Prout 1997: x.
7 See James *et al.* 1998: 27; Jackson 1982: 28; and Jenks 1996.

appropriate and inevitable in contemporary society, but are they? I adopt an approach known as unmasking constructionism,[8] through which I intend to reveal that the construction of innocence in particular has a dubious, if not fallacious, authority. I also intend to expose the purpose of this construction.[9]

The communication of certain social definitions and constructions ensures that they play a significant role in the way in which we define ourselves and interact with the world around us, as explained by Trenholm: 'Coordinated interaction is intimately tied to our ability to create and maintain definitions of self and others … these definitions are created by society and supported by communication.'[10] In other words, constructions of the child and the harms of child pornography and grooming come into being through social and legal structures, culture, politics and, last but not least, the media. Through communicating these constructions to each other, we ensure that they gain further credence and strength. Child pornography and grooming have come to be perceived as social problems through the communication of constructions that reflect a high level of concern about them. In addition, as Searle observes, it is important to be aware that 'social reality is created by us for our purposes and seems as readily intelligible to us as those purposes themselves'.[11] Thus, perceiving children as innocent and vulnerable serves to ensure that we protect them and continue to see them as fundamentally different from adults. Childhood innocence and vulnerability are constructions of the powerful protectionist discourse which currently prevails in the social and legal world. One of the primary concerns of this book is that the taken-for-granted constructions of children we most commonly communicate to each other and accept may, in fact, be creating an unrealistic and dangerous social reality. I am thus utilizing social construction theory to 'raise consciousness' about the societal and legal reaction to child pornography and grooming.[12]

It is when our attention is brought to the crucial communicative tools of language and discourse that the influence of morality becomes apparent. Foucault's discourse analysis encourages reflection upon why we construct and perceive phenomena in the way that we do. Whilst I do not apply a specifically Foucaultian approach to discourse in this book, I draw broadly on the emphasis he places on the power of discourse

[8] See Hacking 1999: 20. [9] Ibid. [10] Trenholm 1991: 9. See also Gergen 1999.
[11] Searle 1995: 4. [12] See Hacking 1999: 6.

to shape our understanding of the object being studied.[13] I apply the concept of discourse to refer to the operation of language, interactions and practices in social, legal and ideological contexts.[14] One particular focus of this book is a discourse of morality. We interpret certain behaviour, especially behaviour that is norm-breaking, through a lens of morality, and discourse enables us to convey our moral judgement of the actor. Bergmann alerts us to the fact that our personal lens of morality is shaped through discourse: 'whenever respect and approval (or disrespect and disapproval) for an individual are communicated, a moral discourse takes place … Morality is constructed in and through social interaction, and the analysis of morality has to focus, accordingly, on the intricacies of everyday discourse.'[15] In other words, discourse and morality go hand in hand.[16]

A discourse of morality surrounds and influences the way in which we perceive and construct child pornography and grooming. As a consequence of this morality discourse, our understandings of and reactions to both phenomena are influenced by juxtaposing constructions such as innocence versus depravity, purity versus corruption, child versus adult, the normal adult versus the abnormal paedophile and protection versus abuse. If, as I will shortly discuss, there has been a disproportionate reaction to child pornography and grooming, it is morality which has given content to this reaction.[17] Morality is capable of invoking such strong emotions and responses that I will argue we may have witnessed a panic about these phenomena, generated by the authorities' reactions, the media and public opinion. In fact, the moral discourse that exists upon child pornography, grooming and child sexual abuse generally is so strong that one cannot choose to reject this discourse without being excluded from the social reality that is so intertwined with it.

Morality also pervades the legal discourses upon child pornography and grooming. Child pornography exists within a moral, ideological framework of indecency. Judicial and legislative condemnations of both phenomena are bolstered by moralistic terminology. Given the nature

[13] Discourses are 'practices that systematically *form* the object of which they speak. Of course discourse is composed of signs; but what they do is more than use these signs to designate things. It is this more that renders them irreducible to language [langue] and to speech. It is this "more" that we must reveal and describe.' Foucault 1972: 49 (my emphasis).

[14] See also Meyer 2007: 22. Generally, I use the term 'discourse' without subscribing to a particular theory.

[15] Bergmann 1998: 286.

[16] See Bergmann on the 'proto-moral' dimension to discourse. Ibid.: 283–5.

[17] Goode and Ben-Yehuda 1994: 142.

of child pornography and grooming and the subject under threat, it is almost inevitable that social and legal understandings of the problem are shaped by morality. Indeed, the presentation of the harm of child pornography and grooming that I support, exploitation,[18] has an inherently moral dimension. However, too much of a focus on morality can detract attention from the main harms of these phenomena. I argue that one of the primary reasons why the placing of indecency at the heart of the current child pornography laws is so problematic is because the concept of indecency does not adequately address the fact that children are exploited and, in some cases, abused. It is around this exploitation that social and legal concerns should be framed.

With this theoretical framework in mind, I will now introduce, in turn, the critical tensions that this book is concerned with: children's vulnerability and the question of harm, childhood innocence, child pornography and grooming as contemporary moral panics and finally, the vulnerability of individual rights.

CRITICAL TENSIONS

Protecting children's vulnerability to exploitation and the crucial question of harm

> Suffering children appear as archetypal victims, since childhood itself is defined by weakness and incapacity.[19]

Any research relating to children inevitably entails a focus on the sacred in society. In social culture, theory and policy, children enjoy a heavily guarded and highly cherished status. Because of the particular characteristics that we attribute to 'the child', behaviour that places children at risk of harm appears more harmful to us than the same behaviour that exposes adults to risk.[20] In the social and legal world, children are categorized as a vulnerable class in need of protection from physical and certain kinds of psychological threats. According to the British Government, for example, children are particularly vulnerable 'because

[18] I explore the concept of exploitation in Chapter 3. I should state from the outset that I apply Feinberg's analysis of harm and exploitation. See Feinberg 1984; and Feinberg 1988. I see exploitation as the harm of child pornography and grooming in a normative sense and because pornographers and groomers set back children's interests.

[19] Holland 2006: 143. [20] See also Jackson and Scott 1999: 90.

of their immaturity of judgement, lack of authority in relation to adults and physical vulnerability'.[21]

Sociological discourses have drawn attention to the question of whether and to what extent the vulnerability that children are seen to possess is an innate or a socially constructed vulnerability. For Lansdown, children's vulnerability is, in part, a structural vulnerability socially constructed by their lack of civil status.[22] Jackson sees claims that children are vulnerable and weak as justifying a social world in which children are unable to make their own decisions, have no ability to exercise rights and remain dependent on adults.[23] Diduck suggests that it is the power of the notion of childhood, coupled with the physical dependency of children, which causes their welfare to be prioritized over protection of their legal rights.[24] It would appear, then, that the social reality of vulnerability that children experience is only partly the result of a natural characteristic of childhood and is largely defined by a society that has accentuated this particular image of the child. Children experience this socially defined vulnerability because it is so prevalent that it permeates their lived reality. Additionally, children's vulnerability to exploitation is not fixed; it is dependent on the way in which both vulnerability and exploitation are defined in the particular social world, the social context and constructions of that social context.

The concept of vulnerability is frequently alluded to when the protection of children is at issue. Whilst protecting children from harm is considered to be a specific parental duty,[25] a broader responsibility is placed on our society, on our lawmakers and adjudicators, for the welfare of all of the children who exist within it.[26] In the American Supreme Court case of *Bellotti* v. *Baird*,[27] for example, which involved the question of whether the requirement of parental consent for minors requesting an abortion was unconstitutional, Justice Powell emphasized '[t]he Court's concern for the vulnerability of children'. He stated that the 'peculiar vulnerability of children' was one of the main reasons that the Supreme Court had previously held that it was not possible to equate children's constitutional rights with those of adults.[28] In the more recent English

[21] Home Office 2000: para. 4.1.2. See also Goodin 1985: 191: the characteristics of 'limited information, understanding, sophistication, etc. – make children inevitably vulnerable'.

[22] See Lansdown 1994: 34–5.

[23] Jackson 1982: 26.

[24] Diduck 1999: 130–1. See also Piper 2000: 40.

[25] See Goodin 1985: 79–83.

[26] See Lansdown 1994: 33; and Diduck 1999: 131.

[27] 443 US 662 (1979).

[28] Ibid.: 633–4.

case of *R. v. Kabir*,[29] the Court of Appeal held that the trial judge's decision that the offender serve a minimum term of thirteen years for the murder of his ten-month-old son was unduly lenient, because an aggravated feature of the crime was that 'the victim in this case was particularly vulnerable because of his age; he was helpless'.[30] Countless more examples exist of an emphasis upon the need to protect children's vulnerability in legal discourses.

The desire to protect what is most vulnerable is particularly apparent when there is a risk of children and behaviour of a sexual nature being brought together.[31] As Kleinhans comments: 'Children and sexuality are western sacred cows of the present age.'[32] Sachsenmaier goes so far as to argue that 'protection of children from harm, particularly sexual abuse, is the moral imperative our society has adopted as the most important'.[33] Children's particular vulnerability to sexual abuse was emphasized when the Sexual Offences Bill (which became the Sexual Offences Act 2003) was being debated in Parliament:

> Sexual crime, and the fear of sexual crime, has a profound and damaging effect on the lives of individuals and communities. A responsibility rests on the Government adequately to protect everyone in society from such crimes, *especially those who are most vulnerable to abuse*: *children* and persons with a mental disorder or learning disability.[34]

Although children and adults with mental disorders are both categorized as vulnerable groups in relation to sexual behaviour, there is a distinction drawn between the *level* of protection that it is considered should be offered to both groups, because of the accepted social and cultural perception that children are unable to consent to involvement in sexual acts. During the Parliamentary debates referred to above, Lord Falconer responded to the question of whether the protection offered by the proposed offence of meeting a child following sexual grooming[35] should also be extended to adults with mental disorders. In his view, extending the scope of the offence in this way would lead to a situation where:

> even though the right of those people who have the capacity to consent is recognised – albeit with some form of mental impairment – nevertheless

[29] [2005] 1 Cr. App. R. (S). [30] Ibid., para. 23, *per* Lord Woolf C. J.

[31] See, e.g. Summit 1990: 64. [32] Kleinhans 2002: 233. [33] Sachsenmaier 1998.

[34] Hansard, HL Deb, 13 February 2003: column 771 (Lord Falconer) (my emphasis).

[35] Now s. 15 of the Sexual Offences Act 2003.

> they are entitled to especial protection and they should not be able to make the kinds of judgments that the rest of us are entitled to make … But because of our profound concern not to prevent people who do have the capacity to consent to be able to court and be courted in the way that other adults are, I am not sure that it would be right to extend this protection to those who do have the capacity to consent.[36]

The difference in the level of protection regarding sexual behaviour is rationalized then, because law and society recognize the autonomy of adults with mental disorders (at least to some degree in this context), and respect for their autonomy outweighs concerns regarding their vulnerability. In contrast, children are seen as non-autonomous in this context; we cannot see them as playing any kind of complicit role in sexual behaviour they are involved in. As a consequence, whereas an adult with a mental disorder will see his right to autonomy protected (assuming he has the capacity to consent to sexually related behaviour),[37] the child's right remains framed around protection from harm.[38] Wendy and Rex Stainton Rogers believe the conception that children are incapable of consent is based on 'a sensibility to their vulnerability to adult power' rather than an understanding derived from a developmental perception of children's intellectual capability.[39] The notion of victimization also plays a role here. King and Piper argue that legal and social constructs of the child present the notion of children as victims and consequently: 'In child protection the concepts of the willing victim or contributory negligence simply do not arise.'[40]

In cases specifically involving child pornography and grooming, the vulnerability of the child victim(s) is commonly emphasized. In referrals or appeals against sentences that have come before the Court of Appeal, for example, judges regularly make references to the child victim being particularly vulnerable.[41] Members of the legislature are also keen to stress this characteristic. When the Bill that would become

[36] Hansard, HL Deb, 1 April 2003: columns 1265–6.

[37] Although cases such as *F. v. West Berkshire Health Authority* [1989] 2 All ER 545 evidence that legal recognition of a mentally incapacitated individual's autonomy regarding sexual behaviour and its possible repercussions is limited.

[38] See also Waites 2005: 38 and 218.

[39] Stainton Rogers and Stainton Rogers 1999: 191.

[40] King and Piper 1995: 65.

[41] See, e.g. *R. v. Mohammed* [2006] EWCA Crim. 1107, para. 13; *R. v. Wilson* [2006] EWCA Crim. 505, para. 12; *Attorney General's Reference (no. 3 of 2006)* [2006] EWCA Crim. 695, para. 10; and *R. v. GA* [2006] EWCA Crim. 1201, para. 13.

the first piece of legislation on child pornography was being debated in the House of Lords, Lord Robertson reminded the other Members of the House that: 'we need to be sure that we do not lose sight of the special qualities, limitations and vulnerability of children'.[42] The concept of vulnerability thus inevitably shapes legal and societal responses to child pornography and grooming, and is consequently an important focus of my analysis within this book. Specifically, I will examine the nature and reality of the threat that child pornography and grooming represent, and consider what exactly makes children so vulnerable in these contexts and ways in which society can tackle this vulnerability. Another necessary element of my focus on the notion of vulnerability is to understand and assess the extent to which there are parallels between the way in which child pornographers and groomers exploit the vulnerability of children.

Whilst the emphasis placed on children's vulnerability plays an important and compelling role in promoting child protection, the powerful nature of the concept of vulnerability creates a tension. Because children are distinguished as a special vulnerable group, as victims in need of protection, it can become difficult to respond objectively to the level of threat posed to them. I will assess whether the legal and social mechanisms that currently exist to combat child pornography and grooming are protecting children appropriately and effectively serving 'society's need to protect vulnerable children'.[43] It also seems that the strength of the desire to protect children causes us to be less inclined to demand proof of real, definite harm before we criminalize behaviour that may pose a threat. Social and legal narratives present the protection of children as imperative. The protectionist discourse has become so powerful and compelling that, when it comes to the legal regulation of the possession of indecent images of children, the fact that there is a risk of potential, more remote, harm to children as a consequence of this behaviour suffices. We do not demand, for example, proof that the possessor of child pornography will be incited to go out and sexually abuse a child. Indeed, the criminalization of the possession of child pornography and of arranging to meet a child following sexual grooming can be seen as examples of the targeting of behaviour that can potentially cause harm to children.[44] Also, if the individual in question has already

[42] Hansard, HL Deb, 5 May 1978: column 566. [43] Home Office 2000: para. 3.6.11.

[44] See generally Husak 2008: 44. This is not to say that the possession of an indecent photograph of a child offence under the Criminal Justice Act 1988 is only targeted at behaviour that is

behaved in a way that we see as being injurious to children, the Sexual Offences Act allows for an application to be made under the law for a Risk of Sexual Harm Order to prevent the individual from posing further potential harm.[45]

It is my contention that whilst we do need to recognize and respond to the fact that children are vulnerable to exploitation, we must address the question of whether we are tackling real harm, or a potential risk of harm, rationally. Specifically, the nature of harm, and hence justification for criminalization, requires careful analysis in the context of possessing child pornography, the creation of pseudo-images[46] and images of naked children and grooming behaviour. In all of these cases, the individual concerned may not have caused any direct harm to the child by his[47] actions and this is a significant parallel between behaviour related to child pornography and grooming that I will explore further in this work. We must also reflect upon how we construe children's vulnerability, and consider whether child pornographers and groomers are able to exploit children as a consequence of social constructions that define and make them more vulnerable. To do this necessitates a move away from the current tendency to structure debates surrounding child pornography and grooming around problematic, morally laden terminology such as the 'sexual corruption' of children. This brings me to a related issue that explains in part why our attention is directed towards children's vulnerability and why we are so determined to protect children from the particular threats which child pornography, grooming and other acts related to child sexual abuse represent. It is to a significant, but potentially dangerous, construction of childhood – innocence – that I now turn.

potentially harmful. As I will discuss in Chapter 3, it can also be argued that criminalizing possession is aimed at the exacerbation of pre-existing harm.

45 These orders and the offences relating to child pornography and sexual grooming are discussed in Chapter 2.

46 Images that are not real images of child sexual abuse. They may involve the manipulation of a real child's image or not feature a real child at all, and are most often computer-generated.

47 I should note at the outset that when referring to child sexual abusers, child pornographers and groomers, I use the masculine pronoun throughout this work. In so doing, I am not making stereotypical assumptions; the existing research indicates that the majority of individuals who engage in behaviour related to child sexual abuse or use child pornography tend to be male, although this is not to say that women do not engage in such activities. See Chapter 1, at 44–5. For clarity of exposition, I use the feminine pronoun when referring to the child, although I recognize that both male and female children can be victims of child sexual abuse.

Childhood innocence

> Innocence makes you vulnerable, badly in need of protection, which is one reason adults like it to be in others.[48]

Innocence has become such an integral part of childhood narratives in contemporary Western society and culture that a child without it appears conspicuous and suspect. Innocence, particularly sexual innocence, clearly demarcates children from adults, fosters a protectionist stance, dictates the correct way for a child to appear and behave and reminds adults of what we once were. A historical construct,[49] it is a notion of childhood that continues to dominate today and its myth endures, notwithstanding the impact of Freud's work upon our understanding of childhood and sexuality.[50] For my purposes here, I will briefly discuss the emphasis that we place on childhood innocence and the tensions that our enduring fascination with this ideal generates.

The prevalence of the construction of childhood innocence is perhaps the primary reason why child sexual abuse is considered to be such an abhorrent evil. Archard observes that: 'The sexual abuse of children is seen as horrific precisely because it robs children of the innocence that is naturally and rightfully theirs.'[51] In the specific contexts of child pornography and grooming, childhood innocence plays a pivotal role in shaping social and legal reactions. Anne Higonnet's work has effectively illustrated how our fixation with childhood innocence determines the way in which we see and respond to images of children.[52] Images that challenge or threaten the idea that children are innocent beings cause controversy and discomfort, the photographs of Sally Mann which hint at child eroticism being a primary exemplar of this.[53]

Allusions to the destruction of childhood innocence are common in the legal arena. For example, in passing sentence in a recent case involving the creation and possession of indecent images of a child and other sexual offences against a child, the judge emphasized that the defendant had stolen the innocence of the child in question.[54] The concept of childhood innocence also permeates discourses surrounding grooming. The very label 'sexual grooming' draws our attention to the notion that it takes away

48 Kincaid 1998: 54. See also Archard 1993: 49.

49 See, e.g. Hendrick 1994.

50 See also on this point Piper 2000: 27.

51 Archard 1993: 40; and Meyer 2007: 58–9.

52 Higonnet 1998.

53 See ibid.: 194–6; 'The notional paedophile now dictates what we can look at', *The Guardian*, 4 October 2007.

54 *R.* v. *O'Brien* [2006] EWCA Crim. 3339, para. 10.

a child's sexual innocence and increases her vulnerability to sexual abuse. Framing the nature of the damage this behaviour poses to the child in this way causes us to be much more likely to support steps taken to criminalize it. Innocence, once lost, cannot be regained. Thus, the avoidance of adult corruption of a child's innocence by way of child pornography or grooming has become paramount, a major societal and legal concern.[55]

The dominant role of innocence in structuring the meaning of the child, and the emphasis placed on preventing the corruption of a child's innocence in social and certain legal discourses, causes tension. To begin with, we should consider why, for adults, innocence is such a vital representation of childhood. Higonnet sees the force of nostalgia behind our attraction to innocence: 'It's about adults who want to look back on a time before their own lives which was supposedly less complicated, more pure and worthy.'[56] Visualizing our children as innocent beings is one part of the battle we fight in vain to prevent them from becoming adults for as long as we can. The notion that children are pure, uncorrupted and dependent on their parents is both comfortable and comforting. But are we, in fact, using the idea of childhood innocence as a curtain to mask a reality of childhood today that is harder for us to accept? Children are increasingly more sexually aware at an early age, are becoming more independent, and may be more eager to escape the over-protection of their parents than we are willing to see.[57] Clinging to the accepted construction of innocence blurs reality.

At the same time as we foster a public image of the child as naive and innocent, we are frequently presented with a reality of childhood by the media that is entirely and starkly different:

> Reports continue of children driven to suicide through bullying; of children who terrorise local estates, stealing cars, breaking windows, starting fires and terrifying elderly inhabitants; of gangs, whose rivalry is based on territory or race; of a growing drugs and gun culture and of suburban youth whose violence is casual and random.[58]

Furthermore, our persistent concentration on innocence overlooks other serious harm that can be caused to children. First, our inability to let go of the powerful notion of innocence may be damaging to the rights of older children who are no longer sexually 'innocent'. Later in this

[55] See also 'Our Anxiety Over the Corruption of Innocence', *The Independent*, 18 July 2003.
[56] Najafi 2002: 2. See also Holland 2006: 16; Mitchell 2001: 115; and Jackson 1982: 28.
[57] See Kitzinger 1997: 175; Boyden 1997: 203; and Piper 2000: 33–4.
[58] Holland 2006: 121.

chapter, I introduce the argument that, in one particular respect, the laws criminalizing behaviour relating to indecent images of children are failing to take into account the autonomy rights of teenagers after they have attained the current age of sexual consent.[59] Secondly, our obsession with innocence produces a particularly dangerous representation of children that research suggests is attractive to paedophiles.[60] There is a real risk that the emphasis placed upon childhood innocence may actually be making children more vulnerable to exploitation. Perversely, at the same time as we promote the damaging and misleading ideology of innocence, the child is sexualized and exploited by contemporary culture and the media, and the female child in particular has become the subject of a fetish for sexualized innocence.[61]

However, the tension that exists in a society that is torn between the child's innocence and his or her sexualization is not new. Edwards has documented the comparable strain that existed during the Victorian era between contemporary conceptions of childhood and sexualized images of children.[62] Notwithstanding this parallel with Victorian society and culture, tensions between childhood innocence and sexuality are even more apparent today. In Kincaid's view, Freud paved the way for the modern-day contradiction of the child who is pure, yet also sexual[63] and, according to Higonnet, the eroticization of children in contemporary society means that the 'ideal of childhood innocence has entered a crisis'.[64]

Concentrating our attention on innocence causes a tension and an overreaction whenever there is a potential threat to children's deemed purity. This can be seen in the reaction apparent in certain tabloid newspapers to a photographic exhibition in 2001 that included images of naked children wearing adult facemasks and urinating in the snow.[65] That such images are seen as dangerous in social discourses reflects the idea that children's nakedness should not be seen, should be shrouded, or otherwise we risk a violation of their bodies.[66] Notions of violation would seem to apply even if the actual body of the child has not been violated, but violation takes the form of the child's nudity being

[59] Whether the age of sexual consent laws themselves are a legitimate infringement of children's autonomy rights is a matter extensively considered by Waites 2005.

[60] See also Kitzinger 1997: 168; and Archard 1993: 40.

[61] Holland 2006; 191–195; and Higonnet 1998: 10–11.

[62] Edwards 2003.

[63] Kincaid 1998: 13–14.

[64] Higonnet 1998: 7.

[65] See Chapter 4, at 186–8.

[66] 'Children's bodies are to be preserved at all costs, any violation signifying a transgressive act of almost unimaginable dimensions.' James *et al.* 1998: 152.

captured on camera and the viewer being sexually aroused by looking at the resulting image: an imagined violation of the child's body. This book is particularly concerned with the social and legal responses to images of naked children without sexual content, the question of whether such images should be criminalized, and the potential consequences of such criminalization for children.

What constructions of childhood innocence also prevent, therefore, is society adopting a more rational, objective approach towards children's exploitation. Thus, I suggest that social and legal discourses should turn aside from constructions of the harms caused by child pornography and grooming which play on a specific corruption of children's assumed innocence. What potentially stands in the way of the adoption of such an approach is the current social reaction to child pornography and grooming, as I will now discuss.

Moral panics surrounding child pornography and stranger grooming

> Sexual predators lurk like spiders on the world-wide web, waiting to catch vulnerable children.[67]

Moral panics are sociological phenomena and significantly, given the theoretical framework of this book, social constructs. The concept of the moral panic can perhaps best be introduced by briefly discussing one example and analysis of what we can now understand to be a historical instance: the societal reaction to the Jack the Ripper murders in Victorian England. Walkowitz effectively demonstrates the way in which the media's coverage of the murders, and public reaction to this coverage, was played out in a theatre where discourses of power, class and gender abounded.[68] This gave rise to a widespread panic that left women in London vulnerable to male fantasies of sexual violence and dependent on men for their protection. Walkowitz explains how the public's impressions and understandings of the Ripper murders were gauged from sensational and compelling media reports which focused on the sexual mutilation of the victims. Stories in the daily press emphasized the immoral occupation of the victims and the squalid, dangerous setting of Whitechapel for the murders. The social and political reaction

[67] Hansard, HL Deb, 13 February 2003: column 872 (Lord Astor of Hever).

[68] Walkowitz 1992: ch. 7. There are numerous other historical examples of moral panics. For just two of these, see Silverman and Wilson 2002: 10–12; and Sutter 2003.

to this coverage entailed calls for greater state control over prostitution and more police patrols, riots by the poor in Whitechapel, night patrols around Whitechapel by its male inhabitants and instances of what Walkowitz terms 'copycat activities'.[69]

The way in which this and other instances of widespread social unrest and alarm are now understood and assessed has been informed by the conceptual analysis of moral panics that appeared in the latter part of the twentieth century. The concept of the 'moral panic' was originally developed by Jock Young and Stan Cohen,[70] who argued that the combined effect of the media's coverage of a phenomenon, public opinion and the reaction of the authorities can have the spiral-like effect of creating a moral panic. Initially, in order for a moral panic to evolve, there must be a belief that there is a threat to 'something held sacred by or fundamental to the society'.[71] To consider how this theory applies to the phenomena of child pornography and grooming perpetrated by a stranger (what I term 'stranger grooming'),[72] first it is fundamentally clear that we have a subject held sacred in our society, the child, who may be at threat. Secondly, child pornography and stranger grooming consistently make headline news. Stories relating to both phenomena frequently appear on television news reports and saturate our newspapers. The stories that appear in the tabloids in particular are couched in sensationalist and frenzied language.[73]

The media are not alone in choosing to highlight child pornography and stranger grooming as matters of great social concern in recent years. There has also been much attention paid to these particular issues in the political arena and, consequently, as I shall discuss in Chapter 2, there

[69] Walkowitz 1992: 218–9. [70] Young 1971; and Cohen 1972. [71] Thompson 1998: 8.

[72] For reasons that are explained in Chapter 4, I apply the idea of a moral panic to the sexual grooming of a child by a stranger rather than sexual grooming in a wider sense.

[73] Some recent examples of headlines include 'Rocketing number of child porn sites reported', *Daily Mail*, 8 March 2006; 'Destruction of innocence; exclusive map reveals huge online child porn trade in Scotland … and it's only the tip of the iceberg', *Daily Record*, 21 January 2008; 'Hall of shame; children in danger from sex beasts', *Sunday Mirror*, 17 June 2007; 'Shock rise in kid porn sites; Irish surfers reporting more paedo filth on net', *The Mirror*, 30 March 2007; 'Police struggle to halt the spread of child porn websites', *Daily Mail*, 21 July 2006; 'Kid porn on web doubles', *The Mirror*, 28 February 2006; 'Police bust biggest child porn ring in the world', *Daily Mail*, 29 November 2001; 'Pervert runs child abuse website from his jail cell', *The Mirror*, 31 August 2005; 'Paedo priest's "300 victims"', *The Mirror*, 29 July 2006; 'Beware internet grooming', News Wales, 3 March 2008, www.newswales.co.uk/?section=Community&F=1&id=13460; 'Warning over net grooming danger', BBC News report, 9 November 2005; http://news.bbc.co.uk/1/hi/scotland/4421604.stm; and 'Stranger danger in cyberspace', BBC News report, 6 January 2003, http://news.bbc.co.uk/1/hi/programmes/breakfast/2630545.stm.

has been an expansion of the criminal law to deal with such matters. In its 2001 Manifesto, for example, the Labour Party pledged to 'take measures to tackle the problem of child pornography on the Internet'[74] and appointed the Taskforce on Child Protection on the Internet in the same year to make recommendations as to how children could be offered protection whilst surfing the World Wide Web. Since the party began its first term in government in 1997, new laws have both criminalized more behaviour relating to child pornography and grooming, and bestowed wider powers upon the police in these areas.[75] The Conservative Party has also put forward specific proposals aimed at improving laws 'governing paedophiles'.[76] By highlighting child pornography and grooming as significant political issues, the main political parties are evidently addressing matters they believe to be important to the public. But at the same time, this political focus can only increase public concern about the threat that both child pornography and stranger grooming represent in our society.

If there has been a moral panic in respect of child pornography and stranger grooming, then it has had, and will have, a longer trajectory than that surrounding Cohen's Mods and Rockers in the 1960s. According to Cohen, 'moral panics have their own internal trajectory – a microphysics of outrage – which, however, is initiated and sustained by wider and social political forces'.[77] As already noted, the primary reason why society attaches such significance to the actual and potential harms of child pornography and stranger grooming is because the victims of the deviance in question are society's most cherished. The protectionist stance that society and law adopt when children are the subject of potential harm has led to a situation where we have a tension between the real level of risk caused by child pornography and stranger grooming and society's reaction to the perceived risk. The law's criminalization of behaviour and the punishments imposed under the criminal justice system also continue to increase. For example, following the extension of the criminal law to pseudo-images of child pornography in the 1990s, social campaigners, the media and politicians chose to call for further criminalization of other deviant behaviour that might also represent

[74] Labour Party 2001: 32.

[75] See the Regulation of Investigatory Powers Act 2000 and the Sexual Offences Act 2003.

[76] See, e.g. Conservative Party 2002; 'Widdecombe gets tough on child porn', *Birmingham Post*, 22 May 2000; and 'Tories call for net paedophile laws', BBC News report, 16 August 2002, http://news.bbc.co.uk/1/hi/uk_politics/2196734.stm.

[77] Cohen 2007: xxxi. See also Critcher 2006: 55.

a threat, such as stranger grooming. The impetus of the protectionist movement, fuelled by an apparent moral panic response, did not encourage an alternative, more rational approach of taking a step back and attempting to objectively assess whether the existing law was already protecting children from real and present dangers.[78] The government's decision in 2002 to take steps to create an offence designed to prevent child sexual abuse before it occurs and thus criminalize behaviour carried out with an ulterior harmful intent towards children[79] could only have been supported in such a social climate. For, as Cohen observes: 'During moral panics … one "doesn't take a chance" or is "rather safe than sorry".'[80]

I also suggest that what appears to be a disproportionate societal response to child pornography and stranger grooming is formed, in part, as a result of an availability cascade. Kuran and Sunstein define availability cascades as: 'cascades, through which expressed perceptions trigger chains of individual responses that make these perceptions appear increasingly plausible through their rising availability in public discourse'.[81] Members of the public do not have all of the precise information or the personal experience to reach a careful, informed judgement about the prevalence of child pornography and stranger grooming. Instead, reliance is placed on the representations most readily available, from the media and politicians, for example. The media's coverage and focus on child pornography and stranger grooming, and the ease with which the public can access this coverage, can lead to a consequent acceptance of this as shorthand to ascertain the extent of these problems. This means that it is easy for the public to bring to mind the prevalence of both phenomena as a real and prominent danger. However, there may in fact be a disparity between the perceived and actual prevalence of child pornography and stranger grooming. This disparity is reinforced by the way in which the government has chosen to fix attention on these phenomena, perhaps because they are forms of child sexual abuse and related behaviour that are somewhat easier to tackle than child sexual abuse which occurs in the home.

Moral panic and availability cascade theories are particularly germane to the concerns of this work. Cohen's analysis informs us that moral panics are 'merely warning signs of the real, much deeper and more

[78] See Chapter 2 at 87–90. [79] Home Office 2002. [80] Cohen 2007: 62.
[81] Kuran and Sunstein 1999: 685.

prevalent condition'.[82] Society views child pornography and stranger grooming through a distorted lens, within a frame of prevalent social constructions of childhood that makes it next to impossible for the legal and societal responses to these phenomena to be objectively rational. As members of society, we are all caught up in this moral panic and symbolic universe. It is difficult to step outside this universe and adopt a more critically reflective approach without fear of being criticized for failing to take seriously the harm that children can suffer as a result of involvement in child pornography, or being subject to grooming perpetrated by a stranger.

The vulnerability of individual rights

It is perhaps unsurprising that in a protectionist social and legal climate such as that surrounding child pornography and grooming, individual rights take second place to the concern of ensuring children are shielded from as many potential risks of harm as possible. In the context of the general social treatment of children, Corsaro opines that: 'Because of their immaturity and dependency on adults, children have limited rights and ... [are seen] as inferior and not worthy of the same respect as adults.'[83] Significance continues to be attached to age as a determinate of children's recognized ability to exercise autonomy in the Western world.[84] However, as children gradually approach adulthood, one might expect that the law would come to recognize their autonomy rights. I argue that older teenagers' autonomy rights are at threat from the way in which we are responding to child pornography and that there is a real tension between rights of protection and autonomy. For instance, a legislative provision I examine in Chapter 2 constrains the autonomy rights of sixteen- and seventeen-year-olds to take what the law constructs to be an indecent photograph of each other. Law and society override their autonomous right to make a decision to be involved in a situation where adults may feel they are exploiting themselves. However, this failure to respect autonomy appears at odds with other laws: sixteen is an age at which older teenagers are considered to possess the maturity to consent to sexual intercourse and to consent to medical treatment and, at seventeen, they are deemed to be mature enough to drive a car.

I contend that it is not just the rights of older teenagers that are being sacrificed in order to achieve the protectionist stance regarding child

[82] Cohen 2007: viii. [83] Corsaro 1997: 199. [84] James and Prout 1997: 235.

pornography and grooming, but also, in some cases, those who are prosecuted for offences. Whilst it would be very difficult to challenge the appropriateness of, for example, the deprivation of liberty where an individual has caused harm to a child, my focus is upon those individuals who have not caused such direct harm. Take, for instance, an individual who has created a completely fabricated pseudo-image depicting a child engaged in sexual activity. Regardless of how repugnant this material may be considered to be, in a society that values individual rights, matters of freedom of expression and privacy should be given greater weight than they currently are. Given the serious stigma attached to child pornography and grooming and any behaviour related to child sex abuse, we should also take note of the severe consequences of being suspected, charged and perhaps found guilty of offences related to these matters, not only for the individual, but also for his family.[85]

OVERVIEW OF THE BOOK

The following chapters provide a comprehensive overview of the legal and social responses to child pornography and sexual grooming, addressing and unpacking in greater detail the themes and critical tensions that I have outlined here. Chapter 1 sets the scene, presenting the objects of the analysis which follows in the rest of the book. I consider what constitutes the modern day phenomena of child pornography and grooming and assess how the grooming process fits into aetiological theories of child sexual abuse. I then turn to the matters of paedophilia and child sexual abuse, exploring theories of sexual offending against children, the medical understanding of paedophilia and popular constructions of the paedophile. I examine parallels between child pornography and grooming before finally considering the impact of the internet upon both phenomena.

In Chapter 2, I embark on a detailed critical examination of the law surrounding child pornography and grooming. I explain and discuss the child pornography offences under the Protection of Children Act 1978 and the possession of child pornography offence under the Criminal

[85] 'There is overwhelming evidence that individuals tried for alleged sexual offences frequently suffer disproportionate publicity and, if acquitted, there are serious consequences when they try to rebuild their lives.' Hansard HC Deb. 15 July 2003: column 193 (Dominic Grieve); 'Paedophile's daughter "crashed while fleeing vigilantes"', BBC News report, 22 August 2000, http://news.bbc.co.uk/1/hi/wales/890360.stm; '"Suspicious" fire at paedophile's home', BBC News report, 20 August 2000, http://news.bbc.co.uk/1/hi/wales/887451.stm; and Critcher 2006: 139.

Justice Act 1988 (CJA). I address the question of whether the newer child pornography offences under the Sexual Offences Act 2003 (SOA) catch more harmful behaviour when considered alongside the pre-existing offences. I consider the potentially serious repercussions that increasing the age of a child from sixteen to eighteen years old (since the advent of the SOA) may cause. In this chapter, I also study the offence of meeting a child following grooming under s. 15 of the SOA and the need to establish an ulterior intent in order for the offence to be made out, on which little research currently exists in the academic literature. In the final part of the chapter, I undertake a theoretical analysis of the legal discourses surrounding child pornography and grooming. As of yet, there has been little reflection on the reasons for the criminalization of behaviour related to child pornography and grooming in the existing literature, and more attention needs to be paid to the problematic ideological legal framework and constructions that surround the phenomena.

Chapter 3 is concerned with discourses of harm. I analyse the research and academic debates upon the harms of child pornography and grooming. I concentrate particularly on the offence of possessing an indecent photograph of a child under the CJA and identify the primary, potential, remote and perceived harms that occur through the possession of such material. Following an analysis of the existing literature and research, I argue that we do not currently have any real evidence that possessing indecent images of children will incite an individual to become an actual abuser, although there may be some evidence of a correlative link between possession and abuse. I argue that possession is a remote harm, underwriting the primary harm caused by those who produce child pornography. However, I critique the argument that criminalization can be legitimated because preventing individuals from possessing child pornography reduces the market in such material. Notwithstanding the powerful desire to protect children's vulnerability, I argue that criminalization must have a rational, defensible basis. I explore the way in which criminalization of behaviour related to grooming as a crime of ulterior intent can be rationalized, and how grooming itself can amount to, or facilitate, the causing of primary harm to the child. Another particular focus of the discussion is the real risk that the harms of grooming may be increased by the way in which the phenomenon is presented by the media, and in legal and social discourses. Finally, it is in this chapter that I present my construction of child pornography and grooming as harmful exploitation.

In Chapter 4, I turn my attention to the matters of morality, moral panics and the construction of childhood innocence. In the first part of this chapter, I provide a detailed assessment of whether there has been a moral panic regarding child pornography and stranger grooming, and the role that availability cascades may have played in this. In the second part, I consider in depth the question of whether the emphasis upon childhood innocence reflected in the social and legal discourses surrounding child pornography is damaging and actually makes children more vulnerable. I argue that children's lived experience of *being* children may be detrimentally affected by the powerful societal desire to protect their innocence and vulnerability being taken too far, and that our current attitude towards childhood nudity damages our perceptions and, even more significantly, children's perceptions of their own bodies.

Both child pornography and grooming are recognized as problems which cannot be confined within legal borders. Chapter 5 provides the international, comparative dimension to this work, with a focus on a discourse of rights. First, I focus on the law in two other jurisdictions. Canadian law merits consideration, not least because of the significant judgment given by the Supreme Court in *R.* v. *Sharpe*,[86] a judgment that involved a balancing of the state's interest in protecting children's rights and vulnerability against the defendant's right to freedom of expression and privacy. Particularly, I analyse Canadian law's expansive definition of child pornography and its potential for sexualizing non-pornographic images of children. I also consider whether the criminalization of written material and works of the imagination is warranted. Unsurprisingly, given the American Constitution's protection of individual freedoms, issues of individual rights have also featured significantly in a number of American cases involving laws surrounding child pornography. Following a discussion of the federal law in America, I highlight the problems caused by the way in which American law requires judges to focus on the sexual elements of an image of a child. Additionally, I briefly examine Canadian and US laws that criminalize the luring and enticement of a child to facilitate a sexual offence (the most similar offences to that under English law relating to grooming). Secondly, I explore individual rights in the context of English law, and the impact upon individuals who are suspected of and arrested for the offences relating to child pornography and grooming. In the final part of this chapter, I address the international protection afforded to children's rights and the protection the international community offers children in the context of child pornography and grooming.

[86] [2001] SCC 2.

Chapter 6 brings together the issues addressed within the book. Here, I critically evaluate the way in which law and society deal with child pornography and grooming, highlighting the main problems with the current societal and legal responses. I offer a number of suggestions for ways in which we can adopt a new approach that will present and tackle the harms of child pornography and grooming more effectively and appropriately. The approach I present is designed to enable children to have a better lived experience of childhood.

One of my intentions in writing this book was to examine how the legal and policing systems work in practice, to explore the interface between legal regulation and social and cultural practices. Thus, as part of my research, I undertook a small qualitative empirical study, interviewing eight police officers working for Lancashire Constabulary in the North West of England during a four-month period in 2008, who are, or have been, involved with cases of child pornography and grooming in their professional duties.[87] I focused the interviews especially upon grooming, as the experiences of law enforcement officers regarding such behaviour have not been explored to any great extent in the existing research. The interviews were semi-structured, lasting between forty minutes to an hour and a half, and I endeavoured to ask questions in an open-ended way to avoid leading the interviewees. I interviewed officers from various ranks: Detective Chief Superintendent, Detective Superintendent, Detective Chief Inspector, Detective Inspector, Detective Sergeant and Constable. As the anonymity of participants was guaranteed, when quoting extracts from their interviews, I simply use a code to refer to the specific interview (RX1, RX2, etc.), and provide the date of each interview in Appendix A. As the aim of qualitative research is not to have a representative sample and results that can therefore be generalized, but, rather, to gain an in-depth, informative insight into social phenomena, my sample size was necessarily small.[88] Furthermore, although I approached two other police forces, obtaining permission to interview appropriate personnel proved to be very difficult and I was not given a reason for permission being refused.

[87] It seemed particularly appropriate to interview officers from the Lancashire Constabulary, since this force has prioritized child sexual exploitation in recent years, as noted by three of the police officers I interviewed (Interviews RX3, RX4 and RX5). See, e.g. the Western Division's *Awaken Project* (http://popcenter.org/library/awards/goldstein/2007/07–24.pdf) and the Eastern Division's *Operation Engage* (www.blackburn.gov.uk/server.php?show=ConWebDoc.39228).

[88] Bowling 1997. I was given approval to conduct my empirical study by Lancaster University's Research Ethics Committee.

The topics addressed in the interviews I conducted with the police officers reflect the central questions and themes of the book. For instance, the question of harm and constructions of harm was addressed through exploring officers' experiences of grooming and the impact upon the child, their personal perceptions of the exploitative nature of child pornography and grooming and offenders, and the risk factors of possessing child pornography. I also asked the officers about their views on what law and society still need to do to tackle the exploitation of children through child pornography and grooming. The theme of moral panics and availability cascades was alluded to by ascertaining officers' opinions on the media's coverage of both phenomena. Importantly, the empirical study also enabled me to discover more about how the offence relating to grooming operates in practice. For instance, officers described whether and how they are able to establish ulterior intent regarding the offence of meeting a child following sexual grooming. Two of the especially interesting revelations of the study relate to the different ways in which young teenagers can be groomed and the fact that, in cases of successful grooming, the young person often does not perceive she is a victim. As the empirical study thus mirrored various themes and concerns of this book, my analysis in various chapters includes discussion of the findings from the study, and the views of the police officers who participated.

CHAPTER ONE

THE MODERN DAY PHENOMENA OF CHILD PORNOGRAPHY AND SEXUAL GROOMING

In order to contextualize the problems of child pornography and sexual grooming in the contemporary social and legal arena, this chapter examines their modern-day presentation, medical definitions of paedophilia, aetiological theories of sexual offending against children and popular social constructions of the 'paedophile'. It also explores parallels between child pornography and grooming, the way in which the internet has shaped their contemporary forms, and further reveals something of the broader framework within which I will be exploring critical tensions throughout the rest of book.

The occurrence of sexual acts involving children is certainly not a new phenomenon. Child prostitution and sexual abuse have occurred throughout antiquity.[1] Since the Middle Ages it has been a criminal offence to have sexual intercourse with girls under the age of consent in England, although until the late nineteenth century the age of sexual consent was much lower than it is today.[2] It is also true that child pornography has existed in various forms throughout history, from Ancient Greece to Victorian England.[3] It is essential, however, to consider child pornography and grooming specifically within the context of the society in which we currently live, given the existence of a number of significant factors that impact on the nature and perceived prevalence of both

1 See also Jenks 1996: 92.

2 The Offences Against the Person Act 1875 raised the age of sexual consent from twelve to thirteen and the Criminal Law Amendment Act 1885 from thirteen to sixteen.

3 See further Tate 1990; Quayle and Taylor 2005: v–vi; Edwards 1994; Edwards 2003; and O'Connell 2000.

phenomena and shape public attitudes towards them. However, at the same time, care needs to be taken when discussing and presenting the contemporary realities of child pornography and grooming. Consider the following way in which I present the problem:

> Child pornography and sexual grooming are prolific, modern-day evils of society that pose an ever-increasing threat to children. Computers and the internet have undoubtedly contributed to the increased prevalence of both child pornography and sexual grooming over the past twenty years. The widespread availability of home computers at ever-decreasing prices has led to 62 per cent of households in the UK now owning a computer, according to the most recent figures.[4] For creators of child pornography, this means that any number of the images they make can be stored in electronic format, and connecting a computer to a printer enables an unlimited number of hard copies of the images to be made. Software programs facilitate the manipulation of images and the creation of pseudo-images. For example, superimposing a child's head upon the body of an adult having graphic sexual intercourse, or turning an innocent image of a naked child into something much more provocative. The fact that all of this can be done in the privacy of an individual's home makes it easier to act in a criminal way with less fear of being detected. The internet offers child sexual abusers, pornographers and groomers real, virtual and international opportunities to achieve their aims.[5] The existence of chatrooms, e-mail, discussion boards and instant messages, for instance, have opened up new global avenues for groomers to make contact with children and provide an anonymity that makes it much easier for groomers to engage in behaviour which they would not otherwise be able to carry out. One recent example is that of Toby Studabaker. Sat at a computer in America, Studabaker used an internet chatroom to groom a twelve-year-old girl in England. After visiting her in Manchester, he took her to France and then on to Germany. Following his arrest in Frankfurt, he was charged with both abduction and incitement to gross indecency.[6] Those who wish to disseminate child pornography can send images as e-mail attachments to as many recipients as they wish with a simple click of the mouse. For those who wish to view child pornography, it is easier to download such material from an internet site than to actively seek it elsewhere and risk exposure. Moreover, the work of police forces across different countries has uncovered a vast

[4] Office for National Statistics 2007, *Regional Patterns in Family Spending 2006*. London: National Statistics: 3.

[5] 52 per cent of UK households now have an internet connection. Ibid.

[6] See 'Ex-marine jailed for child abduction', BBC News report, 2 April 2004, http://news.bbc.co.uk/1/hi/england/manchester/3594235.stm.

> number of international 'Paedophile Rings', membership of which enables individuals to share child pornography and communicate with other like-minded individuals.

Such a presentation of child pornography and stranger grooming as prevalent and growing dangers occurs commonly; in the previous chapter, I alluded to the fact that it is something that can be seen, read and heard about by anyone who has access to the media on an almost daily basis. Indeed, the intense media coverage of both stranger grooming and child pornography certainly suggests that children are increasingly at risk of falling prey to predatory pornographers and groomers. Futhermore, child pornography and stranger grooming are two parts of child sexual abuse and related behaviour that can be seen as real and present dangers, because evidence of both phenomena is available and obtainable (by way of images, texts, chat room conversations, etc.). They are thus threats that society can see, recognize and respond to more effectively than, for example, familial child sexual abuse. Common presentations of the phenomena may, however, provide a one-sided and potentially distorting account of the actual prevalence of child pornography and stranger grooming in modern-day society. It is inevitably true that the internet has increased the availability and accessibility of child pornography and provided new opportunities to groom. However, when child pornography and grooming are presented in the way I have set out above, figures regarding the number of instances of grooming or the actual propagation of child pornography (online and offline) are rarely provided, or are presented in a misleading manner.[7]

The fact that the aforementioned Studabaker case was well publicized in the UK should come as no surprise. Blacker observes that the story had elements that the media like: 'stranger-danger' and 'the "new" phenomenon of Internet grooming'.[8] In the minds of many parents, a scenario where an individual poses as a child in an internet chatroom in order to initiate a relationship with a child and begin a grooming process may be considered the most likely way in which grooming could occur. Yet, whilst the Studabaker case does provide a real example of grooming, Smallbone and Wortley's research involving self-report data completed by 169 convicted child sex offenders reveals that most of the

[7] See also Lanning 2004: 530: 'Presentations and literature with poorly documented or misleading claims about 1 in 3 children being sexually molested, the multibillion-dollar child pornography industry … and 50,000 stranger-abducted children are still common.'

[8] 'Our anxiety over the corruption of innocence', *The Independent*, 18 July 2003. See also Craven *et al.* 2007: 66.

offenders abused a child whom they knew already and had immediate or convenient access to.[9] Using data supplied by America's National Incident-Based Reporting System, Simon and Zgoba found that only 16 per cent of victims of child sex abusers were abused by strangers.[10] Such research supports the implication that many incidents of grooming are not perpetrated by strangers over the internet.[11] It is also important to bear in mind that the modern technology available within our twenty-first-century society can have a positive impact on the prevalence of child pornography and grooming. Whilst computers and the internet can provide the means to facilitate criminal behaviour related to child pornography and grooming, these technologies also provide vital evidence when an individual is prosecuted for a related offence, thereby playing an important role in combating criminal behaviour.[12]

I develop the argument that presentations of child pornography and grooming are distortive throughout the rest of this book. As child pornography and grooming are evils that have such particularly prominent profiles in our modern-day society, one would anticipate that there would be a commonality of understanding as to what amounts to such material and such behaviour in social, public and legal discourses. It is to this matter that I now turn.

CHILD PORNOGRAPHY

The history of modern-day child pornography can be traced back to the late 1960s and 1970s.[13] More liberal obscenity laws in Western Europe during this time paved the way for the commercial production of child pornography, in both film and magazine format. Denmark and Holland were particularly large producers and exporters of this material, and

[9] Smallbone and Wortley 2000; 2001; and Wortley and Smallbone 2006: 12.

[10] Simon and Zgoba 2006: 76. The data in their study related to 42,610 sex crimes reported in one year. 72 per cent of these crimes were committed against individuals aged under eighteen.

[11] See also Conte and Berliner 1981: 601; Elliott *et al.* 1995: 584; Finkelhor 1984: 90; Grosz *et al.* 2000: 11; Knudson 1988: 256; McAlinden 2006; Simon 2000: 286–7; and Craissati and McClurg 1996 (only 13 per cent of the perpetrators of child sexual abuse in their study were strangers to the children whom they committed their offences against).

[12] One way in which technologies and the anonymity offered by the internet can be used against would-be offenders is through the use of police covert sting operations, discussed in the concluding chapter, at n. 22. See also Select Committee on Home Affairs 2003: Appendix 7, para. 5 (Childnet International's memorandum).

[13] See Taylor and Quayle 2003: 42–6; and O'Donnell and Milner 2007: 4–9.

traders in these countries began to distribute to a growing number of producers and traders in the United States in exchange for American material.[14] Taylor and Quayle note that the material produced during this period still constitutes the largest part of child pornography that is currently available, having been transferred into digital format and uploaded onto the internet.[15]

Whilst there is no single universally accepted definition of child pornography, there is at least some general consensus as to what actually constitutes such material.[16] The format child pornography takes is most usually visual, in the form of photographic or filmic images. In the 1970s, when child pornography first began to be perceived as a real social problem posing a serious threat to children, such material most often appeared in magazine, film and video format. Following the criminalization of child pornography, coupled with the development of photographic technologies, material created in recent decades is most likely to be produced in the home and made available to others through the internet.[17]

The content of less hardcore pornographic photographs or videos of children can include images of naked children in provocative poses and images of children's genitalia. Child pornography can then progress from images of the child's body alone to images of the child performing sexual acts upon adults or other children and adults having sexual intercourse with the child. Extreme hardcore child pornography may include images of the infliction of sadistic, physical harm to the child and, occasionally, may even end in a child's death.[18] It is thus apparent that the material which can attract the label of child pornography is extremely broad in scope. The label can even be attached to a pseudo-photograph, generated on a computer without the involvement and abuse of an actual child. Such images can either be morphed (created through the manipulation of an innocuous image of a real child), or completely fabricated, by, for example, being computer-generated. There is, however, one significant limitation to what can legally be defined as

[14] Taylor and Quayle 2003: 43–4. [15] Ibid. 45. See also Jenkins 2001: 84.

[16] Although the question of whether material at the lower end of the scale, particularly images of naked children, should constitute child pornography is a matter that is contested (see, e.g. Higonnet 1998) and will be addressed in this book.

[17] Taylor and Quayle 2003: 45–6.

[18] Taylor and Quayle provide a grading system for the different levels of severity of child pornography images based upon material available on the internet (2003: 32). See also Sentencing Advisory Panel 2002: para. 21 (discussed in Chapter 2); Renvoize 1993: 121; and Tate 1990: 15–16 and 169–71.

child pornography; the material in question must be a photographic image, as I shall discuss in the next chapter. Whilst the current law relating to child pornography does not extend to written material that describes behaviour of a sexual nature involving children, such material could fall under the Obscene Publications Act 1959, or the common law of indecency.

Notwithstanding the broad nature of the material that can amount to child pornography, as Taylor and Quayle observe, there is an important link between all of the images that can be given this classification: 'they in some way serve a sexual purpose … for the producer and viewer'.[19] It is therefore not just the content of the image, but also the *context* in which the image is viewed and used that causes it to be described as child pornography in popular discourse.[20] For instance, parents use a digital camera to take a photograph of their naked child in the bath for their family photograph album. The use of the image in this context is highly unlikely to cause it to be given the label of child pornography.[21] However, when the parents take the camera's memory card to a photographic processing shop in order to obtain a hard copy of it, the person who transfers the digitally stored images into print makes a copy of this photograph and stores it on his computer. He then views it for his sexual gratification and distributes it to others for their gratification. The context in which the same photograph is now viewed, the purpose for which it is being used, may lead to it being labelled as an image of child pornography. The danger of such a popular perception is that, by focusing on the context in which the image is used in the current protectionist, moral-panic climate, it fosters the view that images of naked children are all potentially indecent or pornographic if individuals obtain sexual gratification from viewing them. Whether an image of a naked child is indecent and, crucially, whether a child is *harmed* by the creation of the image, surely depends on the context in which the image was taken. This is an argument I shall return to in Chapter 3. Also, I should note here that whilst popular perceptions of whether material that amounts to child pornography can be shaped by context, the legal question of whether such an image is indecent is not answered by considering the context in which the image is viewed or the intention of the person possessing it.

[19] Taylor and Quayle 2003: 5. [20] Ibid.: 33.

[21] It is also highly improbable that the parents would find themselves faced with prosecution for making an indecent photograph of a child. See *R.* v. *Smethurst* [2002] 1 Cr. App. R. 6, para. 22.

What should be apparent from the way in which we define and understand child pornography is that such material frequently depicts acts of real child sexual abuse. Some commentators simply state that child pornography *is* child sexual abuse.[22] In fact, 'child abuse images' or 'abusive images' are the preferred terms to 'child pornography' for many researchers and practitioners. This is because it is considered that the term 'child pornography' fails to convey the content of some of the material at the more severe end of the spectrum and promotes the idea that the images are merely images of naked children.[23] Thus, the rationale behind the preferred term of 'child abuse images' is predicated upon the nature of the material and the harm caused to the child. A further argument for adopting the term 'child abuse images' is presented in the following statement from the Metropolitan Police Service:

> Child pornography intimates that the child partakes … wilfully and consensually for the purpose of personal or financial gain; this is not the case. Children are usually physically sexually assaulted to create these images or coerced into believing that the pose they perform is normal. The images are in no way done for the benefit of the child. [24]

For similar reasons, in a 2007 Press Release, G-8 Ministers state that the term pornography 'mischaracterizes sexual representations where children are involved, and its continued use causes misunderstanding'.[25]

If it were indeed true that 'child pornography' is popularly understood to relate to images of naked children, there would be grounds to support the more widespread re-labelling of such material as 'child abuse images'. However, the use of the phrase 'child pornography' or 'child porn' in tabloid newspapers would surely not have the same impact if this were the case.[26] I share the same view as Ryder, who notes that it is images that record the actual sexual abuse of children which are generally thought of as child pornography.[27] Furthermore, the insertion of the word 'child' before the more general term 'pornography' undoubtedly causes a very

[22] See Watson and Lefever 2004: 198; Akdeniz 1997b: 2; and Oswell 2006: 246.

[23] See Gallagher *et al.* 2003: 353, n. 4; and Taylor and Quayle 2003: 7.

[24] Select Committee on Home Affairs 2003: Appendix 22, para. 18.

[25] 'Ministers' Declaration: Reinforcing the International Fight Against Child Pornography', Press Release, 24 May 2007, http://virtualglobaltaskforce.org/news/article_24052007.html.

[26] See, e.g. the tabloid headlines listed in the previous chapter, in n. 73. Taylor and Quayle note that: 'The media accounts of child pornography quite properly emphasise [the] extreme sexual quality of the pictures, and draw the inference that all child pornography is necessarily related to ongoing sexual assaults on children.' 2003: 4.

[27] Ryder 2003: 109.

different meaning to be attached to it than if it is preceded by the word 'adult'. Although there may be at least some truth in the argument that the term 'pornography' connotes the consensual participation of all of the parties involved, the idea that the child's involvement in child pornography can ever be consensual is not something that society would be likely to accept. As Taylor and Quayle note:

> In the case of child pornography, as with child sexual abuse, we tend to conclude that there is an imbalance of power between the child in the picture and the adult who produced it, such that the child cannot in any meaningful sense 'choose' whether or not to be in the photograph.[28]

In legal discourses, the issue of valid consent also plays a vital role in differentiating adult and child pornography. Provided both parties consent to lawful sexual activity in adult pornography, no crime is depicted. In contrast, even where a child who features in child pornography appears to consent to sexual activity, the adult involved still commits an offence.

For reasons I will elaborate on later in this book, I would argue that if the harm caused by child pornography is to be emphasized, it is more appropriate to refer to such images as exploitative images of child pornography. However, child pornography continues to be the commonly applied term, and it is the one I apply throughout this book.[29]

SEXUAL GROOMING

Grooming behaviour can share a relationship with the wider phenomenon of child sexual abuse; research has shown that an opportunity to sexually abuse a child is more likely to emerge following an act of grooming.[30] Grooming can be conceived as a predatory act committed in order to facilitate sexual abuse and, thus, the issue of context – particularly the motivation behind the behaviour – is highly relevant. The context in which initial, seemingly innocent behaviour of making contact with and forming a relationship with a child occurs is crucial in separating harmless behaviour from grooming behaviour.[31]

Finkelhor's 'Precondition Model' of child sexual abuse,[32] and theories of sex offending against children that focus on the offence process,

[28] Taylor and Quayle 2003: 2. [29] See also O'Donnell and Milner 2007: 68.

[30] Durkin 1997; Lanning 1984; Tate 1990; and Gillespie 2002: 412.

[31] See also Craven *et al.* 2006: 292. [32] Finkelhor: 1984.

provide revealing insights into the part that the grooming process can play in child sexual abuse. According to Finkelhor's model, there are four preconditions to child sex abuse. The first is a motivation to sexually abuse a child, which may exist because, for example, the individual develops emotional congruence with children, or has deviant sexual preferences. The second is overcoming the individual's inhibitions. Thirdly, the individual must also surmount any external obstacles to committing the abuse. These could include, for example, parental supervision of the child. Finally, the individual must overcome the child's resistance. As will become evident, a successful course of grooming could facilitate Finkelhor's second, third and fourth preconditions.

Research carried out by Proulx and Ouimet focuses on the decision-making process that child sex offenders engage in, and the authors found that offenders made a number of rational choices.[33] Initially, offenders decide on their 'hunting field', the place(s) where they consider it most likely that potential victims will be found. They will then consider the time that offers the best opportunity for their offending. Next, they choose their victim 'type' on the basis of her erotic value, vulnerability and familiarity. They must then choose the strategy they will employ to approach the victim and, subsequently, to have sexual contact with her. Applying this model, if the offender engages in a grooming process before committing a sexual offence against a child, the rational choices he makes about how to approach the victim and how to best facilitate sexual contact could well shape this process.

Ward *et al.* offer a particularly comprehensive and empirically informed 'Descriptive Model of the Offense Chain'.[34] Based upon the descriptions and experiences of convicted child sex offenders, the model reveals nine distinct stages to the child sex abuse offence chain. First, the initial stage in the offence chain relates to the offender's background, his lifestyle and circumstances and positive and negative 'affected states'. These background factors impact on the later stages in the chain. At the second stage, the offender engages in distal planning, covertly or explicitly arranging contact or unintentionally coming into contact with the child to facilitate the offence. Stage three is the occurrence of non-sexual contact with the child and this is followed by the offender consciously or unconsciously restructuring perceptions of the situation, and perhaps his relationship with the child, at stage four. The fifth stage

[33] Proulx and Ouimet 1995: 294–310. Discussed in Beauregard and Leclerc 2007: 117.

[34] Ward *et al.* 1995. See also Craven *et al.* 2006: 291.

relates to the seduction process, 'the immediate precursors to the sexual offense'.[35] This stage is influenced by cognitive distortions in which the offender focuses on his own needs, the needs of the child, or mutual needs. The actual offence occurs at stage six. At stage seven, further cognitive restructuring occurs and the offender engages in positive or negative evaluations of what has occurred. The final two stages involve the offender's future resolutions about future offending, based upon the negative or positive evaluation of his behaviour.[36]

The grooming process could, then, be enabled at the second stage, begin at the third stage and be completed at the fifth stage of the chain. Grooming of another child could occur afterwards, if the offender's evaluations of the offence in the seventh stage are positive and the resolutions he makes in the final two stages are to continue offending. There is no explicit discussion of grooming in the authors' presentation of the model, but this is not an unusual absence in models of sex offending against children. Craven *et al.* argue that it is vital for such theories as have been discussed here to encompass the grooming process in order to facilitate a greater understanding of the whole process of child sexual abuse. However, their analysis of the current research leads them to conclude that these theories have largely neglected to account for the role that grooming plays, since they were formulated before grooming was recognized as a distinct stage in sexual offending.[37]

What, then, does the existing research reveal about the phenomenon of grooming? Gillespie notes that grooming is increasingly seen as being a 'distinct behavioural type',[38] as behaviour that can be identified and targeted in order to reduce the occurrence of child sexual abuse. It seems that, in a similar vein to child pornography, 'sexual grooming' is a label that has a very broad application. Any behaviour that is designed to build up a relationship of trust with a child with the longer-term goal of involving the child in some sexually related act or acts could constitute grooming. Groomers often target vulnerable children lacking in confidence, with low self-esteem or who are emotionally deprived.[39] Craven *et al.* differentiate between physical grooming, which they define as the actual sexualization of the relationship between the groomer and the child, and psychological grooming, which enables the relationship to

[35] Ward *et al.* 1995: 463. [36] Ibid.: 461–5. [37] Craven *et al.* 2006: 291 and 297.

[38] Gillespie 2006: 412.

[39] Conte *et al.* 1989: 298–9; Elliott *et al.* 1995: 584; Kaufman *et al.* 2006: 119; Marshall *et al.* 2006: 40; McAlinden 2006: 349; and Wortley and Smallbone 2006: 24.

become sexual.[40] Psychological grooming strategies include convincing the child that the suggested behaviour is both natural and commonplace, the presentation of abuse as a game, bribery and coercion, giving gifts and gradually introducing and desensitizing the child to sexual activities.[41] A police officer I interviewed highlighted the grooming tactics he tended to encounter in his work:

> Gifts, drugs ... A lot of the time, it's vulnerable young people who don't get any love at home [and] are out there, looking for some sort of affection. And some of these predators recognise that. So a lot of the time, it's in return for a bit of attention ... But, gifts are really prevalent ... It depends on the individual circumstances of that particular victim. [Groomers] pick up on ... [young] people's vulnerabilities and exploit them for their own ends.[42]

Other officers gave examples of the giving of gifts and alcohol,[43] flattery, attention, monetary rewards, threats and blackmail.[44] The variety of forms of psychological grooming that can occur is further demonstrated by an Australian study, which revealed that the convicted child sex offenders who took part in the study used a variety of strategies for getting the child to go with them to the place where sexual contact occurred. These included promising rewards or privileges, telling the child they (the offenders) could be trusted and giving the child money.[45]

A successful course of grooming the child should, therefore, fulfil Finkelhor's fourth precondition, namely overcoming the child's resistance. Psychological grooming can continue after sexual abuse has occurred, in order to facilitate further abuse and to prevent the child from disclosing what has happened. The groomer may, for example, tell the child that she is responsible for the abuse because she did not stop it occurring.[46] If the groomer is a family member, he may threaten the child about repercussions for the family if she reveals the abuse.[47]

The powerful nature of the grooming process was emphasized by two of the police officers in my study. One referred to a case involving a young teenage girl who had been groomed. She had met the man and gone to

[40] Craven *et al.* 2006: 295. Coercive, manipulative and non-persuasive strategies (the latter being where the groomer waits for an opportunity to abuse to present itself, rather than utilizing particular strategies) can be involved in the grooming process. See further Leclerc *et al.* 2006.

[41] Elliott *et al.* 1995: 585–6.

[42] Interview RX4.

[43] Interviews RX3, RX5 and RX7.

[44] Interviews RX2, RX5, RX6 and RX8.

[45] Smallbone and Wortley 2000.

[46] Craven *et al.* 2006: 296.

[47] Christiansen and Blake 1990: 96.

a hotel with him on numerous prior occasions. When the police became aware of what was happening and went to arrest the individual concerned, the officer was amazed that he had been able to hold such power over the girl: 'Even to this point where this person was horribly unkempt and unhygienic, she was still prepared to go along with him. I think that astonished me in relation to the power when somebody grooms somebody and gets them to the point where they're unable to break that cycle of grooming and abuse.'[48] Another officer discussed a case that had also involved the grooming of a young teenage girl. He stated that:

> The grooming process is very subtle, it changes kids in ways you wouldn't expect them to be changed sometimes. Even though there are strong motivational factors not to do what they're doing, so much so that she completely broke down after the offence had been found. Her parents did the same. The whole family unit needed building back up which is a massive motivational factor not to do it. She'd lied about it when she was doing it, so she must have had that inkling, but wasn't strong enough to do anything. [49]

Recent research evidences that it is not just the child who is targeted by grooming behaviour. Individuals must also groom themselves, the community and 'significant others'. 'Self grooming' involves the individual justifying or denying their behaviour.[50] This could be seen as an aspect of Finkelhor's second precondition of the individual overcoming his own inhibitions, a necessary precursor in order for the individual to proceed, and as an example of behaviour occurring during the fourth and seventh stage in Ward *et al.*'s 'Descriptive Model'. Grooming the community and significant others, such as parents and teachers, enables a groomer to gradually place himself in a position of trust that will present opportunities to have access to and groom children,[51] reflecting the second stage in the 'Descriptive Model'. Research also indicates that child sex abusers hone in on single-parent families or otherwise vulnerable families. They may undertake babysitting responsibilities or look to embed themselves more firmly within the family unit by becoming involved in a relationship with the child's parent.[52] This is supported by the experiences of police officers who participated in my study. One commented: 'Grooming in the home … we get repeat offenders. There are people who move on from one family to another and within a period

[48] Interview RX2. [49] Interview RX5. [50] Craven *et al.* 2006: 292.
[51] Ibid.: 293; Salter 2004: 42–44; and van Dam 2001.
[52] Elliott *et al.* 1995: 585; and McAlinden 2006: 349.

of time ingratiate themselves within that family and get access to the children. Then they commit serious offences against those children and then they move on to somewhere else.'[53]

Once intrafamilial status is gained, the child's parent can then be groomed further by being encouraged to go out more and leave the child in the abuser's care.[54] Child sex abusers may look for particular types of employment in which such opportunities are more likely to exist, working in schools, nursery schools and residential homes, for example.[55] It is also possible that community grooming can conceal a successful child sex abuser's offending since, if a child does subsequently expose the abuse, the community may have become so convinced that the abuser is a trustworthy individual that he is more likely to be believed than the child.[56] Thus, grooming significant others and the community could realize the third of Finkelhor's preconditions: removing external barriers to committing the abuse.

Careful to offer a definition of grooming that encompasses all the dimensions and variations of the phenomenon, Craven *et al.* propose that it amounts to:

> A process by which a person prepares a child, significant adults and the environment for the abuse of this child. Specific goals include gaining access to the child, gaining the child's compliance and maintaining the child's secrecy to avoid disclosure. This process serves to strengthen the offender's abusive pattern, as it may be used as a means of justifying or denying their actions.[57]

An example of grooming given particular prominence in recent media coverage is the sending of text messages to a child's mobile phone.[58] Such texts may initially be seemingly innocent messages that enable the groomer to strike up a relationship with the child. Once this relationship is in place and the groomer has gained the child's trust, the texts can then become more flirtatious and suggestive in nature and, ultimately, the groomer may request a meeting with the child so that the relationship can be taken forward. Another popular example of grooming is that involving the use of internet chatrooms to make initial contact with a

[53] Interview RX3. Two other officers made similar observations: Interviews RX5 and RX8.

[54] Craven *et al.* 2006: 293. [55] Sullivan and Beech 2002: 163; and McAlinden 2006: 349–50.

[56] Craven *et al.* 2006: 293. [57] Ibid.: 297.

[58] See, e.g. 'Text error led to "sex grooming"', BBC News report, 22 August 2005, http://news.bbc.co.uk/1/hi/wales/4174064.stm; 'Children groomed by phone', *Oxford Mail*, 3 March 2008; 'Teacher "groomed" vulnerable schoolboys with lewd text messages', *Irish Examiner*, 6 January 2004; and 'Girl, 14 groomed for sex', *Manchester Evening News*, 7 November 2007.

child. When the groomer has attracted the child's attention, he can, for example, move the communications to a private chatroom that he has created exclusively for himself and the child.[59] A similar process of gaining the child's trust through online conversations with the ultimate aim of instigating a meeting can then occur. Both of these examples of grooming behaviour offer the groomer a valuable tool to achieve his purposes – anonymity. The ability to conceal his identity, and perhaps to pose as another child, can enable him to convince the child to meet him following a successful course of grooming.[60] What needs to be borne in mind, however, is that despite the media's focus on the use of modern technologies to groom, this is not the only method through which grooming can occur. In fact, taking into account the evidence that the majority of child sexual abuse is perpetrated by someone known to the child,[61] it is much more likely that grooming in other contexts occurs more commonly.[62] Indeed, McAlinden has argued that significant others or 'familial' grooming and institutional grooming are phenomena that legal and social responses have so far failed to address.[63]

Given the vast array of grooming strategies and opportunities which are utilized, there is no such thing as a 'typical' groomer, either in terms of the grooming method employed or the groomer's background. This was a matter discussed by four of the officers I interviewed:

> I don't think there is one general groomer. People with … no previous convictions for sexual offending, they'll come across the child in the street, the child might start some conversation and then they'll continue as if it's an ordinary relationship but for the age of the child. But then you see others, within the home, a member of the family who starts grooming for instance. They will use different strategies. They might

[59] See O'Connell 2003; and Gallagher *et al.* 2003. O'Connell's empirical research reveals five possible stages of online grooming: friendship forming, relationship forming, risk assessment, exclusivity and sexual stages (8–9).

[60] In *R.* v. *Mansfield* [2005] EWCA Crim. 927, *R.* v. *Kingsley* [2006] EWCA Crim. 546; and *Attorney General's Reference (no. 64 of 2003)* [2003] EWCA Crim. 3948, each of the groomers initially deceived their child victims about their age and identity.

[61] See the discussion in the next section.

[62] One of the police officers involved in my study commented that: 'Not all grooming occurs over the Internet. Most grooming doesn't occur over the Internet from what I've seen.' Interview RX5. In the experience of another: 'Internet grooming may occur, but it's in the minority rather than the majority of cases that I deal with.' Interview RX8.

[63] McAlinden 2006. McAlinden uses the phrase 'institutional grooming' to refer to the grooming of organizations and employment settings which will provide the individual with access to children (2006: 352–3).

> leave pornographic literature lying around to decrease the sensitisation of the child. I don't think there's one homogeneous grooming group.[64]
>
> If you're looking at it demographically, who are the most likely people to commit this, I've [seen people] right across the board. From somebody with no previous convictions whatsoever who was just completely leading a double life … a family at home, wife at home … daughters the same age as the person they're grooming and the wife who was oblivious to the fact this was going on behind the scenes … To the point where I've also dealt with predatory sex offenders who have also been previously convicted of targeting children.[65]

As I will now discuss, this accords with the findings of the existing research that child sex abusers are not a homogenous group.

THE PAEDOPHILE AND THE CHILD SEXUAL ABUSER

It is beyond the scope of this book to engage in an in-depth analysis of medical understandings of paedophilia and aetiological aspects of sexual offending against children. However, I present a brief examination of paedophilia as a sexual orientation, of various theories on sexual offending against children and studies on the characteristics of creators and consumers of child pornography and groomers, and of popular constructions of the paedophile here, in order to place my research in the wider setting.

One characteristic that the child pornographer and the groomer may have in common is a paedophilic interest in children.[66] Narratives involving the 'paedophile' make regular appearances in newspaper articles and in news reports on the television and radio, and thus it is unsurprising that certain constructions about individuals who are ascribed this label have been formed. A paedophile can be defined in ordinary layman's terms as 'a person feeling sexual attraction to children'.[67] Psychiatric definitions focus on a sexual attraction to children, one example being 'a person with a perversion in relation to sexual interest in children'.[68] According to the diagnostic criteria for paedophilia, the object of the

64 Interview RX1. Similar comments were made by other officers: Interviews RX5 and RX7.

65 Interview RX2.

66 According to research by Seto *et al.*, child pornography offending is a strong indicator of paedophilia. Seto *et al.* 2006.

67 Oxford Dictionary and Thesaurus 1997. Oxford University Press.

68 Glasser 1990: 739–48. Paedophiles may (or may not) also have a sexual attraction to adults. See the American Psychiatric Association 1994: 527. For a useful consideration of the definition of a 'paedophile', see Araji and Finkelhor 1986: 89–90. Cowburn and Dominelli provide a num-

paedophile's interest is generally a prepubescent child aged thirteen or younger.[69] This medical understanding of the term indicates inaccuracies in other available definitions of a paedophile, such as the following: 'any adult who shows an active interest in sexually engaging with a child below the legal age of consent'.[70] Thus, to be described as a paedophile, an individual must find children – usually prepubescent children – sexually attractive. The paedophile's personality is manifested in sexual thoughts and desires. Although paedophiles might subsequently act out their sexual fantasies and commit child sexual abuse, committing child sexual abuse is not a requisite element of the paedophilic personality according to the standard dictionary definition, medical definitions of the term and clinical diagnosis.[71] Craven *et al.* caution against labelling all child sex offenders as paedophiles, since this could prevent some offenders from recognizing and accepting their grooming behaviour, and leave individuals oblivious to the risk posed by offenders who do not meet the common perception of the paedophile.[72]

Recent psychological and criminological research reveals that child sex abusers may not be driven to commit sexual offences against children by a powerful paedophilic sexual desire, that there are other factors that lead to the occurrence of child sex abuse.[73] Wortley and Smallbone's research found that, at the time of their first sexual contact with a child, the offenders' mean age was thirty-two years. This suggests to the authors that 'strong sexually deviant motivations' to sexually abuse children cannot be so influential, given that the offenders must have been able to resist them for so long, as did the fact that less than a quarter of the

ber of definitions adopted by psychologists, clinical practitioners and sociologists. Cowburn and Dominelli 2001: 401–3.

69 American Psychiatric Association, 1994: 528.

70 Carr 2003: 1, n. 7. The limitation of a paedophile's attraction to a child below the legal age of sexual consent in Carr's definition may pose additional difficulties, given that this age differs depending upon jurisdiction. Carr provided an alternative and equally problematic definition of a paedophile as 'someone who sexually abuses children' in 'Net blamed for rise in child porn', BBC News report, 12 January 2004, http://news.bbc.co.uk/1/hi/technology/3387377.stm.

71 See also Lanning 2004: 542; and Taylor and Quayle 2003: 12. Simon and Zgoba state that: 'for a clinical diagnosis of … pedophilia [sic], an individual does not need to engage in sexual activity with a child … an individual needs to have fantasized about sexual activity with a prepubescent child for at least six months, so long as the fantasies or sexual urges cause clinically significant distress or impairment in social, occupational, or other important areas of functioning'. Simon and Zgoba 2006: 91.

72 Craven *et al.* 2006: 288. See also Salter 2004: 71.

73 See Simon *et al.* 1992; Simon and Zgoba 2006: 68–9; and Smallbone and Wortley 2004. Only between 8.5 and 14 per cent of child sexual abusers in Simon's study had been diagnosed as paedophiles. Simon 2000: 287.

offenders had prior convictions for sexual offences.[74] Nearly one-half of them had offended against one victim only and 60 per cent had previous convictions for non-sexual offences, leading the authors to argue that: 'For these offenders, the problem seems to be less some special motivation to sexually abuse children than a more general problem involving the failure to inhibit urges and impulses, especially within the interpersonal domain.'[75] In their view, the findings tend to support the argument that it is a control model rather than a sexual deviance model that best fits many child sex offenders.[76] Under such a model, the primary cause of criminal behaviour is a lack of restraint. Individuals become unable to resist the temptation to commit crime due to the absence or failure of controlling factors which prevent them from offending.[77] There may then be a significant hedonistic aspect to child sex offenders' behaviour, although other research indicates that they can be rational decision-makers.[78]

Perhaps most importantly, the existing research reveals that there is no 'typical' child sex abuser, that individuals who sexually abuse children have differing life experiences, personal characteristics and criminal histories.[79] In the 1980s, work began on providing taxonomic models of child sex abusers, and a division was drawn between regressed or fixated offenders.[80] Regressed offenders are described as being likely to have age-appropriate sexual relationships, before regressing to a sexual interest in children. Their offending against children tends to be prompted by external stressors such as marital difficulties or unemployment. They may also be led to offend because of negative emotional states, including anxiety and loneliness. Such offenders are usually attracted to adults and their sexual interest in children is temporary.[81] Fixated offenders are hypothesized to focus their sexual interest on children and to be unlikely to have age-appropriate sexual relationships. According to the existing research, fixated offenders tend to commit premeditated actions and, thus, they are likely to undertake a grooming process prior to beginning a sexual relationship with a child. They are also more likely to be diagnosed with paedophilia.[82]

However, further research has indicated that the regressed/fixated typologies are not homogenous and do not account for all child sexual

[74] Wortley and Smallbone 2006: 11. [75] Ibid.: 12. [76] Ibid.: 12–13.

[77] See, e.g. Gottfredson and Hirschi 1990; and Hirschi 1969.

[78] See Beauregard and Leclerc 2007: 117 and 126–7; and Simon and Zgoba 2006: 69. I should make it clear here that I am not claiming that it is a sudden, impulsive lack of control that causes individuals to groom children for sexual abuse. As the earlier section on grooming should confirm, the nature of the process evidences careful, premeditated planning.

[79] Prentky *et al.* 1997: 2. [80] Quayle *et al.* 2006: 21. [81] Ibid.: 22. [82] Ibid.: 21.

abusers.[83] In 1989, Knight *et al.* offered a multi-dimensional typologies model which concentrates on the degree to which offenders are sexually interested in children, the offenders' level of social competence (Axis 1 typology), their amount of contact with children and the degree of violence involved in offenders' contact with children (Axis 2 typology).[84] An offender is assigned a separate typology under each axis. In a later study replicating this model, only offenders who fell within the high fixation–low social competence under Axis 1 had a definite sexual preference for children.[85]

Ward and Keenan argue that child sex offenders show cognitive distortions which are generated by five core implicit theories that offenders have about themselves, their victims, the non-harmful impact their behaviour has on their victims and their environment.[86] These theories are: seeing children as sexual objects, entitlement to special consideration, a dangerous world, uncontrollability and the nature of harm.[87] According to Quayle *et al.*, existing research suggests that child sex abusers justify their behaviour 'by neutralizing their guilt, through claims that they are helping the child to learn about sex, that sexual education is good for the child, that the child enjoys it, that there is no harm being done to the child, that the child initiated the sexual contact and that the child acts older than they are'.[88] Such justifications serve to free offenders of any remorse or guilt for their actions.[89] More recently, research has evidenced that it is not only various predispositions and implicit theories which play a role in sex offenders' behaviour, but also situational factors, such as the victim's response to their actions.[90] For example, Ward and Siegert's 'Pathways Model'[91] suggests that there are five different pathways that lead to child sexual abuse.[92] Each pathway features primary psychological mechanisms caused by interacting learning events, biological and cultural factors that make an individual vulnerable to committing child sexual abuse. In each of the pathways, 'situational triggers interact with the various predispositions of individuals to violate children, and thus result in sexually abusive behaviour'.[93]

[83] Ibid.: 22; Finkelhor and Araji 1986; Prentky *et al.* 1997: 5; and Ward *et al.* 1995: 468.

[84] Knight *et al.* 1989; Prentky *et al.* 1997: 6–7; and Quayle *et al.* 2006: 22.

[85] Looman *et al.* 2001: 763. See also Quayle *et al.* 2006: 22.

[86] Ward and Keenan 1999. See also Proulx and Ouimet 1999: 125.

[87] Ward and Keenan 1999: 827–32. [88] Quayle *et al.* 2006: 19. [89] Ibid.

[90] Beauregard and Leclerc 2007. [91] Ward and Siegert 2002.

[92] The five pathways are as follows: intimacy deficits, deviant sexual scripts, emotional disregulation, anti-social cognitions and multiple dysfunctional mechanisms. Ibid.: 335–9.

[93] Ibid.: 341.

Specific research has been conducted regarding offenders who use the internet to facilitate child sexual abuse. In their study of American internet-related sex crimes against children, Wolak *et al.* found that 37 per cent of those individuals who produced child pornography were family members and 36 per cent were acquaintances. Strangers who created child pornography accounted for just 5 per cent of the 122 internet-related cases of producing child pornography that featured in the authors' study.[94] Middleton *et al.* have recently applied Ward and Siegert's 'Pathways Model' of offending in their study involving offenders convicted of creating, distributing and possessing indecent images of children offences, who had made use of the internet. Their findings reveal that such individuals may reflect a range of different offender types, from low to high deviance.[95] They conclude that: 'The research supports the suggestion that men who use the Internet to obtain indecent images of children are not a homogeneous group.'[96] This conclusion is also supported by Quayle *et al.*'s research, which found that such individuals were of all different ages, from varying social backgrounds. While some had a history of sexual offending, some did not and some had not previously acknowledged any sexual interest in children.[97]

Other researchers have created typologies of offenders who use the internet for offences related to child pornography and grooming. Beech *et al.* provide an overview of these typologies, concluding that four broad classificatory groups for internet offenders emerge:

> (1) Individuals who access abusive images sporadically, impulsively and/or out of curiosity; (2) individuals who access/trade abusive images of children to fuel their sexual interest in children; (3) individuals who use the Internet as part of a pattern of offline contact offending, including (i) those who use the Internet as a tool for locating and/or grooming contact victims and (ii) those who use the Internet to disseminate images that they have produced; and (4) individuals who access abusive images for seemingly non-sexual reasons (eg, for financial profit).[98]

As with child sex abusers, it thus seems that internet offenders have varying backgrounds and motivations for their use of the internet.

It is clearly apparent that the existing research findings do not reflect one of the most common popular perceptions of child sex abusers, that the 'usual' sexual abuser of children is a stranger.[99] The existing research

[94] Wolak *et al.* 2005: 35. [95] Middleton *et al.* 2005: 106. [96] Ibid.

[97] Quayle *et al.* 2006: 2. [98] Beech *et al.* 2008: 225.

[99] Kitzinger 2004: 157. See also Bell 2002: 87.

overwhelmingly demonstrates that child sexual abusers are most commonly individuals known to the child.[100] It is no doubt disturbing for us to accept this reality, as we must then recognize the fact that individuals who sexually abuse children are 'normal' people, like ourselves, people who we see as having a responsibility to nurture and protect children. It is much easier to shield ourselves with the belief that paedophiles are 'others' in our society, strangers and abnormal individuals harbouring socially unacceptable, immoral sexual desires for children whom we can easily distance ourselves from.[101] Kitzinger argues that it is the media that is partly responsible for this conception, given that news reports tend to focus by and large on 'stranger-attacks'. Her empirical research also demonstrates, however, that public discourses and social interaction play a significant role in bolstering the commonly held belief that strangers pose more of a threat than someone the child knows.[102] In addition, people often believe that they should somehow just *know* if a person in their community is a paedophile and simply would not suspect that a normal, respectable individual in their social circle could pose a threat to children.[103]

In light of the research findings currently available, therefore, I do not want to underestimate the occurrence of behaviour related to child pornography and grooming in the domestic setting. This is especially because intrafamilial child sexual abuse tends to be of a longer duration than extrafamilial abuse and progresses more quickly to more serious forms of abuse, according to Fischer and McDonald's research.[104] Taylor and Quayle conclude that: 'The regrettable reality is … that people who have legitimate access to a child produce most child pornography in domestic settings.'[105] Their research also indicates that the person who creates the image of child pornography is most likely to be someone close to the child, a member of their family or a family friend.[106]

A social construction that is in fact borne out by the existing research is that the child sex abuser is most commonly male.[107] As Kleinhans notes: 'while female sexual predators do exist, their representation among

100 See the references in nn. 9–11 above.

101 See also Bell 2002: 96–7; Craven *et al.* 2006: 292; Lanning 2004: 532; and Meyer 2007: 2.

102 Kitzinger 2004: ch. 7. See also Cowburn and Dominelli 2001: 404; and Surette and Otto 2001: 150.

103 Kitzinger 2004: 137.

104 Fischer and McDonald 1998: 926.

105 Taylor and Quayle 2003: 206.

106 Ibid.: 23.

107 Wortley and Smallbone 2006: 5. In the specific context of child pornography offenders, in their study of 205 convicted offenders on the Ontario Sex Offender Registry, Seto and Eke found that only one offender was female. Seto and Eke 2005: 203.

paedophilic sexual offenders is so minimal as to preclude the use of gender-inclusive language in referring to these offenders'.[108] Consequently, as already noted, throughout this book I refer to the child sex abuser, child pornographer or groomer as 'he' rather than 'she'. I disagree with Cowburn and Dominelli that the media's heavy reliance on the label of the 'paedophile' is problematic, since it 'ignores the importance of gender and obscures the reality that most sex offenders are men'.[109] There would be a certain truth to this contention if representations of 'paedophiles' and child sexual offenders in the media were disproportionately focused on women. However, in recent years, relevant headlines in the press and news reports on the television and radio have, by and large, related to men.[110]

A particular focus of contemporary stories in the press involving the 'paedophile' is the question of whether the danger posed by child sex offenders is being adequately assessed.[111] Media campaigns have given rise to calls that communities should have a right to know when a convicted and released child sex offender is living in their midst.[112] Sensationalist media coverage of the danger posed by paedophiles has also fuelled community protests and a more radical, vigilante public response in certain cases.[113] Significantly, in the light of this work's focus on constructed vulnerability, the targeting of child sex offenders with threats and acts of violence has caused *them* to become a vulnerable

[108] Kleinhans 2002: 251, n. 1. It should be borne in mind, however, that child sexual abuse perpetrated by women may be under-reported and women often have easier access to child victims because of accepted cultural norms. See Taylor and Quayle 2003: 66–8; and Salter 2004: 76–9.

[109] Cowburn and Dominelli 2001: 408.

[110] I could find only three notable cases involving female paedophiles that featured in the press in the past four-and-a-half years. The first is that of Tanya French who played a part in her partner's rape of a baby. See 'Baby fiend's jail terror', *The Sun*, 3 April 2006. The second is that of Kelly Trueman, who was convicted for the indecent assault of a twelve-year-old girl. See 'Lesbian jailed for assault', *The Sun*, 8 March 2004. The third case is that of Tammy Fuller, convicted for indecently assaulting a ten-year-old boy. See 'The woman paedophile who stole my son's innocence', *The Mirror*, 22 August 2005.

[111] A point also made by Cowburn and Dominelli 2001. See, e.g. 'Police blunders freed paedophile to strike again', *Daily Mail*, 8 September 2006; 'Schools failing to protect children from paedophiles', *The Independent*, 20 June 2006; 'Paedo in family hotel room', *The Sun*, 30 June 2006; 'Freed paedo snatches tot', *The Sun*, 8 April 2006; 'Paedophile was set free to rape young children in their homes', *The Observer*, 23 July 2006; and 'On the run – the child snatcher', *Daily Mirror*, 25 May 2006.

[112] The most prominent being the *News of the World* newspaper's campaign for 'Sarah's Law' in the wake of the abduction and murder of Sarah Payne. See www.forsarah.com/html/sarahslaw.html.

[113] See Kitzinger 2004: 145–8; and Bell 2002: 85–6.

group in society, in direct contrast to their status as the powerful party in the context of the abuser/victim relationship.

Just as some, but not all, paedophiles are actual child sexual abusers and not all child sexual offenders are paedophiles, it is important to note that not all people who are involved in child pornography or grooming will necessarily be child sex offenders.[114] The individual who attempts to groom a child may be unsuccessful in his grooming technique and, consequently, not become a child sex offender. The person who distributes child pornography is not necessarily involved in the actual abuse that took place to create the image, and the individual who downloads such material might have no engagement with any contact sexual offences.[115] Unless they are involved with child pornography purely for commercial purposes or their involvement is forced, however, the creator and distributor might share a paedophilic interest in children, as may the individual who seeks child pornography to keep in his personal possession. However, there is at least one circumstance in which an individual without any motivation or desire to sexually abuse a child can come into contact with child pornography. It is possible for an individual to innocently come across such material by, for example, downloading an e-mail attachment when he is completely unaware that it contains child pornography. I will consider whether an individual in these circumstances would have a defence if charged with offences relating to child pornography in the following chapter.

EXPLORING PARALLELS BETWEEN CHILD PORNOGRAPHY AND SEXUAL GROOMING

Whilst child pornography and sexual grooming are clearly distinct phenomena, there is an obvious parallel between them: both are methods of exploiting children's vulnerability. One way in which pornographers and groomers can exploit children's vulnerability revolves around the issue of consent. In legal discourses, a child is deemed incapable of giving consent to an act of sexual intercourse until she reaches the age of sexual consent and she is unable to consent to being the subject of an indecent

[114] In fact, Taylor and Quayle's clinical model of child pornography offending focuses upon the processes of such offending within the broader spectrum of criminal behaviour on the internet, rather than exploring the sexual qualities of offences. Taylor and Quayle 2006: 183–5.

[115] Interestingly, recent research has suggested that a significant number of internet offenders do not have the psychological vulnerabilities that sexual contact offenders display. See Middleton *et al.* 2006; and Taylor and Quayle 2003: 173.

image until she reaches the age of eighteen. Thus, the child pornographer either forces the child to be the subject of the image, or obtains the child's invalid and coerced consent. If the groomer is successful, the consent he obtains from the child to engage in sexual activity would also not be recognized by law, and this consent may have been obtained through coercion, deception or a breach of trust. Moreover, social discourses reject the idea that children can give valid consent to sexual activity and/or involvement in child pornography to a person who is much older than them.

Sometimes there can also be a significant physical link between child pornography and grooming. If an individual is successful in his attempts to groom a child, one of the subsequent offences could involve the recording of any sexual abuse which does takes place.[116] A groomer who gains a child's trust may convince her to take pornographic images of herself and send these images to him.[117] Furthermore, research suggests that pornography is sometimes used as a 'seduction method' during the grooming process, to convince a child that taking part in sexual activities is both normal and acceptable.[118] There is also research indicating that some individuals who produce child pornography may utilize methods used by groomers to gain access to children. Some of the ways in which the child pornography producers in the study conducted by Wolak *et al.* acquired access to children were by associating themselves with schools and youth organizations and by becoming close to families by taking a special interest in the children.[119] There are numerous reported cases where there is evidence of a possible correlative link between child pornography and grooming.[120] According to one of the police officers I interviewed: 'It's unusual to find somebody who has groomed an individual who hasn't got indecent images of children on their computer as well.'[121]

[116] See, e.g. *HM Advocate* v. *Millbank (Joseph) (Sentencing)* [2002] SLT 1116; *Attorney General's Reference (no. 3 of 2006)* [2006] EWCA Crim. 695; *Robertson* v. *HM Advocate* (2004) JC 155; *Attorney General's Reference (no. 64 of 2003)*; and *R.* v. *Wilson*.

[117] See Wolak *et al.* 2008: 120.

[118] See Kaufman *et al.* 2006: 121; Marshall *et al.* 2006: 52; O'Connell 2003: 11; and Taylor and Quayle 2003: 23. Note that most of the available research reveals that it is adult pornography which tends to be used.

[119] Wolak *et al.* 2005: 35.

[120] See, e.g. 'Man, 54, jailed for web grooming', BBC News report, 1 March 2007, http://news.bbc.co.uk/1/hi/wales/north_west/6410013.stm. A search on the BBC News website (http://news.bbc.co.uk) for grooming cases reveals a large number of reported cases where the defendant was charged with meeting a child following a sexual grooming offence and one or more child pornography offences.

[121] Interview RX2.

I should note, however, that whilst a physical association between the two phenomena is indicated by some of the existing research,[122] it is not proven. Also, it would be inaccurate to claim that there is a definite and necessary link between child pornography and grooming – only some individuals who possess child pornography will groom children, and only some groomers will collect child pornography, for example.

There is an additional parallel regarding the way in which the harms of possessing child pornography and grooming can be constructed. As I noted in the previous chapter, criminalizing possession can be perceived as taking action primarily to avoid potential and more remote forms of harm. Unless the individual actually created the child pornography he possesses, most of the arguments in favour of criminalization do not start from the premise that his behaviour has caused direct harm to the child. As I will discuss in Chapter 3, the 'market reduction' argument is essentially concerned with potential harm to other children, as are the claims that the possessor will be incited to commit child sexual abuse by viewing child pornography and that his and society's shared morality will be corrupted if possession is permitted. The only construction of harm argument that is premised on the possessor's behaviour actually having harmed a child is that the knowledge that the image is being distributed and possessed by others causes additional and continued psychological suffering to the child involved.

THE INTERNET AND THE CHILD: A DOUBLE VULNERABILITY?

> [The Internet] is not responsible for the 'invention' of abuse images, nor has it created a demand that wasn't already there. Children were being sexually exploited before the Internet, and no doubt when we have solved the problems of the Internet, other forms of exploitation will emerge. What the Internet does do is to make abuse images of children relatively easily available, at little or no cost, in circumstances of perceived anonymity.[123]

It is impossible to examine the modern-day phenomena of child pornography and grooming without considering the impact of the internet

[122] Taylor and Quayle provide a case study example of an individual who attempted to groom children over the internet after his desire to make contact with a child was increased by accessing child pornography. Taylor and Quayle 2003: 108–14. See also Alexy *et al.* 2005.

[123] Quayle and Taylor 2005: vi.

and its utilization by producers, distributors and possessors of child pornography and groomers to achieve their aims. The advent of the internet may have led to the existence of a double vulnerability in the context of child pornography and grooming. The internet is a site of vulnerability because of the difficulty of regulation across national boundaries[124] and the relative anonymity of users. When the internet's susceptibility to abuse is presented alongside the vulnerable status of children using it, there would appear to be attractive opportunities available to child pornographers and groomers. These opportunities may be particularly attractive because of the added security the internet provides as a means of facilitating criminal behaviour, such as the ability to conceal the identification of the location and computer that is used to upload child pornography onto the internet. As I have already noted, being able to conceal one's identity could assist groomers in reaching their ultimate goal. They can wait until a later stage in the grooming process to uncover their true identity, when they are confident that the relationship they have forged with the child is strong enough to withstand this revelation. Futhermore, groomers who use the internet can place their computer in a secure environment where they can have sustained access to communications such as e-mail, chatrooms and instant messaging.[125] Using such communications, groomers can look to meet and develop a relationship with a child, gaining the child's trust and confidence.[126]

It is of significant note that groomers who utilize the internet tend to pursue adolescents rather than younger children and thus, as Wolak *et al.* observe, they may not fit the clinical definition of a paedophile as someone who is attracted to prepubescent children.[127] Groomers utilizing the internet can target particular vulnerabilities, such as a young adolescent's naivety or insecurity. One police officer I interviewed stated that, in his experience, groomers take advantage of:

> the naivety of young girls who would perhaps send an explicit picture of themselves, either clothed or revealing an intimate part of themselves, and then as soon as that happens, [the groomer has] got the potential for blackmail. [He] can impose complete command and control over that person by way of the veiled threats, proper threats, blackmail ... 'I'll send this to your friends, I'll put them on posters all around where you live'

[124] See, e.g. Taylor and Quayle 2006: 173; and Jenkins 2001: 183.

[125] Quayle *et al.* 2006: 76; and Wolak *et al.* 2008: 112.

[126] Wolak *et al.* 2008: 116.

[127] Ibid.: 118–19.

> ... [Or there is] the insecure thirteen or fourteen-year-old girl who's not particularly well liked at school, doesn't have many friends and the internet becomes a pseudo-friend of theirs. They search the internet and are flattered by the attention that's showered upon them by this unknown person and very quickly, they're being groomed.[128]

We should also consider, however, that in terms of their technological skills, children's online vulnerabilities to groomers could be constructed rather than real.[129] Children may often have greater skills than parents, and might be better able to block unwanted, unsolicited contact. Meyer argues that, although research indicates that children are skilled internet users and are aware of the dangers of internet use, the powerful discourse of innocence prevents adult recognition of this. Instead, children's vulnerability is emphasized, as is the need to increase the protection offered to them online.[130] Thus, children's constructed vulnerability in this context can enable the protectionist discourse to prevail.

In 2007, the results were reported of the Eurobarometer on Safer Internet for Children qualitative study, which covered twenty-nine countries and involved children aged between nine and ten, and twelve and fourteen, who regularly use the internet at least once a month.[131] One of the main focuses of the study was the participants' perception of risks involved in online behaviour. The greatest risk the children identified was using the internet in a way that could give rise to contact with adult strangers, such as participating in open chats or discussion forums and responding to blogs or websites of someone they had never met.[132] Despite the children's awareness of this risk, the findings of the study also tended to reveal that some of them adopted more risky behaviour than they thought and could be too confident in their abilities to realize when someone was posing under a false identity.[133]

For those adolescents who are successfully targeted by groomers online, important issues of autonomy and consent are raised. Radin has tackled the issue of consent and the internet in the context of online contracts, arguing that: 'At minimum, consent involves a knowing understanding of what one is doing.'[134] In the context of internet grooming, where a would-be abuser pretends he is a child and asks to meet the adolescent

[128] Interview RX2. [129] Wolak *et al.* 2008: 115.

[130] Meyer 2007: 38–9. As an example, see Watson and Lefever 2004: 199.

[131] European Commission May 2007. *Safer Internet for Children: Qualitative Study in 29 European Countries, Summary Report*, http://ec.europa.eu/information_society/activities/sip/eurobarometer/index_en.htm.

[132] Ibid.: 8. [133] Ibid.: 9. [134] Radin 2000: 1126.

with whom he is communicating, the adolescent who agrees to this in no way comprehends who she has actually agreed to meet. The fact that screen names and online personas can be used as shields behind which would-be abusers conceal their real identities arguably makes real, truly informed consent to meet the person with whom the adolescent has been in communication impossible. However, Wolak *et al.*'s recent overview of the existing research suggests that this form of deception may be less prominent than is thought to be the case. The authors state that: 'In the great majority of cases, victims are aware they are conversing online with adults … Also, offenders rarely deceive victims about their sexual interests … When deception does occur, it often involves promises of love and romance by offenders whose intentions are primarily sexual.'[135]

Groomers operating online can become proficient at communicating with adolescents in a way that enables them quickly to gain the adolescent's trust and move the conversation towards sexual matters. According to one police officer involved in work in this area:

> One of the things we found particularly disturbing [was] how quickly an offender would turn an initial contact into one of a sexual nature and you're talking about possibly two or three questions. They seem to have an inbuilt sense of understanding the vulnerability of the person they're communicating with … so quickly are those questions turned into ones of an intimate nature … they perfect the art of being able to identify the vulnerabilities of the individual and when you examine an individual's computer who has … groomed someone on the internet … there may well be twenty or twenty-five occasions where they've crashed and burned. They've asked the wrong question. They've got a little bit clumsy. They've been a bit heavy handed … And then they suddenly perfect the art.[136]

Again, however, I wish to emphasize here that online stranger grooming is not the only way, or the main way, that children are groomed. In America, surveys by the National Center for Missing and Exploited Children conducted in 2000 and 2006 did not reveal the high prevalence of online grooming one would expect from media coverage and prevailing constructions of grooming.[137] In 2000, 19 per cent of the 1,501 ten-to seventeen-year-olds who participated in the survey reported that they had received unwanted online sexual solicitations. In 2006, this figure had dropped to just 13 per cent. It is also important to note that groomers who already know the child may take advantage of the particular

135 Wolak *et al.* 2008: 112–13.
136 Interview RX2. See also ibid.: 119.
137 Finkelhor *et al.* 2000; and Wolak *et al.* 2006.

vulnerability the child possesses because of the groomer's relationship of trust with the parent, a relationship that the online groomer simply does not have the advantage of.[138]

Computer child pornography and the way in which the internet can be used for exchanging child pornography has recently been the subject of important academic analysis.[139] Taylor's and Quayle's research has found that accessing and trading child pornography tends to occur through applications found at the edges of the network.[140] Due to the illegality of these activities in many jurisdictions, users interested in child pornography and in communicating with others who share the same interest select methods of internet communication that best ensure privacy and limit the risks of monitoring, such as Usenet newsgroups, Internet Relay Chat, Peer-to-Peer networks and Bulletin Board Systems.[141] Researchers have found that Usenet newsgroups provide one of the main sources for those interested in child pornography.[142]

The utilization of the internet to disseminate and acquire child pornography transnationally has posed challenges for law enforcement agencies,[143] and this has given rise to international cooperation between police forces to combat computer-based related crimes.[144] One well-publicized international police investigation, Operation Cathedral, related to an internet child pornography ring named the 'W0nderland Club' with around 200 members. On 2 September 1998, this investigation uncovered 750,000 indecent photographs of children that were distributed by and to W0nderland Club members across the world. In a series of simultaneous raids, 107 members of the club in different countries were arrested. As a further example, an international investigation entitled Operation Avalanche targeted Landslide Promotions, an American-based gateway to a network of child pornography websites.[145]

138 Research also suggests that, besides trust, familial abusers can take advantage of favouritism and alienation tactics which, again, would not be available to the online stranger groomer. See Christiansen and Blake 1990.

139 See Akdeniz 2008; Jenkins 2001; O'Donnell and Milner 2007; Taylor and Quayle 2003.

140 Taylor and Quayle 2006: 172–3.

141 Taylor and Quayle 2006: 179; Beech *et al.* 2008; Jenkins 2001: ch. 3.

142 Akdeniz 2008: 6; Jenkins 2001: ch. 3; and Taylor and Quayle 2006: 188.

143 See Jenkins 2001: 153 and 183.

144 Most recently, see Operation Orangebill: 'Swoop on Austria child porn rings', BBC News report, 2 January 2008, http://news.bbc.co.uk/1/hi/world/europe/7167711.stm and Operation Chandler: 'Police identify 200 paedophile suspects in Britain after smashing online ring', *The Times*, 19 June 2007.

145 'Operation Avalanche: Tracking child porn', BBC News report, 11 November 2002, http://news.bbc.co.uk/1/hi/uk/2445065.stm.

The UK's national investigation which was the result of Operation Avalanche, namely Operation Ore, was launched when FBI agents gave British police credit card details of the British subscribers to Landslide. I will discuss whether Operation Ore effectively targeted those who subscribed to the gateway and the impact of the investigation on individuals who were suspects and later cleared of any involvement in Chapter 5.

Thus, the internet does clearly offer opportunities for engaging in behaviour related to child pornography and grooming. However, we should not be quick to assume that what makes children – especially teenagers – vulnerable when using the internet is an innate vulnerability that cannot be overcome, or that they lack the technical skills required to navigate the internet safely. Rather, attention should be given to providing children with the information they need to develop avoidance skills and, therefore, make it much harder for individuals to groom them online.[146] When it comes to combating internet child pornography, continued international collaboration between law enforcement agencies, the assistance of ISP providers[147] and ensuring that successful international and national investigations are well publicized should go some way to help tackle the problem.

It is also essential, of course, that national laws enable the successful prosecution of those individuals who represent a threat to children, whether online or offline. However, equally, national laws must respond to child pornography and grooming in a rational and proportionate manner. It is the legal response to these phenomena in England and Wales that is the focus of the next chapter.

[146] See the concluding chapter for reference to one example of such an education programme.

[147] Akdeniz 2008: pt. 3; and Taylor and Quayle 2003: 202–3.

CHAPTER TWO

CRIMINALIZING CHILD PORNOGRAPHY AND BEHAVIOUR RELATED TO SEXUAL GROOMING

Despite the number of existing offences that can apply to behaviour related to child pornography or sexual grooming, it is only relatively recently that the law has specifically targeted these phenomena. In 1978, the first piece of legislation directed at individuals involved in the creation and distribution of indecent images of children was introduced, namely the Protection of Children Act (PCA). The specific criminalization of behaviour relating to grooming has occurred even more recently, under the Sexual Offences Act 2003 (SOA).

Initially in this chapter, I analyse the legal response to child pornography. The relevant statutory provisions to be found in the PCA, the Criminal Justice Act 1988 (CJA) and the SOA and case law surrounding child pornography are elucidated and analysed in section one. Then, in section two, I examine and assess the scope of the offence of meeting a child following sexual grooming to be found in the SOA. Finally, in the third section, I explore what lies beneath the surface of the law's response to child pornography and grooming. Here, I identify a number of societal and legal concerns that have been the driving force behind the creation of the current statutory provisions aimed at child pornography and grooming and the way in which the harms of both phenomena have been legally constructed.

CRIMINALIZING CHILD PORNOGRAPHY

The offences under the Protection of Children Act 1978

Various statutory offences relating primarily to the creation and distribution of child pornography are to be found under the PCA. An individual commits an offence if he takes or makes, or permits to be taken, an indecent photograph or pseudo-photograph of a child (s. 1(1)(a)), distributes or shows such a photograph or has such a photograph in his possession for the purpose of showing or distributing it (s. 1(1)(b) and (c)), or publishes an advert that gives the impression that the advertiser distributes or shows such photographs or intends to do so (s. 1(1)(d)). Therefore, although the PCA catches indecent photographic material, it does not extend to written material or drawings taken from an individual's imagination that portray behaviour of a sexual nature involving a child.[1] A defence is available to a person charged with an offence under s. 1(1)(b) and (c) of the PCA if he had a legitimate reason for distributing or showing or having in his possession the photographs in question, or if he had not seen the photographs and did not know or have cause to suspect that they were indecent.[2]

Judicial interpretation of the word 'make' was provided in the case of *Atkins* v. *DPP*, in which Brown LJ held that the word was to be given its 'natural and ordinary meaning'. In this context, this meant 'to cause to exist; to produce by action, to bring about'.[3] He further held that whilst it is possible to make an indecent photograph of a child through intentional copying, an offence is not committed under s. 1(1)(a) if the individual unintentionally copies a photograph.[4] In *R.* v. *Smith, R* v. *Jayson*,[5] the Court of Appeal provided further clarification of when the *mens rea* element of the s. 1(1)(a) offence is made out in the context of indecent images of children accessed from the internet. It was held that, provided the individual is aware that an e-mail attachment contains or is likely to contain indecent images of children, he makes an indecent image of a child when he opens it and it is saved in his computer's temporary cache.[6] The Court of Appeal also held that if an individual views an image on the internet, then, as soon as it appears on his computer screen, he has made an indecent image

[1] As noted in the previous chapter, such material could be caught under other obscenity and indecency laws. I will discuss the recent Home Office proposals on criminalizing obscene drawings and non-photographic computer-generated images in the concluding chapter.

[2] See PCA, s. 1(1)(4).

[3] *Atkins* v. *Director of Public Prosecutions* [2000] 1 WLR 1427, 1437 (Brown LJ quoting the Oxford English Dictionary).

[4] Ibid.: 1438. [5] [2002] EWCA Crim. 683.

[6] Ormerod argues that in circumstances where an individual does not realize the image she or he clicks on or downloads is an indecent image of child, the possession offence may be committed, but a defence will be available if the e-mail is unsolicited and the individual does not realize the image is an indecent image of a child. (Ormerod 2002). However, this is dependent upon the individual deleting the image promptly from the cache and the obvious potential difficulty is that she or he may not know how to do this.

of the child regardless of whether he intended to save the images. In this scenario, the individual must again have knowledge of the content of the image by, for example, having seen a thumbnail miniature of the image before he views and/or downloads it.[7] Thus, it is apparent that although the actual statutory provisions under s. 1 of the PCA do not include a *mens rea* requirement of knowledge, the judiciary has been required to interpret the offences in light of the methods by which indecent images can be created today. In the late 1970s, legislators were unlikely to have anticipated that the advent of modern technology would lead to the possibility that an individual could potentially 'make' an indecent image of a child by downloading it from the internet, with no knowledge of its contents.[8] Yet it remains questionable whether the act of downloading an image from the internet with knowledge of the image's contents would have been intended to be categorized as making an indecent image of a child by the legislature.[9] This is especially the case given the differentiation made between the acts of making and possession (the latter of which, as will shortly be discussed, is an offence criminalized by the CJA). Sentencing guidelines have been produced highlighting the much more severe nature of making an original indecent image and advising judges to equate making through downloading with the possession offence in terms of the sentence passed.[10] However, the merging of the making and possession offences through judicial interpretation of statutory law should, I submit, still be a matter for concern with regard to fair labelling and the importance of drawing distinctions between different levels of wrongdoing.[11]

Explication of the meaning of the word 'indecent' was provided in the Court of Appeal case of *R.* v. *Graham–Kerr*,[12] where it was stated that photographs of children are considered indecent under the PCA if ordinary people would view them as such, by applying recognized standards of propriety. Whilst we do not have a legal definition of 'indecent', what is clear is that in deciding whether the material in question is indecent, the jury focuses on the content of the image rather than the maker's intention or the context in which it was taken.[13] The seemingly

[7] See also *R.* v. *Beaney* [2004] 2 Cr. App. R. (S) 82.

[8] See also on this point, Gillespie 2005.

[9] See also Akdeniz 2008: 50–1 and 55–7.

[10] Sentencing Advisory Panel 2002: para. 23. See also *R.* v. *Saunders* [2004] EWCA Crim. 777, para. 8.

[11] On the matter of fair labelling, see Chalmers and Leverick 2008, and Chapter 5, at 221–2.

[12] [1988] 1 WLR 1098.

[13] See *R.* v. *Smethurst* [2002] 1 Cr. App. R. 6, para. 16; and *R.* v. *Nicklass* [2006] EWCA Crim. 2613. See also Gillespie 2005.

objective, jury-based test of indecency has been subject to criticism in the context of indecency laws generally. Authors such as Childs have claimed that the test is in fact largely subjective to the particular jury, and this makes it difficult for an individual to know if he has committed an indecency offence.[14] Indeed, a reasonable argument can be made that offences which rely on this indecency test may breach Art. 10 of the European Convention on Human Rights (ECHR),[15] which states that any limitation to the right to freedom of expression must be prescribed by law. The argument could proceed along the lines that the indecency test is not certain or precise enough for citizens to foresee when they are acting criminally. However, when such an argument was raised specifically in the context of the PCA offences, the Court of Appeal confirmed that these offences are sufficiently certain to avoid a breach of the Human Rights Act 1998.[16] Moreover, the jury-based test of indecency has been confirmed by the European Court of Human Rights' decision in *O'Carroll* v. *UK*.[17] Here, the defendant argued that leaving the jury to decide upon the matter of indecency breached Art. 7 of the ECHR,[18] as it did not sufficiently enable an individual to know in advance whether his conduct is criminal. The court held that such an approach was in fact 'perfectly compatible' with the Convention, provided that the judge indicates to the jury 'with sufficient clarity' the scope of its discretion.[19]

Whilst I would argue that in most cases what amounts to an indecent photograph of a child will be fairly clear cut, a jury's view as to whether a photograph of a child is indecent may be less predictable where the image in question is at the lower end of the child pornography scale, featuring, for example, a naked child and no sexual activity. The question of whether a photograph of a naked child without any sexual activity or posing can and should be capable of being defined as legally indecent is a crucial one. As I will discuss in Chapter 4, perceiving such images as indecent, as sexualized, raises serious questions about the way in which society and law view children's naked bodies.

[14] Childs 1991: 25.

[15] The Article's protection of individuals' freedom of expression includes the freedom to 'receive and impart information and ideas without interference by public authority'.

[16] *R.* v. *Smethurst*. [17] (2005) 41 EHRR SE1.

[18] Which reads: 'No one shall be held guilty of any criminal offence on account of any act or omission which did not constitute a criminal offence under national or international law at the time when it was committed.'

[19] At 5.

The Sentencing Advisory Panel's league table, which describes different levels of child pornography, offers an indication of whether material that features a naked child with no sexual content could potentially be defined as indecent.[20] The table was adapted from the Copine typology scale[21] and was created in order to assist the judiciary when passing sentence for offences relating to indecent photographs of children. It lists: (1) images depicting nudity or erotic posing with no sexual activity; (2) sexual activity between children, or solo masturbation by a child; (3) non-penetrative sexual activity between adults and children; (4) penetrative sexual activity between children and adults; and (5) sadism or bestiality. It was adopted by the Court of Appeal when providing sentencing guidelines in *R.* v. *Oliver*,[22] with one alteration. The Court of Appeal judged that an image of a naked or semi-naked child in a legitimate setting, or an erotic or surreptitious image showing underwear[23] would not, of itself, amount to 'a pornographic image'.[24] Thus, applying this ruling, the depiction of deliberate posing suggesting sexual content[25] would be the minimum level at which images could be defined as indecent and, consequently, images of naked children with no actual or suggested sexual content would not seem to be capable of being legally indecent. However, this may not be the case. Gillespie argues that the subsequent Court of Appeal judgment in *R.* v. *Carr*[26] has brought the decision in *Oliver* into question. Some of the images taken by and possessed by the appellant amounted to material that would fall under levels two and three of the Copine scale; yet, whilst the court quashed the sentences relating to these images, it did not address the defendant's convictions in respect of them.[27] Moreover, the court's explanation that it was quashing the sentences 'to demonstrate the necessity for the activity depicted in the photograph … to pass the custody threshold, set out in the Copine guidelines relied on in *Oliver*'[28] is somewhat ambiguous. Is the court referring to the minimum level in the Copine guidelines, or the Copine level that the Court of Appeal in *Oliver* felt appropriate to apply as the minimum legal threshold of indecency? In *R.* v. *O'Carroll*,[29]

20 Sentencing Advisory Panel 2002: para. 21.

21 See Taylor *et al.* 2001: 101.

22 [2003] 1 Cr. App. R. 28.

23 Levels two and three of the Copine typology scale.

24 At para. 10.

25 Level four of the Copine typology scale. Such as, for instance, the photograph that formed the basis of the appellant's conviction for taking an indecent image of a child in *R.* v. *Gosling* [2005] EWCA Crim. 3300 (an image of a child sitting naked on a bed, with her back to the camera, wearing stockings).

26 [2003] EWCA Crim. 2416.

27 Gillespie 2005: 33.

28 At para. 27.

29 [2003] EWCA Crim. 2338.

the images in question (photographs of naked young boys playing outdoors) would also appear to fall under level two of the Copine scale.[30] Whilst the Court of Appeal quashed the sentence passed by the trial judge, finding it to be 'manifestly excessive', the Court of Appeal later dismissed O'Carroll's application for leave to appeal against his conviction.[31] As I will argue in Chapter 3, there are alternative approaches that could be taken to images of naked children without suggested or explicit sexual content, which would avoid the problems encountered when the law remains focused on whether the image is indecent.

The PCA's definition of a photograph includes: 'an indecent film, a copy of an indecent photograph or film, and an indecent photograph comprised in a film'.[32] In order to address the exploitation of an expanding loophole in the law by producers of computer child pornography in the 1990s, the Criminal Justice and Public Order Act 1994 (CJPOA) amended s. 7 of the PCA. Thus, the definition of a photograph was extended to include 'the negative as well as the positive version and data stored on a computer disc or by other electronic means which is capable of conversion into a photograph'.[33] Furthermore, the CJPOA ensured that pseudo-images, whether computerized or created through other means, also come within the scope of the offences under the PCA.[34] Provided that the predominant impression conveyed by the pseudo-photograph is that the person depicted is a child, then it will be construed to be an indecent photograph of a child 'notwithstanding that some of the physical characteristics shown are those of an adult'.[35] The inclusion of pseudo-photographs in the legislation is largely targeted at sophisticated, computer-generated images which convincingly appear to be real images. In the case of *Goodland* v. *DPP*,[36] Brown LJ held that a pseudo-photograph could not be said to be created as a result of taping together two different photographs in a crude fashion, although a photocopy of these two photographs could amount to a pseudo-photograph.

30 See Gillespie and Bettinson 2006.

31 See *O'Carroll* v. *UK* (2005) 41 EHRR SE1, 2. See also *R.* v. *McKain* [2007] EWCA Crim. 1145. Again, this was an appeal against sentence. The images in question featured 'no suggestion of sexual behaviour' (para. 9). Although the Court of Appeal quashed the original sentence of six months imprisonment, it was replaced with a three months prison sentence.

32 S. 7(2). 33 S. 7(4). 34 S. 7(7).

35 PCA, s. 7(8). For judicial interpretation of what can amount to a pseudo-photograph, see *Goodland* v. *DPP* [2000] 1 WLR 1427.

36 Ibid.

Finally, an individual convicted on indictment of an offence under the PCA can face a prison sentence of up to ten years.[37] Previously, until January 2001, the maximum sentence that could be imposed on an individual who was convicted of one of the PCA offences was three years.[38] In the case of *R. v. Toomer*,[39] the Court of Appeal held that following the principles which had emerged from previous cases, factors such as any evidence of commercial exploitation, the nature of the material, the character of the defendant and whether a plea of guilty had been lodged should be taken into account when considering the length of sentence which should be imposed.

The offence of possessing child pornography

The PCA does not criminalize the act of possessing indecent photographs of a child *unless* such possession is with a view to showing or distributing the photographs. That the possession of indecent photographs of children is only one possible element of these offences indicates that, when the PCA was enacted, simple possession was not considered to represent a significant enough threat to warrant its legal prohibition when carried out in isolation from producing and distributing child pornography.[40]

In 1988, however, further legislation criminalized the mere possession of child pornography. Section 160 of the CJA states that: 'It is an offence for a person to have any indecent photograph of a child in his possession', and this mere possession offence was extended by the CJPOA to cover pseudo-photographs.[41] Furthermore, the maximum sentence for a person convicted of the possession offence on indictment has been increased from six months to five years.[42] Identical defences exist for an individual charged with the possession offence as under s. 1(1)(b) and (c) of the PCA.[43] A further defence for the possession offence exists if

[37] PCA, s. 6(2).

[38] Parliament increased this maximum sentence through an amendment made to the PCA by the Criminal Justice and Court Services Act 2000 (CJCSA).

[39] See *R.* v. *Toomer, R.* v. *Powell and R.* v. *Mould*, The Times, 21 November 2000.

[40] In fact, Cyril Townsend, the Tory MP who introduced the Private Member's Bill that became the PCA, initially sought to include a clause prohibiting possession within the Bill. This clause was later dropped. The Home Secretary advised that: 'Possession alone as an offence may not be easy to justify, both because of circumstances in which possession alone would not be blameworthy and because of inroads into private behaviour.' Letter from Brynmor John to Cyril Townsend, 30 January 1978. Held in NVALA Archives, Box 19.

[41] See the CJPOA, s. 84(4)(a).

[42] See the CJA, s. 160(2A), as inserted by the CJCSA 2000, art. 2(a).

[43] That is, that the individual had a legitimate reason for having the photograph in his possession, or that he had not seen the photograph and had no reason to suspect it was indecent. S. 160 (2)(a) and (b).

the individual can prove that the photograph was sent to him without any request, and that he did not keep it for an unreasonable time.[44] An unsuccessful attempt to rely on the 'legitimate reason' defence in response to a charge of the possession offence was made in the case of *Atkins* v. *DPP*. Atkins, a university lecturer, was discovered to have indecent photographs of children which he had viewed on the internet at work and inadvertently stored in his computer's cache. In his defence, he argued that he had a legitimate reason for being in possession of the photographs, as he was conducting research into the sexuality of children. The High Court held that possessing indecent photographs of children for the purposes of academic research in this case did not constitute a legitimate reason for being in possession of such material. On the issue of the applicability of the defence, Brown LJ commented:

> The central question where the defence is legitimate research will be whether the defendant is essentially a person of unhealthy interests in possession of indecent photographs in the pretence of undertaking research, or by contrast a genuine researcher with no alternative but to have this sort of unpleasant material in his possession.[45]

Atkins was unable to rely on the legitimate reason defence, as it could not be proven that his academic research was legitimate. However, his appeal against his conviction for the offence of possession was allowed. Atkins had no knowledge that the photographs had been stored in his computer's cache and Brown LJ reached the conclusion that Parliament did not intend to criminalize the unknowing possession of indecent photographs, as indicated by the existence of the defence available to individuals who reasonably do not know that photographs in their possession are indecent.[46] This requisite *mens rea* element of knowledge was affirmed in *R.* v. *Collier*.[47]

I explore judicial attitudes towards the possession of child pornography in the following chapter. What it is important to emphasize here

[44] CJA, s. 160(2)(c). [45] At 1435. [46] At 1440.

[47] [2004] EWCA Crim. 1411. The presence of deleted files containing indecent images of children on computer hard drives has posed other important questions regarding *mens rea* and the possession offence. In *R.* v. *Porter* [2006] 2 Cr. App. R. 25, the Court of Appeal was required to decide whether an individual has committed the possession offence when deleted indecent images are still present on his computer, but can only be accessed through the use of special techniques unavailable to him. The court favoured the interpretation of possession applied in cases involving the possession of drugs; the defendant possesses whatever he knows to be in his custody or control (at para. 20). If an individual cannot access or retrieve images stored upon his computer's hard drive, as in the case before them, the Court of Appeal held that he no longer has control or custody of them.

is that the criminalization of possessing child pornography reveals that, in the space of ten years, the legislature's perception of the level of threat caused by possession substantially altered. I will explore the reasons for this modification in stance later in this chapter.

Extending legal constructions of the 'child'

Until the coming into force of the SOA, the PCA defined a 'child' as an individual under the age of sixteen. However, the SOA revised the PCA, re-defining a child as being under the age of eighteen.[48] This re-definition of a child brought English law in this area in line with the UN Convention on the Rights of the Child and the European Council Framework Decision on Combating the Sexual Exploitation of Children and Child Pornography, which both define a child as a person who is less than eighteen years old.[49] There are, however, negative repercussions that result from increasing the age of a child from under sixteen to under eighteen. Particularly, this expansion of the definition of a child raises a significant issue regarding the sexual liberty rights of sixteen- and seventeen-year-old adolescents, a matter to which I will turn shortly. Also, whilst the extension of a 'child' from under sixteen to under eighteen is consistent with the general approach under the SOA, it creates something of a discrepancy and illogicality within the law, given that sixteen-year-old adolescents can give lawful consent to sexual intercourse, but are now unable to give consent to the creation of a pornographic photograph or video of any such act in which they partake. The law thus presents a state of affairs in which an act is lawful, but the representation and recording of that act is not.[50] As Gillespie notes, 'two 17-year-olds can give their consent to have sexual intercourse with as many people as they want, in whatever style they want, but cannot give consent to take an intimate photograph of each other'.[51] It is also not outside the realms of possibility that the seventeen-year-old's consent to have sexual intercourse could be for unprotected sexual intercourse on each occasion. Thus, an adolescent of this age can freely give valid consent to

[48] SOA, S.45, revising s. 7(6) of the PCA. The SOA shifted the age boundary from under-sixteens to under-eighteens in the context of a number of other offences, such as abuse of trust offences (ss. 16–19) and familial child sex offences (ss. 25–9). See further Waites 2005: ch. 8; Ashworth 2006: 355–7; and Home Office 2000: para. 7.6.2.

[49] Art. 1 of the UN Convention on the Rights of the Child; Council Framework Decision 2004/68/JHA, Art. 1(a), [2004] OJ L13.

[50] For a parallel observation regarding Canadian law, see Ryder 2003: 105.

[51] Gillespie 2004: 364.

any number of acts that potentially could be very harmful indeed, yet is prevented from consenting to, and perhaps requesting, her partner to take a pornographic photograph of her which she intends to keep in her own possession.

There is an exception to the offences under the PCA in a case where the child is aged over sixteen and either married to or living together as partners with the defendant in an 'enduring relationship'.[52] However, this does not encompass all situations where a sixteen- or seventeen-year-old might see the making of a pornographic image of herself as an expression of her sexual liberty. It also appears to make the law less clear regarding the question of whether the child who is the subject of the photograph behaves in a criminal manner. Gillespie identifies a situation where two seventeen-year-olds have been engaged for two years, but do not live together.[53] Say that in this situation, the girlfriend takes a pornographic photograph of her boyfriend, to which he consents. She has, on the face of it, committed the offence of taking an indecent photograph of a child. As the couple do not live together, she would not appear to be able to rely on the new exception under the PCA. Moreover, there is also the matter of whether her boyfriend, by permitting her to take the photograph, has also committed an offence.[54] If he has, then the *victim* of the crime, the person whom the legislation was designed to protect, can also be guilty as co-principal to the offence.[55] In the context of the example above, it is thus to be hoped that if the fact that the photograph has been made becomes known to the authorities, as a matter of policy, the prosecution of neither individuals would be brought. In *Setting the Boundaries* and *Protecting the Public*,[56] the government emphasized that the SOA's extension of prohibitions from under-sixteens to under-eighteens would be accompanied by discretionary enforcement and implementation of the law. Notwithstanding this, the appropriateness

[52] See s. 1A of PCA, inserted by the SOA. The exception applies to the offences under s. 1(1)(a), (b) and (c). It also applies to the possession of an indecent photograph of a child offence under s. 160 of the CJA (see s. 160A). The exception does not apply when an individual in the photograph is someone other than the child or the individual who takes the photograph. See s. 1A(3) of the PCA and s. 160A(3) of the CJA.

[53] Gillespie 2004: 364.

[54] Again, under s. 1(1)(a) of the PCA – it is an offence to '*permit to be taken* ... any indecent photograph ... of a child' (my emphasis). Whilst the assumption would be that the legislature was looking to target an adult who permits another to take an indecent image of the child, this is not made clear in the legislation itself.

[55] Interestingly, according to the principle in *R.* v. *Tyrrell* [1894] 1 QB 710, the victim of a crime whom the law was intended to protect cannot be guilty as *accessory* to the offence in question.

[56] Home Office 2000; and Home Office 2002.

of a blanket approach to criminalization concerned a wide range of Parliamentary Members.[57]

In the House of Commons debates on the Sexual Offences Bill, a major concern of the proposed legislation was highlighted as being to target 'predatory behaviour' and this was a reason why the legislature wished to avoid criminalizing 'effectively consensual', 'minimal sexual activity' between children aged thirteen to sixteen.[58] If 'predatory behaviour' was the main mischief targeted by the legislature, and bearing in mind that the original purpose of the PCA was to prevent the exploitation of children,[59] the currently defined exception that applies to sixteen- and seventeen-year-olds is unnecessarily limited by the need for marriage or an 'enduring relationship'. An alternative approach to that discussed above which would also better recognize the sexual liberty rights of sixteen- and seventeen-year-olds, and at the same time reflect the purpose of the PCA, would be to have allowed a defence where an individual could establish that the image had not been created in an exploitative situation and had not caused harm.[60]

Because the exception is so limited it may be that, by increasing the age of a child, the PCA is incompatible with the UN Convention on the Rights of the Child, the Human Rights Act 1998 (HRA) and the ECHR. According to Art. 12 of the Convention on the Rights of the Child: 'States parties shall assure to the child who is capable of forming his or her own views the right to express those views freely in all matters affecting the child, the views of the child being given due weight in accordance with the age and maturity of the child.' The failure to take into account autonomy and sexual liberty rights of sixteen- and seventeen-year-olds could breach Art. 12, particularly as there is no evidence to suggest that the views of such older children were sufficiently taken into account when the child pornography offences were extended to their age group.[61]

[57] See Waites 2005: 199 and 202; and Ashworth 2006: 354 and 359. In an earlier draft of the particular clause relating to this exception in the Sexual Offences Bill, no offence would have been committed if the child depicted in the photograph was aged sixteen or over, provided the photograph was made with the child's consent. There was no need for the child to be married to the defendant, or for an enduring relationship to exist between them. See cl. 52, at www.publications.parliament.uk/pa/ld200203/ldbills/026/03026.24–30.html#j413. Interestingly, the aforementioned European Council Framework Decision provides that Member States may exclude from criminal liability the production and possession of images of children who have reached the age of sexual consent when the image is taken with the child's consent and is solely for private use (see above, n. 49, Art. 3.2(b)).

[58] Hansard HC Deb. 15 July 2003: column 202 (Simon Hughes).

[59] See the later discussion at 83–4 and 99.

[60] See Ryder 2003: 105.

[61] See generally, Spencer 2004: 360; and Home Office 2000: para. 3.3.9.

Gillespie observes that the right to a sexual life is protected under the umbrella of the Art. 8 right to privacy and family life under the ECHR, as confirmed by *Dudgeon* v. *UK*.[62] He also notes, however, that there are a number of circumstances under which Art. 8 can legitimately be breached.[63] These include where the breach is necessary for the protection of the rights or freedoms of others or to protect morals. The need to protect children from exploitation has already been highlighted as a legitimate reason for infringing Art. 8 and 10 of the ECHR.[64] However, if the seventeen-year-old who takes a pornographic image of her boyfriend, to which he consents, simply keeps this image in her possession, can it really be argued that criminalization of this act is necessary in order to protect other children from exploitation? I acknowledge that some might perceive the situation as being different if she intends to show and distribute this photograph to others. It may be contended that the autonomy of the sixteen-or seventeen-year-old who wishes an indecent photo of her boyfriend or herself to be distributed to others can *legitimately* be restricted by the law, if allowing such an exercise of autonomy could potentially threaten other children.[65] Certainly, in our courts of law, infringing autonomy in order to protect other vulnerable individuals in society is likely to be deemed a justifiable violation of Art. 8 of the ECHR.[66]

Undoubtedly, it is the protectionist stance fostered by a society that is anxious to cover all children with the same shield against potential and perceived harm which has served to extend the child pornography offences to older adolescents.[67] Couple this with the fact that the subject in question relates to children's involvement in sexual acts, and it is apparent why it so difficult for society and law to recognize the autonomy rights of older children in this respect.[68] It seems that in this context, a discourse of morality prevails. Society and law may have been able to move away from conservative moral attitudes concerning youth sexuality sufficiently to allow the homosexual age of consent to be reduced to sixteen. However, Parliament has chosen to allow morality and an

62 (1982) 4 EHRR 149. Article 8 reads: 'Everyone has the right to respect for his private and family life, his home and his correspondence.'

63 Gillespie 2004: 364. See Art. 8(2) of the ECHR.

64 See *R.* v. *Smethurst*, para. 24.

65 By, e.g. encouraging the market – commercial or otherwise – in indecent images of children. See Chapter 3, at 113–18.

66 See, for instance, the reasoning behind the decision in *DPP* v. *Pretty* [2001] 1 All ER 1, 18, *per* Lord Bingham.

67 See Home Office 2000: para. 7.6.3.

68 See Stainton Rogers and Stainton Rogers 1999: 182, 193 and 195.

'adults know best' philosophy to re-shape the definition of a child under the child pornography law. In other areas, in contrast, the law does allow concerns about older children's autonomy to take precedence over concerns for their protection. The consent of a child who is aged sixteen or above to medical treatment is legally effective under the Family Law Reform Act 1969, s. 8(1). The mature minor aged under sixteen can also consent to treatment provided she demonstrates sufficient maturity to be able to reach an intelligent choice.[69] Therefore, framed in its earlier form as discussed above,[70] the provision providing an exception to the inclusion of sixteen- and seventeen-year-olds where the photograph was made with the subject's consent would have reflected existing legislation and case law on older children's consent to medical treatment. When it comes to the child pornography provisions, however, society is dealing with a subject that does not fall within the 'same kind of sanitized domain'[71] as older adolescents consenting to medical treatment. Moreover, statutory and common law's recognition of a more mature minor's autonomy does not extend to a situation where the minor refuses medical treatment. The decision to allow the force-feeding of a sixteen-year-old girl suffering from anorexia nervosa in *Re W. (Minor) (Medical Treatment)*,[72] if necessary, evidences the greater reluctance to respect an older child's autonomy when the decision she reaches is not in accordance with what adults deem to be her best interests. Thus, the extension of the child pornography offences to sixteen- and seventeen-year-olds is a reflection of a broader legal approach in which children's personal autonomy rights can be ignored when adults consider their decisions to be harmful or dangerous to their wellbeing.

In sum here, as Persky and Dixon observe: 'There's something deeply anomalous about a law that criminalizes the representation of a non-criminal act. Since two sixteen-year-olds are legally free to engage in sexual acts, why should it be a crime to represent those acts?'[73] The only convincing answer would seem to be that this aspect of the child pornography law is an example of the criminalization of adolescent behaviour that adults consider to be wrong or inappropriate.

[69] *Gillick* v. *West Norfolk and Wisbech AHA* [1985] 3 All ER 402. Of course, supporting the autonomy rights of the mature child under the age of sixteen is more problematic in the context of the child pornography offences whilst the age of sexual consent remains at sixteen.

[70] See above, n. 57.

[71] Stainton Rogers and Stainton Rogers 1999: 194.

[72] [1992] 4 All ER 627. See also *Re R. (A Minor)* [1991] 4 All ER 177; and Brazier and Bridge 1996.

[73] Persky and Dixon 2001: 210 and see also 60–1 (referring to Canadian law).

Widening the net: the creation of further child pornography offences

The SOA brought wide-reaching changes to the current legislation on sexual offences. One of the government's main aims in introducing the legislation was to give children 'the greatest possible protection under the law from sexual abuse'.[74] Consequently, there are a number of specific sexual offences against children that feature within Pt. I of the Act, including the 'meeting a child following sexual grooming' offence which I explore later in this chapter. The offences I examine here relate to encouraging, arranging or causing the involvement of a child in prostitution or pornography. These offences exist alongside the afore-discussed offences relating to child pornography. Under s. 48, it is an offence to intentionally cause or incite a child to become involved in child pornography. Under s. 49, it is an offence to intentionally control a child who is involved in child pornography, and an individual's behaviour is criminalized under s. 50 if he intentionally arranges or facilitates a child's involvement in pornography.[74a]

It is significant that the SOA is the first statute to make direct reference to child pornography, as opposed to indecent photographs of children,[75] although the reference to child pornography sits alongside the pre-existing legal terminology of an indecent photograph of a child. It is stated in the SOA that a child is involved in pornography if an indecent image of the child is recorded.[76] The legislation's reference to child pornography raises two interesting questions. First, why did the legislature prefer the legal terminology 'indecent photographs of children' until this time rather than child pornography? Secondly, why, in 2003, did the legislature decide to adopt different terminology? In considering the first question, the legislature may have avoided utilizing terms such as 'pornography' and 'pornographic' when drafting the PCA to avoid association with the Obscene Publications Act 1959 and the type of material often caught by this Act.[77] The legal test for obscenity requires that the material would have a tendency to deprave and corrupt its audience,[78] often a difficult issue for the jury to decide. Placing

[74] Hansard, HL Deb. 13 February 2003: column 772. See also Home Office 2002.

[74a] The offences are not made out if an individual reasonably believes that a child is eighteen or over, provided that the child is actually over thirteen.

[75] See the titles of the SOA offences.

[76] S. 51(1).

[77] 'This Bill is a children's Bill. It is not a Bill directed primarily against obscenity; it is a Bill to safeguard children.' Baroness Faithfull, Hansard, HL Deb. 5 May 1978: column 536.

[78] See s. 1 of the 1959 Act and *R. v. Martin Secker & Warburg* [1954] 2 All ER 683, for example.

pornographic photographs of children under the umbrella of indecency rather than obscenity avoided the need to consider the subjective effect on the mind of the images in question in order to establish that they are unlawful. Moreover, the indecency test is an easier test to satisfy than the obscenity test. The answer to the second question posed above may lie in the fact that today's public is much more aware of child pornography than it was when the PCA was enacted, particularly in the light of substantial and persistent media coverage and national and international police investigations into the creation, distribution and possession of such material. The government may, then, have decided to modernize the legal terminology used to label images of children of a sexual nature in 2003 to reflect popular discourses.

No doubt because the pre-existing indecency framework remains, the SOA provides no statutory indication of the type of material that can be deemed to be pornography involving a child. The introduction of these offences did seem to offer the perfect opportunity to provide an indication of the varying content of material which can be deemed to be child pornography. What is more, the government would not have had to start from scratch in providing an indication of what can amount to child pornography. The SOA could have incorporated, for example, the afore-mentioned Sentence Advisory Panel's league table of classes of child pornography to illustrate the varying content of material which could fall under this heading. By explaining what can amount to child pornography in this way, the SOA would have clarified the wide range of material that can fall under the label of child pornography.[79]

The intention behind the creation of the new offences was obviously to extend the law's ability to catch more of the people involved in child pornography, including individuals who do not commit existing offences by actually recording or carrying out the sexual abuse. However, the relationship between these proposed offences and the existing offences relating to indecent images of children is somewhat unclear. Gillespie contends that there is 'significant overlap' between the new and old offences, thereby creating confusion in the law.[80] The confusion could have been avoided had the new offences retained an element that was present in the relevant clauses in earlier drafts of the Sexual Offences Bill. Under the originally worded clauses in the Bill when presented before the House of Lords, it was necessary for an individual to commit one of the acts listed under the clauses for gain. The definition of gain provided was fairly broad,

[79] See also, generally Gillespie 2004. [80] Gillespie 2004: 366–7.

being any kind of financial advantage or the goodwill of any person which it is likely will produce a financial advantage in time. The government chose to focus on a motivation of gain in the originally drafted clauses under the Bill because it was trying to tackle primarily the commercial aspects of the child pornography market.[81] However, the sub-section of the clause that stated the element and definition of gain was removed following concern expressed by Baroness Noakes in the House of Lords that including an element of gain would result in fewer convictions for the offences.[82] Removing the gain element has indeed resulted in offences that have much broader application. Gillespie comments that: 'It is difficult to conceive of a non-commercial situation that could come within ss. 48–50 and would not already be covered by s. 1 [of the PCA] using inchoate or secondary liability.'[83] It may be contended that it is simply easier to charge the individual with the new offences rather than relying on inchoate or secondary liability. The fact remains, however, that since such liability in relation to the PCA and the CJA offences exists, it is harder to argue that making an intention of gain a necessary element of the new offences would have failed to protect children from individuals who cause, control, incite or arrange for them to become involved in pornography for non-financial gain.

One final point is that liability for the SOA child pornography offences extends beyond England, Wales and Northern Ireland. Each offence criminalizes the relevant behaviour 'in any part of the world'. Moreover, the potential reach of all the offences relating to indecent images of children has been extended by s. 72 of the SOA. This provision provides that if a British citizen commits what would constitute a sexual offence in this jurisdiction outside the UK and in the jurisdiction in which the act was committed it constituted an offence, the individual has also committed an offence under the law in this jurisdiction.[84] This should make it easier to prosecute British citizens who, for example,

81 'We should extend the law, whether on pornography or prostitution, to make it easier to take decisive action to protect people against exploitation for commercial gain.' Hansard, HC Deb. 15 July 2003: column 186 (Home Secretary). Also note that a maximum sentence of fourteen years' imprisonment can be imposed on conviction for the SOA offences (as noted earlier, the maximum sentence for the PCA offences is currently ten years). See also Gillespie 2004: 367.

82 The gain element was laid down in cl. 58(3) and can be seen in the Sexual Offences Bill, HL Bill 68, available at www.publications.parliament.uk/pa/ld200203/ldbills/068/03068.25–31.html#j418. For the debates regarding the removal of the sub-section, see Hansard, HL Deb. 13 May 2003: columns 176–81 and HL Deb. 9 June 2003: column 60.

83 Gillespie 2004: 367.

84 Sch. 2, para. 1 of the SOA lists the PCA and CJA child pornography offences as constituting sexual offences.

upload indecent images of children elsewhere than in this jurisdiction under our law, and seems to be in line with other case law which suggests that the possibility of bringing a prosecution when an offence is committed elsewhere than in the UK is widening.[85]

CRIMINALIZING BEHAVIOUR RELATED TO SEXUAL GROOMING

The main focus of analysis in this part of the chapter is the offence relating to grooming under s. 15 of the SOA. The introduction of this offence followed calls for such legal reform by both the Taskforce on Child Protection on the Internet and child protection groups,[86] and demonstrates the increased societal awareness of the way in which grooming can occur via the internet. Moreover, in the period prior to the introduction of the SOA, the harms of grooming were being recognized by the judiciary. In *Re Attorney General's Reference (No. 41 of 2000)*,[87] one of the reasons why the Court of Appeal increased the defendant's original sentence for indecent assault and making indecent photographs of a child was because he had groomed a vulnerable child with special needs.[88]

The offence relating to grooming

A question which initially begs consideration is why the creation of a specific offence relating to grooming was thought to be a better step forward than simply utilizing the law of attempt – why not simply arrest an individual who intends to commit a sexual offence against a child and charge him with attempt to commit that particular offence? The answer is that there are commonly known and inherent difficulties when relying on the law of attempt, in terms of ascertaining the stage at which a preparatory act becomes an attempt to commit an actual offence. It is necessary to prove that an individual has gone beyond committing merely preparatory acts in order to satisfy the necessary elements of the offence of attempt under the Criminal Attempts Act 1981.[89] The creation of the offence of meeting a child following sexual grooming enables the police to charge an individual in circumstances where, previously, there

[85] See, e.g. *R.* v. *Perrin* [2002] EWCA Crim. 747. [86] See the next section, at 90.

[87] [2001] 1 Cr. App. R. (S) 372.

[88] Ibid.: 375. See more recently *R.* v. *Kingsley, Attorney General's Reference (no. 64 of 2003); Attorney General's Reference (no. 78 of 2003)* [2004] EWCA Crim. 418; and *Robertson* v. *HM Advocate*.

[89] S. 1(1).

may have been insufficient evidence to establish that the individual had committed more than preparatory acts to the relevant offence under the existing law.[90]

The offence relating to grooming can be found under s. 15(1) of the SOA, which provides that an individual aged eighteen or over (A) commits the offence of 'meeting a child following sexual grooming etc' if:

(1) having met or communicated with another person (B) on at least two earlier occasions, he:
  (i) intentionally meets B, or
  (ii) travels with the intention of meeting B in any part of the world;
(2) at the time, he intends to do anything to or in respect of B, during or after the meeting and in any part of the world, which if done will involve the commission by A of a relevant offence;[91]
(3) B is under 16;[92] and
(4) A does not reasonably believe that B is 16 or over.

The maximum sentence that can be imposed following conviction on indictment is ten years. The courts can also impose sentences for public protection for the s. 15 offence, as is permitted by the Criminal Justice Act 2003.[93]

It initially appears, then, that there is a significant difference between the offence relating to grooming and the child pornography offences. The former is pre-emptive, aimed at tackling preparatory behaviour to the act of child sexual abuse, thereby avoiding the child suffering more serious harm. In contrast, the child pornography offences under the PCA and SOA criminalize a harm that has already occurred to the

90 For further discussion, see Ost 2004: 150–1.

91 Any offence under Pt. 1 of the SOA amounts to a 'relevant offence'. A number of other sexual offences are listed under Sch. 3, paras. 61–92.

92 Given that the s. 15 offence only applies where the child is under sixteen, the appropriateness of revising the definition of a child under the PCA and CJA child pornography offences to encompass sixteen- and seventeen-year-olds is again brought into question. If sixteen- and seventeen-year-olds are thought to be less vulnerable to grooming or more capable of resisting attempts to groom, why should they be considered more vulnerable in the case of child pornography?

93 See, e.g. *Attorney General's Reference (no. 3 of 2006)*. For the court to impose such a sentence under s. 225(4), which is for an indeterminate time, the offender must have committed a serious offence and there must be 'a significant risk to members of the public of serious harm occasioned by the commission by [the offender] of further specified offences'. S. 225(1)(b). The offender can be considered for release when he is no longer considered to pose a danger to children.

child. However, notwithstanding this, I suggest that there is an interesting and important parallel between the offence related to grooming and the possession of child pornography offence; the latter can also be seen to be, in significant part, aimed at preventing potential harm.[94]

Although no actual definition of grooming is provided in the legislation, the explanatory notes that accompany the SOA provide some indication of the form of behaviour that the government considers can amount to grooming. The notes make reference to conduct which may have:

> an explicitly sexual content, such as A [the adult] entering into conversations with the child about the sexual acts he wants to engage her in when they meet, or sending images of adult pornography. However, the prior meetings or communication need not have an explicitly sexual content and could for example simply be A giving the child swimming lessons or meeting her incidentally through a friend.[95]

The lack of any statutory indication of what can amount to grooming through meeting or communication with the child does beg the question of whether s. 15 was intended to be a 'catch all' offence, covering any contact with the child provided that the individual subsequently sets out to meet her. The breadth of s. 15 has led civil rights campaign group Liberty to express concern that people will be less willing to intervene and talk to a child where they suspect that some form of abuse in the home has occurred. Individuals may fear that their intent in communicating with the child will be misinterpreted as harmful.[96]

It is significant that s. 15 does not criminalize an act of grooming *per se*, despite the government's statement in *Protecting the Public* that the offence would be that of grooming.[97] Are there not grounds to argue that, besides being a necessary element of the offence of meeting the child or travelling with the intention of meeting the child under s. 15, the grooming itself should constitute an offence? It is surely arguable that the same threat is posed by a person who grooms a child, but does not then travel to meet the child because, for example, the child informs him that she has decided not to go. If the individual was unsuccessful the first time, he is likely to develop his grooming technique and try to meet a child again. Thus, if one of the main purposes of the legislation is to protect children *before* abuse occurs, then criminalizing the very act of

[94] See the discussion later in this chapter, at 91.

[95] See the explanatory note to s. 15 in *Sexual Offences Act: Explanatory Notes* 2004: para. 27.

[96] Select Committee on Home Affairs 2003: App. 21, para. 18.

[97] Home Office 2002: para. 54. See also Gillespie 2006: 412.

grooming would further meet this aim. This argument has even greater weight if the act of grooming is viewed as *part of* a pattern of abusive behaviour.[98] However, Gillespie comments that 'the creation of … an offence [criminalizing the specific act of grooming] would be virtually impossible as the grooming process takes such a long time and covers so many areas that, if criminalised, it would lead to innocent conversations and actions being brought within the remit too'.[99] Whilst this is undoubtedly true, the offence of *meeting* a child following sexual grooming also raises challenges for the police in terms of gaining sufficient evidence of the harmful intent required.

The crucial question of ulterior intent and the practical utilization of the s. 15 offence

> The act constituting a crime may in some circumstances be objectively innocent, and take its criminal colouring entirely from the intent with which it is done.[100]

In the context of the s. 15 offence, intent is the crucial issue that separates behaviour that is potentially harmful to children from non-harmful behaviour. In order to satisfy the element of an intent to commit an offence against a child, the prosecution must prove beyond all reasonable doubt that an individual arranged the meeting with the child with a harmful purpose in mind. This will depend on the extent to which all of the circumstances surrounding the previous grooming, and perhaps the meeting itself, reveal such a purpose.

Prior to the enactment of the SOA, senior police and probation officers identified difficulties regarding the issue of proving harmful intent and expressed concern that the s. 15 offence might be impossible to use in practice, particularly in cases where the individual has no prior convictions for child sex offences.[101] The practical utilization of s. 15 may reveal that such concerns were well placed. One police officer I interviewed commented that:

> to prove that intent to twelve good men and true in the jury is really difficult. You've really got to have the explicit email before they set off [regarding] what they intend to do in graphic detail … And I think the

98 See Robins 2000; and Chapter 1, 32–9.
99 Gillespie 2002: 419.
100 Williams 1961: 22.
101 'Grooming law is unworkable, police warn', *The Guardian*, 26 November 2002.

> Crown Prosecution Service sometimes appreciate how difficult it is to prove and as a result of that, become reluctant to refer charges.[102]

In the words of another:

> the Government are very good at [creating] offences, but they can't legislate for how you investigate such offences. We have proved a few, but not very many. There haven't been very many prosecutions actually as I understand it.[103]

It may be easier for the police and Crown Prosecution Service (CPS) to establish harmful intent evidence as a result of the changes brought by the Criminal Justice Act 2003 regarding the admissibility of evidence relating to the defendant's prior convictions.[104] Communications of an explicit, sexual nature also provide strong evidence of intent, even where the individual does not have any past convictions for relevant offences.[105] In *R.* v. *Mohammed*,[106] the defendant had no such convictions, although he did have a number of convictions for other unrelated offences. He had been charged with child abduction and the s. 15 offence and the jury found him guilty on both counts. Mohammed had been introduced to the victim, a thirteen-year-old girl with severe learning difficulties and behavioural problems, by one of her friends and they exchanged telephone numbers. There then followed a number of telephone calls and text messages over a period of several months, which were of a suggestive and intimate nature. The victim visited the defendant at his house and stayed overnight. The defendant was arrested after he had collected the victim from a telephone box in his van, this event having being witnessed by her foster sister who, together with her partner, had followed

102 Interview RX2. Similar views were expressed by the officer in Interview RX8. Another stated that: 'There are easier offences to prosecute because you have to know that he wants to go there to have sex, which is why it tends to be done over the internet. You tend to have something written down and then you can prove what his intent was.' Interview RX5. In this officer's experience, the easier offence to prove was that of child abduction under the Child Abduction Act 1984, s. 2, since it is not necessary to establish what the individual's intentions are. However, he saw the negative consequences of this offence as being that sentencing powers 'are perhaps less than a grooming offence should be'.

103 Interview RX3.

104 See Chapter 5. According to one of the police officers I interviewed, 'we've now got evidence of bad character that we can use, if the offender has previous convictions'. Interview RX4. Another officer also made this point: Interview RX6.

105 'We can look at the computer traffic ... If we can get our hands on the victim's and perpetrator's computers, we can look at what traffic has gone between them and maybe adduce evidence from there. There may be telephone contact that we could look at.' Interview RX4.

106 See also *R.* v. *Mansfield*.

the vehicle and alerted the police. Whilst the jury did not have prior convictions for sexual offences from which they could infer that the defendant had a harmful intention when he met his victim, the evidence of the text messages in particular satisfied the majority that the requisite intention to commit an offence was present.[107]

The legislation provides no explicit explanation of *why* the content of communications or the events that take place during a prior meeting with the child may be deemed to amount to grooming, and could thus be indicative of an intention to commit an offence at the subsequently arranged meeting. The Act simply provides a broad definition of an act of prior communication, or a prior meeting with the child, leaving it to the jury to make the decision as to the intention behind the defendant's actions.[108] In some cases, all of the surrounding circumstances could provide evidence of a course of grooming and a harmful ulterior intention. For example, in *R.* v. *Wilson*, the appellant had met a number of girls under the age of sixteen after he had made contact with them on a website. He was charged with various offences alongside the s. 15 offence, relating to sexual intercourse with a girl under sixteen, sexual activity with a child, making indecent photographs of a child, possessing such photographs, and indecent assault on a female. Wilson pleaded guilty to all of the offences. The evidence relating to Wilson's use of the website to meet young teenage girls, his sexual activities with his victims and the indecent photographs of children he had taken could have been convincing evidence of a harmful intention had a jury been required to reach a verdict as to whether he had committed the s. 15 offence.[109]

A well-publicized case in which the conduct in question occurred prior to the SOA coming into force seems to offer another example of the type of evidence which could be enough to demonstrate harmful intent. In August 2003, a man was convicted of attempting to incite another to procure a nine-year-old girl for sex. He had used a website set up by American law enforcement agents to procure a young girl in the UK. When he was arrested on his way to what he thought would be a meeting with a girl, he was found to have in his possession a gun, a teddy bear and a condom.[110] However, such evidence is unlikely to be

[107] Ibid., particularly paras. 6 and 8. [108] See s. 15(2).

[109] See 'Man, 54, jailed for web grooming', BBC News report, 1 March 2007, http://news.bbc.co.uk/1/hi/wales/north_west/6410013.stm for a further recent example of persuasive evidence of an ulterior intent.

[110] See 'Student jailed after child sex sting', BBC News report, 11 August 2003, http://news.bbc.co.uk/1/hi/uk/3141803.stm. In the explanatory note to s. 15, an individual travelling to a

available in all cases since some groomers may take care to ensure that they are not in possession of incriminating evidence. One of the officers I interviewed stated that, in his experience, groomers 'are well versed and practised in the art of deception and they're not going to travel with a … sexual grooming kit that is so obvious and overt that they're going to get themselves charged. They're going to prepare properly and they're going to take [the child] to a hotel or another place or somewhere where that equipment may be.'[111]

The cases discussed above indicate that a harmful ulterior intention can be inferred prior to the individual meeting the child, particularly where explicit communications exist. The broad scope of the offence also means that it can apply in circumstances where sufficient evidence of an intention to commit an offence only materializes when the individual actually meets the child. However, it is highly unlikely that the police would permit such a meeting to occur. Representatives of the Metropolitan Police Service have stated that police officers would never allow a child to physically meet an adult believed to be a danger to her, citing a case where one individual sexually abused three children within fifteen minutes of meeting them.[112] This is further substantiated by the same police officer involved in my study as quoted above:

> You can't … say, 'Well, we'll just let that happen' and then intercept them at the point of contact. Because, what if you get lost? What if they do meet up and you don't make that interception … You're effectively really condoning or allowing an offence. So it's really hard.[113]

Inevitably, there will be cases where the necessary intent cannot be proven without a meeting taking place. For example, an officer working undercover may encounter an individual who, believing the officer is a child, enters into communications with her, the content of which are not overtly sexual. If the individual then arranges to meet the 'child', there is insufficient evidence here to prove an intent to commit a sexual offence. By way of another example, in *Re Attorney General's Reference (No. 41 of 2000)*, the defendant groomed a thirteen-year-old boy prior to committing the offence of making indecent photographs of him by providing

meeting he has arranged with the child with ropes, condoms and lubricants is given as an example of evidence from which the intent to commit an offence could be drawn. See *Sexual Offences Act: Explanatory Notes* 2004: para. 29. One of the officers involved in my study also highlighted this as a way in which intent could be evidenced: Interview RX4.

111 Interview RX2. 112 Select Committee on Home Affairs 2003: App. 22, para. 7.

113 Interview RX2.

him with numerous gifts and money. However, the giving of gifts and money is not behaviour which could, in itself, be indicative of an intent to commit a sexual offence against a child at a subsequent meeting.[114] In such cases, it seems that the s. 15 offence would not be made out, given that the police would be unwilling to allow a subsequent meeting with the child to take place because of the danger that this could pose.

A successful prosecution also depends on a cooperative victim. Where grooming is effective, this is problematic since: 'Many victims profess love or close feelings for offenders.'[115] A police officer who participated in my study discussed the problem of uncooperative victims:

> You've got a young, fifteen year old girl who might not appreciate that [she is a] victim … That is very, very difficult to manage … And then … also, because of the effects of grooming, you sometimes get to the situation where they don't want [the offender] to be punished and they feel that they're still in love with this person. Or they don't want the embarrassment of going to court. Or their parents bring influence to bear because they don't want the family embarrassed by the case going through the courts.[116]

Furthermore, the police often only learn about the occurrence of grooming after the child has been sexually abused. According to one police officer, children 'don't realize they're being groomed … so they don't come forward until something goes wrong. The police are very good at investigating after sexual grooming has taken place and somebody's actually been abused in some way, shape or form. But identifying the signs earlier and being able to prevent it, that's where we're trying to be at.'[117] In his experience, the s. 15 offence only tends to be used: 'a) where parents get access to the computer and find something or b) where we get access online and realize that [we can] actually target somebody using the undercover type work'.[118] Another officer explained why there are not many police statistics available for the s. 15 offence: 'Invariably, a

[114] Consider again the variety of grooming methods discussed in the previous chapter.

[115] Wolak *et al.* 2008: 113.

[116] Interview RX2. The difficulty of the victim not realizing she is a victim was highlighted by other officers (Interviews RX3, RX5 and RX6). Other officers emphasized the need for full disclosure from the victim (Interviews RX4 and RX8).

[117] Interview RX3.

[118] Ibid. For examples of recent police undercover work that has caught groomers, see the following links to reports on the BBC News website: http://news.bbc.co.uk/1/hi/england/norfolk/7296552.stm; http://news.bbc.co.uk/1/hi/england/devon/7410599.stm; http://news.bbc.co.uk/1/hi/england/berkshire/7095947.stm; and http://news.bbc.co.uk/1/hi/england/sussex/6402279.stm. See also *R.* v. *S.* [2008] EWCA Crim. 600.

further substantive criminal offence has been committed ... as opposed to the grooming ... a physical offence, like indecent assault or underage sex with a child ... or a rape ... and so that offence gets crimed and not the grooming.'[119]

Whilst the need to prove an ulterior, harmful intent in respect of the s. 15 offence does pose clear difficulties, the cases discussed above demonstrate that convincing evidence of this intention can be obtained from all of the circumstances surrounding the defendant's actions. It seems that especially where evidence of explicit prior communications exists, the police can successfully utilize the s. 15 offence, although I have highlighted limitations in terms of the police being able to uncover acts of grooming before actual abuse occurs. Whether the introduction of this criminal offence is the most effective means of combating grooming in the contexts it most often occurs is another matter. This is a question I address in the final section of this chapter, and also return to in Chapter 3.

The criminalization of grooming under other statutory provisions

I have noted the fact that the act of grooming itself is not specifically criminalized under the SOA. Thus, it is also necessary to examine other provisions under the SOA that criminalize specific acts which could form a part of the grooming process.

The act of causing a child to watch a sexual act, which includes causing a child to look at a photograph or pseudo-photograph of a person engaging in sexual activity, is criminalized under s. 12, which reads:

A person aged 18 or over (A) commits an offence if –

(a) for the purpose of obtaining sexual gratification, he intentionally causes another person (B) to watch a third person engaging in an activity, or to look at an image of any person engaging in an activity,
(b) the activity is sexual, and
(c) either –
(i) B is under 16 and A does not reasonably believe that B is 16 or over, or
(ii) B is under 13.[120]

[119] Interview RX2.

[120] Conviction for the s. 12 offence can lead to a maximum sentence of ten years' imprisonment. Note also the s. 19 offence, which mirrors the s. 12 offence where the individual is in a position of trust in relation to the victim and the victim is under eighteen.

Crucially, then, it must be proven that this act is carried out for the purpose of sexual gratification in order for the offence to be committed. It would seem that the government felt it necessary to include a specific *mens rea* element within the s. 12 offence in order to exclude from its ambit acts of, for example, showing children material of a sexual content for the purposes of sexual education. One particular method of grooming can be to show a child photographs of other children taking part in sexual activities, in order to convince her that what the individual is asking her to do is the norm. In a study conducted by Elliott *et al.*, 14 per cent of the child sex abusers interviewed by the authors stated that they used pornography to develop strategies to approach children.[121] Prior to judicial interpretation of s. 12, I made the case that if an individual showed a child photographs of other children taking part in sexual activities for the purpose of grooming rather than sexual gratification, he would not have committed an offence under s. 12.[122] However, in *R.* v. *Abdullahi*,[123] it was held that sexual gratification does not need to occur immediately for the s. 12 offence to be made out. The courts have thus extended the sexual gratification element of the offence to a distant, future-intended purpose. This interpretation of the requirement of sexual gratification to include gratification obtained at some later point encompasses a situation where, for instance, the individual continues to successfully groom the child and receives gratification from some subsequent behaviour.[124]

The s. 12 offence follows offences under ss. 9, 10 and 11, which relate to sexual activity with a child, inciting a child to engage in sexual activity and engaging in sexual activity in the presence of a child.[125] Another of the offences under Pt. 1 of the SOA could also be interpreted to apply to a situation in which an individual grooms a child. Under s. 14, it is an offence for an individual to intentionally arrange or facilitate any action which he intends to do or intends another person to do or believes that another person will do, in any part of the

[121] Elliott *et al.* 1995: 585. See also O'Connell 2003: 11; and Taylor and Quayle 2003: 23.

[122] Ost 2004: 154. The individual would not be guilty of an offence under s. 15 in these circumstances, provided that he does not subsequently meet the child and there is insufficient evidence to charge him with attempt. Whilst the individual would commit the offence of showing indecent images of children under the PCA, charging him with this offence would fail to address the fact that he committed this act with a specific, harmful purpose.

[123] [2007] 1 WLR 225.

[124] See also Gillespie 2006: 414; and Ormerod 2007.

[125] For an argument that the s. 10 offence may catch behaviour that involves showing a child pornography, see Gillespie 2006: 415–6. See Ost 2004: 155–156, for a discussion of the way in which the offences under ss. 9–11 cast a wider net than that cast by the now repealed Indecency with Children Act 1960.

world, if this action will involve the commission of an offence under ss. 9 to 13. In *R.* v. *Harrison*,[126] the appellant groomed a child with the intention of causing or inciting her to engage in sexual activity (masturbation of herself whilst she was on the telephone to him), the s. 10 offence. He was charged and pleaded guilty to the offence of arranging or facilitating the commission of a child sex offence under s. 14. The application of s. 14 to behaviour that amounts to grooming in this case is significant because, in a situation such as that in *Harrison*, no meeting between the individual and the child actually took place, nor did the appellant set out with the intention of meeting the child. Thus, the s. 15 offence would not be made out. However, provided that the intended action that the individual arranges or facilitates amounts to or will amount to an offence under the relevant sections, then he commits the s. 14 offence. The s. 14 offence could also apply where, for example, the individual arranges to cause the child to watch a sexual act he will perform through the use of a webcam, for the purpose of grooming (the intention being to commit the s. 12 offence). Again, the s. 14 offence is made out before the behaviour criminalized under s. 12 occurs, and without any meeting between the individual and the child being planned or taking place. That the s. 14 offence criminalizes behaviour which can amount to grooming without the need for a meeting to occur or even to have been intended by the individual, could provide wider protection to children from sexual groomers and abusers.

It is of interest that in giving judgment as to the appropriateness of the sentence passed in *Harrison*, the Court of Appeal actually referred to the s. 14 offence as an 'offence of grooming',[127] although there is nothing within the Explanatory Note to s. 14 to suggest that the legislature was targeting grooming behaviour. The effective utilization of the s. 14 offence in the context of grooming is dependent, however, on the child disclosing the groomer's behaviour. As already discussed, children may be reluctant to come forward with this information. Child sex offenders might use threats or violence to control children when preparing to abuse them and other methods to prevent the child from disclosing after the abuse.[128] Whether the s. 14 offence can be used to criminalize grooming behaviour is also dependent on the existence of evidence that the action which the groomer intended amounted to an offence. Offenders involved in Elliott *et al.*'s study revealed that their grooming

[126] [2005] EWCA Crim. 3458. [127] Ibid.: para. 13. [128] Elliot *et al.* 1995: 585–6.

strategies included telling stories, teaching the child a sport or how to play a musical instrument and playing games.[129] None of these activities in themselves could provide evidence that the groomer was intentionally arranging or facilitating a relevant offence.

Finally, here, there is a further provision under the SOA that could potentially apply to acts of grooming. Steps can be taken to prohibit an individual from carrying out certain acts against children that may be undertaken for the purpose of grooming by virtue of s. 123 of the SOA. This provision enables the police to apply to a magistrates' court for a Risk of Sexual Harm Order (RSHO) to be brought against an individual who has committed certain specified acts on at least two occasions. These acts include communicating with a child where the content of such communication is sexual and causing a child to look at a moving or still image that is sexual.[130] Such an order prohibits the individual from doing anything described in it, with the proviso that any prohibitions imposed must be necessary for the purpose of protecting children generally or any child from harm from the defendant. The harm can be physical or psychological.[131] The individual will commit an offence if he does anything he is prohibited from doing under the order.[132] Therefore, if such an order is made against an individual who, for example, sends e-mails with a sexual content to a child and the order prohibits him from entering into any further communication with children, any subsequent communication will amount to an offence.[133]

The RSHO could effectively criminalize acts which may be carried out for the purposes of grooming, but only *after* an individual has been identified as posing a threat to children. Thus, it is the individual's prior conduct which causes such acts to constitute an offence, rather than these acts being offences in themselves. However, the introduction of the RSHO has certainly extended the reach of the law. Previously, the police could apply to a magistrates' court for a Sex Offender Order if they had reasonable cause to believe that a convicted sex offender was acting in a way that posed serious harm to members of the public.[134] The offender was then prohibited from carrying out the acts named in the order for a minimum of five years. The new order is available at a

129 Ibid. 130 S. 123(3). 131 Ss.123(6) and 124(2). 132 S. 128.

133 Note also the Sexual Offence Prevention Orders that can be imposed upon an individual convicted of any of the offences relating to child pornography, meeting a child following sexual grooming and the ss. 9–12 offences under the SOA, where there is evidence of a risk of him causing serious sexual harm. See s. 104 of the SOA.

134 Under the Crime and Disorder Act 1998, s. 2, repealed by the SOA.

much earlier stage and can be brought against *any* individual, not only convicted sex offenders.[135]

THE LAW'S FRAMING AND CONSTRUCTION OF CHILD PORNOGRAPHY AND SEXUAL GROOMING

Having analysed the relevant offences, in order now to uncover the law's ideological framing of child pornography and grooming, it is necessary to engage in a theoretical analysis of the way in which the law 'thinks' about and constructs the dangers represented by these phenomena. This final section provides the beginnings of my moral panic analysis of the legal and social response to child pornography and grooming, which will be developed in Chapter 4, and offers an introduction to the crucial question of harm to be addressed in the next chapter. It examines the impulsion that steered Parliament towards legislation and assesses what the increased criminalization of behaviour reveals about the law's construction of the harms of child pornography and grooming. It also considers the effects of increased criminalization. It concludes by drawing attention to the problematical legal construct and framework of indecency that surrounds the child pornography laws, and the potential dangers of a generalized legal construction of grooming as stranger grooming through the use of modern technologies.

The impetus behind the introduction of the laws relating to child pornography and grooming and the law's construction of harm

Persak has recently reminded us that the state's power to render behaviour criminal, with all the consequences this brings for the individual concerned, is a vast and dangerous power for a liberal society.[136] Arguably, the main check that can be placed upon this power is to ensure that the behaviour in question has first been socially categorized as seriously harmful. Further, as Ashworth remarks, the 'chief concern of the criminal law is to prohibit behaviour that represents a serious wrong against an individual or against some fundamental social value or institution'.[137] To simply see the criminal law as reflecting a social understanding that certain behaviour is both harmful and wrongful, however, would be

[135] See further Shute 2004: 417–40.

[136] Persak 2007: 12. See also Husak 2008: vii; and Schonsheck 1994: 1.

[137] Ashworth 2006: 1. See also Simester and Smith 1996: 4–6. Duff highlights the criminal law's concern with moral wrongs. Duff 2007: 80.

to take a narrow view. Legislation criminalizing behaviour must pass through the filter of politics in order to become a recognized source of law: 'Criminalisation is, first and foremost, a political process; a process, through which the world of politics *via* criminal policy penetrates into the world of law.'[138] With this in mind, the discussion here focuses on the political impetuses that compelled the legislature to take action against child pornography and grooming, and influenced legal constructions of harm.

The Protection of Children Bill (PCB) began its rapid journey through Parliament during a time when a less tolerant, more restrictive approach was being adopted towards 'corruptive' behaviour, such as the publication of obscene material and behaviour that offended public decency. As McCarthy and Moodie observe, in the wake of more liberal statutes in the 1960s,[139] 'the trend of legislation had swung against "permissive social behaviour"' in the 1970s.[140] The government's concern about the legal regulation of obscene and indecent material was evidenced by the Home Secretary's appointment of a committee chaired by Bernard Williams to review obscenity and indecency laws in 1977.[141]

Much of the propulsion behind the criminalization of behaviour related to child pornography and grooming is revealed by the debates that preceded the enactment of the legislation. My starting point is the background to and introduction of the Private Member's Bill that became the PCA into the House of Commons in 1978. Cyril Townsend, the Conservative MP who introduced the PCB, emphasized the need to eradicate the harm of exploitation caused by child pornography from the start.[142] In MP Michael Alison's view, the PCB was solely concerned 'with the children used in the production of pornography' and the 'appalling damage' they suffer due to their involvement.[143] A number of other

[138] Persak 2007: 5.

[139] Such as the Abortion Act 1967, the Suicide Act 1961 and the Sexual Offences Act 1967. The latter decriminalized homosexual conduct occurring in private where individuals were over the age of twenty-one in light of the conclusions of the Wolfenden Committee. See Committee on Homosexual Offences and Prostitution 1957.

[140] McCarthy and Moodie 1981: 48.

[141] See Committee on Obscenity and Film Censorship 1979 and Hansard, HC Deb. 10 February 1978: column 1851.

[142] Hansard, HC Deb. 10 February 1978: column 1827. See also Townsend 1979, in which Townsend states that his Bill was designed 'to strengthen the law against the exploitation of children for pornographic purposes', at 2.

[143] Ibid.: columns 1854 and 1856.

MPs also highlighted the exploitation of children as the primary harm of child pornography during the 1978 Parliamentary debates.[144]

In the year prior to the debates, the problem of child pornography had increasingly been a matter of media attention and calls for legal action had been made by prominent moral campaigner Mary Whitehouse and the National Viewers' and Listeners' Association (NVALA). Their ABUSE (Action to Ban Sexual Exploitation of Children) campaign was backed by a one-and-a-half-million signature petition.[145] The strong public support for the ABUSE campaign was ensured by Whitehouse writing to editors of 270 regional and religious newspapers to publicize the cause and urging readers to lobby their MPs for their support for the PCB. When the Labour Government failed to support the ABUSE campaign, Whitehouse targeted the Conservative Party, a party that was keen to further its political interests by backing a cause that would cast the government as being soft on behaviour that threatened societal values.[146] Whitehouse also enlisted the help of American child pornography expert, lawyer and psychiatrist Judianne Densen-Gerber. Just before the PCB was due to be read for the second time, Densen-Gerber spoke at press conferences and to MPs, and gave televized interviews about her perception of the enormity of the problem of child pornography in America and internationally.[147]

In introducing the PCB, Cyril Townsend took great pains to emphasize the public pressure and support for a bill of its kind. His justification for a new law targeting child pornography involved reference to expert opinion, newspaper and television coverage, religious opinion, statements from child welfare organizations, and letters from a General of the Salvation Army and the Chief Constable of the Greater Manchester Police.[148] The latter was particularly significant, given the Chief Constable's statement that: 'There is clear evidence from several

[144] Ibid.: columns 1857, 1876–8, 1883, 1885–6, 1889, 1897, 1905, 1909 and 1918. Hansard, HL Deb. 5 May 1978: column 536.

[145] See the NVALA Archives, Boxes 114 and 115; Hansard, HL Deb. 5 May 1978: column 565; and Jenkins 1992: 73.

[146] McCarthy and Moodie 1981: 50 and 54–5.

[147] Ibid.: 50 and 58. See also NVALA Archives, Box 115. For a critical discussion of Densen-Gerber's claims and the evidence relied upon by Mary Whitehouse, see Chapter 4, at 158–60.

[148] Hansard, HC Deb. 10 February 1978: columns 1827–31 and 1840–1. Townsend later commented: 'if there had not been massive public opinion and, in particular, some one and a half million signatures on a petition collected by the ABUSE campaign, I do not believe we would have the Bill on the Statute Book'. Quoted in McCarthy and Moodie 1981: 57. See also Townsend 1979: 3.

of my police divisions that more and more pornographic material seized by my officers depicts young children.'[149] He also noted that, according to Vice Squad officers' estimations, about 5 per cent of all of the material seized from hard pornography bookshops in Greater Manchester was child pornography.[150] Armed with this and other evidence obtained through his nationwide investigation into child pornography, Townsend informed the House of Commons that:

> It is impossible to prove beyond a shadow of a doubt that the photographing of children for pornographic purposes is on the increase in Britain, although the majority of those whom I have consulted believe that that is so ... But there can be no doubt that the photographing of children for such purposes is widespread in this country ...[151]

Other MPs seemed uncertain about how long the problem of child pornography had been developing, with one believing that it had been around for 'the last ten years', another for 'these past two years' and another for even longer than ten years.[152] Townsend's evidence that there had been a recent increase in the prevalence of child pornography was challenged by the Home Secretary, Brynmor John. His consultation with the same Chief Constable revealed that there were no hard figures to back up the 5 per cent figure quoted. Research conducted by the Home Office indicated that contrary to press coverage, the majority of hard pornography was not home-produced, but imported from foreign jurisdictions. The Home Office's research, which involved consultations with many police forces throughout the country, also brought into question newspaper reports that the amount of hard pornography being brought into the country was increasing. According to Customs authorities and police forces, the amount of such material 'is not great and does not show a rapid increase in recent times'.[153] Consequently, the Home Office concluded that existing legislation was sufficient to deal with child pornography.[154] In contrast, those strongly in favour of the PCB presented a construction of the harms caused by child pornography that challenged the ability of the existing law to deal with the problem. MP Michael Alison argued that the law failed to catch the evil of child pornography following a Court of Appeal judgment in 1977 that it

[149] Hansard, ibid.: column 1831. [150] Ibid.

[151] Ibid.: column 1829. Note also Robert Hicks's statement that 'the police believe that child pornography is a problem that may be increasing'. Ibid.: column 1889.

[152] Ibid.: column 1862. [153] Ibid.: columns 1845–6. [154] Ibid.

did not amount to an indecent assault to photograph naked children.[155] Further, in his view, the Obscene Publications Act 1959 was not aimed at the main evil of child pornography, which was again presented as the damage suffered by the child in the image. Townsend highlighted the fact that the Indecency with Children Act 1960 only extended to children under the age of fourteen.[156]

Despite the government's cautious reaction to the PCB,[157] they chose not to oppose it given the nature of the public reaction in light of the ABUSE campaign.[158] In the words of Lord Houghton: 'the Government have connived for political reasons in foisting this Bill onto Parliament, because I believe they are afraid of the Campaign that would be waged against them if the Bill were not passed and they could be accused of having failed to protect the nation's children'.[159] Lord Houghton offered what appears to have been very much the minority view in Parliament, expressing concern that the Bill was being rushed through with little debate and as a consequence of aggressive public pressure.[160]

Moving forward to the criminalization of possessing child pornography in 1988, a large part of the impetus for this extension of the law came from the police and the pressure they placed on the government. Beginning in 1986, Scotland Yard had chosen to make child pornography a 'number one target' and police officers called for the criminalization of possession in order to enable prosecutions to be brought where material was found, but evidence of intended distribution was lacking.[161] This supports Dubber's view that: 'Possession is the ideal fall-back, or charge-down option in today's criminal process. If nothing else sticks, possession will.'[162] The rationalization for making possession an offence was accompanied by the construction of possession as harmful in itself, and this construction is the one that has become cemented in the law thereafter.

One way in which possession was constructed as a harmful act was to blur the distinction between the production and possession of child pornography. For example, the Home Secretary was quick to challenge any

[155] Ibid.: columns 1853–6. [156] Ibid.: column 1834.

[157] Ibid.: columns 1841, 1843, 1848 and 1849–52. [158] See McCarthy and Moodie 1981.

[159] Hansard, HL Deb. 28 June 1978: column 346. See also Gibbons 1995: 87.

[160] Hansard, HL Deb. 5 May 1978: columns 553 and 556. See further Chapter 4, at 161–2 and 164; and McCarthy and Moodie 1981: 60.

[161] See 'Yard officers seek more help to fight child pornography', *The Times*, 4 April 1988; 'Labour backs Hurd on child pornography', *The Times*, 17 October 1987; and 'Obscenity call', *The Times*, 8 October 1987. See also Williams 2004: 256.

[162] Dubber 2005: 96.

argument against criminalization of the possession of child pornography on the basis of infringing individual freedoms when no harm was caused by the behaviour in the following way: 'I am not persuaded in the case of material which exploits children this position stands close scrutiny. Such material can only be produced through exploiting and violating children and sometimes subjecting them to appalling degradation.'[163] His main justification for removing the individual freedom to possess child pornography – that this behaviour was harmful – was presented as and merged with the harm that the production of such material causes children. To use Best's terminology, the possession of child pornography was presented within the domain of the existing problem.[164] Arguing that the creation of child pornography involves the exploitation of a child and that the possession of the image exacerbates and encourages this exploitation can lend further legitimation to such a fusion of harm construct. In a newspaper article, the Minister of State (David Maclean) explained that it was appropriate to criminalize possession 'because it contributed to the exploitation of children' and stated that the only way to bring an end to this exploitation was to 'act against those without whom it would not exist – the people who actually buy child pornography'.[165] As a second validating factor behind criminalization, both the Home Secretary and the Minister of State stated that possession 'fed the instincts which gave rise to sexual abuse'.[166] Such a claim, which appears to be predicated upon the existence of a causal link between possessing child pornography and committing child sexual abuse, is still far from proven today, some twenty years after the government confidently relied on this construction of harm.[167]

Moving forward again to 1994, the objective behind the criminalization of pseudo-images was to expand the law to address what was perceived as another, newer threat.[168] The justification given for broadening the criminal law to catch pseudo-images was that such images were a further part of the larger problem of child pornography as a consequence of new technologies, and the law had to be expanded in

[163] 'Labour backs Hurd on child pornography', above, n. 161. [164] Best 1990: 65–6.

[165] 'New penalty to curb child porn', *The Guardian*, 1 March 1988; and see the Home Secretary's similar statement in the House of Commons debates: Hansard, HC Deb. 18 January 1988: column 689.

[166] Ibid. [167] See Chapter 3, at 108–13.

[168] According to Lady Maitland, 'computer technology has become a tremendous curse in the hands of the pornography industry, and when it is used to exploit children it is of great concern to us all'. Hansard, HC Standing Committee B: Criminal Justice and Public Order Bill, 15 February 1994: column 740. See also Home Affairs Committee 1994: para. 1.

order to keep up.[169] According to the Minister of State, the government was 'trying to ensure that anyone who uses a pseudo-photograph cannot use the excuse that somehow it is not an image'.[170] However, the government provided Parliament with few arguments as to *why* children were at risk of harm from the creation, distribution and possession of such images and, therefore, why the fact that the image was fabricated should not be an 'excuse'. How, then, did Parliament construe pseudo-images as harmful? When the CJPO Bill was at Committee stage, Labour MP Mike O'Brien stated that, although taking a pseudo-photograph of a child could amount to a 'victimless crime', if a photograph of a child's face from a magazine was used to create the pseudo-image, the child could be perceived to be a victim as the photograph was being used without consent, and that 'he or she is abused in another sense'.[171] He also referred to research by Catherine Itzin, which suggested that using 'such material' incited paedophiles to seek stronger stimuli and might lead them closer to committing indecent acts.[172] Both of these arguments are based upon assumptions. In the case of the former, for the child to suffer some form of actual harm, she or others she knows would need to be aware of the existence of the pseudo-image and, in the latter case, there is a supposition that viewing pseudo-images provokes an individual to behave in a certain way.

The 'abuse in another sense' of the child in the original image did not appear to be a construction of harm that impacted on the government. Rather, the Minister of State preferred to offer up another possible threat that pseudo-images represent: 'the problem is that certain people might use the photograph to lure children or to convince them that what is happening is all right … We are concerned that such material will be used to persuade children that something which we all know is wrong is, in fact, correct.'[173] This risk of harm was not substantiated with any evidence or research.[174] As had occurred when the criminalization of

[169] See Chapter 4, at 166–7; and 'Crackdown on computer porn', *The Guardian*, 26 November 1993.

[170] Hansard, HC Standing Committee B: Criminal Justice and Public Order Bill, 15 February 1994: column 733.

[171] Ibid.: column 742.

[172] Ibid. Additionally, O'Brien highlighted a practical difficulty: prosecutions could not be brought in cases where the police were unable to establish that the image was real rather than fabricated, an argument that will be addressed in the next chapter, at 131.

[173] Ibid.: column 745.

[174] The 'compelling' arguments accepted by the Home Affairs Committee in support of the criminalization of pseudo-images were also uncorroborated. See Home Affairs Committee 1994: para. 13.

possession was legitimized, an important distinction was again obscured; this time, the distinction between the production of real and virtual child pornography. Home Secretary Michael Howard, for instance, stated that he would not hesitate to act when individuals who degraded children found new methods to sell their material.[175] The obvious difference between the harm caused when a real child is forced to be involved in child pornography and the non-involvement of a child in the creation of a pseudo-image was left unaddressed. Instead, real and virtual images were placed into the same category and presented as giving rise to the same harm of degrading children.

Just as real child pornography and pseudo-images were given the same classification in the 1990s, so were all children presented as being at the same risk of harm from sexual predators in the early 2000s. By downplaying the maturity, sexual awareness and knowledge possessed by older children, the government was able to legitimate the further expansion of the child pornography laws to sixteen- and seventeen-year-olds brought into being by the SOA.[176] Moreover, the gradual amplification of both law and the construction of harm meant that an increase in the penalties that can be imposed upon conviction for child pornography offences was almost inevitably on the cards.

So, where has all this criminalization taken us? Contemporary child pornography law is not limiting itself towards the main harm of visual depictions that exploit real children, but is now directed towards exploitation of the non-existent child, possible future harm that could be caused to other children, and non-exploitative relationships involving sixteen- and seventeen-year-olds. It would seem that the original legislative purpose of preventing the exploitation of real children has gradually metamorphosed into a more all-encompassing construction of harm. Any behaviour related to child pornography, whether real, potential, remote or virtual, is thought to give rise to a risk of 'harm'.[177] This gradual but major shift in the legal discourses surrounding child pornography has been able to occur because the desire to protect the subject at risk has become so compelling. That there is no overwhelming evidence to suggest that children are at definite risk of harm from pseudo-images, or that there was a lack of considered Parliamentary debate as to whether the taking of a pornographic image of a sixteen- or seventeen-year-old is

175 See 'Crackdown on computer porn', above, n. 169.

176 See Home Office 2000: para. 7.6.3.

177 For a compelling critique of American law that is based in part upon a move away from its original purpose of preventing child sexual abuse to broader purposes that are not constitutionally defensible, see Adler 2001a.

always exploitative, has not mattered. Furthermore, the huge expansion of the legal construct of harm has been made practically possible because of the fluid concept of indecency which frames child pornography law, as I will discuss later.[178]

As with the more recent child pornography offences, in choosing to tackle the problem of grooming, the legislature was not directing itself towards criminalizing behaviour that causes primary harm in itself. Rather, it took a pre-emptive strike, rendering behaviour that could lead to harm unlawful. The harm of grooming was constructed as potential, anticipated harm.[179] This was the notion of harm promulgated by Childnet International, a children's internet charity, which provided much of the impetus and pressure for the introduction of a specific offence relating to online grooming. According to Childnet's Research and Policy Manager, the 'grooming offence' enables 'the law to step in before the physical harm and damage at the end of the grooming process has been wreaked on the child'.[180]

By and large, when the government and Parliament turned their attention to grooming, the main focus was on online, stranger grooming.[181] In the explanatory note to s. 15, it is stated that the offence is 'intended to cover situations where an adult establishes contact with a child through, for example, meetings, telephone conversations or communications on the Internet, and gains the child's trust and confidence so that he can arrange to meet the child for the purpose of committing a "relevant offence" against the child'.[182] Although the offence can cover offline grooming, it was designed to specifically target internet grooming due to Childnet's concentration on 'online sexual predators' and the fact that the offence was also largely brought about with the assistance and recommendations of the Task Force on Child Protection on the Internet.[183]

Thus far, I have examined the legislature's framing of child pornography and grooming, but the judiciary's role in extending criminalization should also be noted. Ashworth comments that judges 'retain a central place in the development of the criminal law. They seem to bear the major responsibility for developing the conditions and the scope of criminal liability, and also exert considerable influence on the shape of

[178] See the final section in this chapter, at 98–101. [179] See, e.g. Home Office 2002: para. 54.
[180] See Gardner 2003: 6. [181] See also McAlinden 2006: 342.
[182] *Sexual Offences Act: Explanatory Notes* 2004: 27.
[183] See Hansard, HL Deb. 19 November 2002: column 286; and Childnet's memorandum to the Select Committee on Home Affairs 2003: App. 7.

criminal law through their interpretation of statutory offences.'[184] This is clearly evidenced by the judiciary's merger of the making and possession of child pornography offences in the context of downloading material from the internet. Consider also the judicial extension of the sexual gratification element of the s. 12 offence under the SOA to a more remote future intended purpose, and the judicial interpretation of the s. 14 offence as an offence of grooming in *Harrison*. These latter developments indicate that the judiciary is following the government's lead, enabling the prevention of potential harm to children before it occurs by interpreting the law in a broad way.

The legislative measures and judicial interpretation discussed in this chapter clearly demonstrate that, in tackling child pornography and grooming, the law is responding to the wider societal desire to protect the group in society considered to be most vulnerable to sexual harm. Once the legislature chose to react to this societal pressure by going down the path of criminalizing the creation and dissemination of child pornography, it became very difficult to stop the trajectory towards criminalization of other behaviour. Thus, successive governments have been keen to enable more prosecutions of individuals who could not be successfully prosecuted under existing law, and to criminalize behaviour that might *potentially* cause harm; expansions of the criminal law which may be harder to legitimate.

Whilst, then, on the face of it, the offences relating to child pornography and grooming might appear to be designed to tackle different mischiefs, this is not necessarily the case. They are all framed around avoiding a risk of harm. Although it is true that a child may already have been harmed through the creation of child pornography, the PCB was introduced to avoid a predicted increase in the child pornography problem, and thus a future increase in the number of children harmed.[185] Criminalizing possession was considered to be a way of reducing the market for child pornography and, consequently, reducing the potential risk of other children being sexually abused through future involvement. As such, even if the mischiefs behind the offences relating to child pornography and grooming can initially be conceived to be different, they all serve to further a broader political, protectionist agenda of safeguarding children from potential, future harm.

The effects of the steady increase in criminalization

As more law has appeared on the statute book, is it also the case that prosecutions for offences regarding child pornography and grooming

[184] Ashworth 2006: 7. See also Husak 2008: 10–11.

[185] See Chapter 4, at 156 and 162–3.

have increased? Does the increase in criminalization reflect an increase in the prevalence of the phenomena? Table 1 provides the official figures for those individuals cautioned, prosecuted and found guilty for the offences of taking an indecent image of a child, possessing such an image and meeting a child after sexual grooming between 1996 and 2006.

What these figures indicate is that there has been an increase in the number of individuals cautioned, prosecuted and convicted in relation to making child pornography during this ten-year period. For instance, over four times as many people were convicted for this offence in 2001 than in 1996 and, in comparison with 2002, the number of people convicted in 2006 rose by over 65 per cent. The significant increase in cautions, prosecutions and offenders found guilty in 2003 for the two child pornography offences is the consequence of Operation Ore.[186] The peak in 2003 for the making offence has descended in more recent years, although the figures remain much higher in 2006 than they were in 2002. As Akdeniz notes, a further reason for this marked increase may be that prosecutors have preferred to bring charges for the making offence rather than the possession offence in light of the judicial categorization of downloading child pornography from the internet as 'making' indecent images of children.[187]

Turning to the possession offence, there was actually a decrease in the number of people found guilty between 1996 (seventy-nine) and 2001 (fifty-one). Since 2004, the figures for those cautioned and convicted for possession have not changed greatly; in fact, there was a decrease in these figures in 2006 compared with 2004. Certainly in the case of possession, none of these figures is staggering, suggesting a 'tide' of child pornography.[188] Turning to the s. 15 offence, although there has been an increase in prosecutions between 2004 and 2006, the figures are notably low. As would be expected, these figures are lower than the total amount of crime measured relating to the s. 15 offence in the same period. The *Crime in England and Wales 2006/7* Home Office Statistical Bulletin records 186 instances of crime in 2004/5, 237 in 2005/6 and 322 in 2006/7.[189] The difference in these figures may support the views of

[186] See Chapter 1, at 53 and Chapter 5, at 215. [187] Akdeniz 2008: 55.

[188] Caution should be taken when discussing official statistics as a guide to the prevalence of behaviour in question as of course, these statistics only reveal the behaviour that has been discovered and the cases where law enforcement action has been taken to at least the stage of issuing a caution. What should also be borne in mind is the difficulty of ascertaining the true prevalence of crimes related to child pornography and grooming. See Quayle *et al.* 2006: 2.

[189] Nicholas *et al.* 2007: Table 2.04. The figures in this bulletin are a combination of statistics from both the British Crime Survey and the police. The crimes recorded by the British Crime

TABLE 1. Number of defendants cautioned, prosecuted and found guilty at all courts for offences relating to child pornography and sexual grooming, 1996-2006

Offence description	Disposal[(1)]	1996	1997	1998	1999	2000	2001
Take/make indecent photographs of children	Cautioned	15	14	26	31	35	38
	Prosecuted	80	111	116	175	284	398
	Convicted	69	103	82	139	218	289
Possession of an indecent photograph of a child	Cautioned	16	17	19	34	25	25
	Prosecuted	125	124	167	163	129	88
	Convicted	79	81	105	99	77	51

Offence description	Disposal	2002	2003	2004	2005	2006
Take/make indecent photographs of children	Cautioned	63	239	201	195	168
	Prosecuted	582	1,464	1,097	1,101	937
	Convicted	434	1,048	978	958	768
Possession of an indecent photograph of a child	Cautioned	53	205	162	151	147
	Prosecuted	156	326	200	184	171
	Convicted	97	239	184	196	166
Meeting a child after sexual grooming	Cautioned	*	*	2	5	10
	Prosecuted	*	*	9	28	43
	Convicted	*	*	3	25	36

(1) The convicted column may sometimes exceed the number prosecuted in cases where a defendant has been prosecuted in earlier years or for a different offence.
* Not applicable.
Source: RDS – Offending and Criminal Justice Group, Home Office, Ref: IOS 503-03 (for 1996-2001), RDS – Office for Criminal Justice Reform, Ref: IOS 078-08 (for 2002-6).

police officers I interviewed regarding the difficulty of proving the s. 15 offence, emphasized by one officer's statement that when sexual activity has already occurred, the individual tends to be charged with a contact offence rather than the s. 15 offence.

Survey include crimes not reported to the police and crimes that have not been recorded by the police.

A consideration of these statistics produces more questions than answers. Can the criminal law really be having a deterrent effect if the occurrence of crimes regarding child pornography and grooming is on the increase? Are these crimes really, in fact, on the increase? Could it not be that the police are getting better at uncovering the occurrence of crime, as four of the officers I interviewed suggested,[190] or are these increasing figures simply the result of the ever-widening scope of behaviour that is criminalized?[191] What the statistics certainly do not and cannot prove is that increased criminalization has deterred individuals from committing crime related to child pornography and grooming.

If the legislature's aim is to offer better protection to children, is increasing criminalization to enable more prosecutions and escalating penal consequences the most effective approach? The supposition at work here is that the criminal law deters; would-be child pornographers and groomers will be discouraged from acting in a way that violates the criminal law for fear of the consequences if caught.[192] However, in Ashworth's view: 'The evidence ... does not support the belief that there is a hydraulic relationship between behaviour on the one hand and criminal laws and sentencing, on the other hand.'[193] Robinson and Darley's behavioural science assessment of whether criminal law deters leads them to conclude that assumptions that the existence of criminal law rules influences behaviour are 'disturbing' and 'dangerous'.[194] The research relied upon by Robinson and Darley reveals that many potential offenders are unaware of the criminal rules assumed to influence their behaviour.[195] What they do know about the rules may be inaccurate information acquired through 'indirect communication', 'experience and gossip'.[196] A major source of information about the criminal law rules

[190] Interviews RX1, RX3, RX4 and RX8. For example, one officer commented that since the introduction of two police operations in Lancashire focused upon child sexual exploitation, more instances of grooming are being found because they are now being looked for (Interview RX4).

[191] See also Adler 2001a: 231.

[192] For an analysis of the role that deterrence plays in justifying the criminal law, see Ashworth 2006: 16–17.

[193] Ibid.: 16.

[194] Robinson and Darley 2004: 173. The authors are 'profoundly sceptical that the formulation of criminal law rules or even sentencing policies or practices can have the deterrent effect that common wisdom assumes it has': 197.

[195] This is significant in light of research which reveals that there are five preconditions in order for criminal deterrence to be successfully achieved, all of which require the potential offender's subjective awareness of the criminal law penalties that can be imposed. See von Hirsch *et al.* 2000: 7.

[196] Robinson and Darley 2004: 178.

pertaining to child pornography and behaviour related to grooming for potential offenders is the media. It may be particularly important, then, that media news reports are littered with misleading references to the s. 15 offence as the 'grooming offence' and tend to focus on cases involving online grooming.[197] The knowledge that potential offenders derive from these reports is likely to be incomplete and inaccurate.

When prospective offenders do have accurate information about the criminal law rules, Robinson and Darley argue that their cost-benefit analysis directs them towards violation rather than compliance.[198] There will, however, be cases where their cost-benefit analysis does incentivize potential offenders to comply with the criminal law. This may be because their analysis takes into account not only the detriment they will suffer by the imposition of a sanction, but broader negative consequences, such as stigma, loss of reputation, social disapproval and the effects of 'naming and shaming'.[199] The latter is particularly relevant in the case of offences relating to child pornography and grooming. This is reflected by Earl Ferrers's observation that criminalizing the possession of child pornography should reduce the market for such material because individuals would not wish to experience the public shame that could follow conviction.[200] As von Hirsch *et al.* observe: 'The stigmatising and

[197] The following are just some of the many examples: 'Man charged with grooming offence', BBC News report, 4 June 2006, http://news.bbc.co.uk/1/hi/england/coventry_warwickshire/5046164.stm; 'Man is convicted of internet grooming', *Bristol Evening Post*, 15 February 2007; 'Online grooming', *The Times*, 26 January 2007: 'A Flying Squad officer pleaded guilty at Southwark Crown Court to online child grooming offences.' 'Law lets paedophiles slip through net', *Scotland on Sunday*, 23 May 2004, in which it is stated that: 'The new legislation makes grooming a child an offence'; 'Radical reform of sex laws to protect children', *Coventry Evening Telegraph*, 3 May 2004, in which it is stated that: 'A new grooming offence means that anyone convicted of contacting a child – including on the Internet – with the intention of committing a sex offence will face up to 10 years in jail.' Almost identical wording to this appears in 'New get-tough move against sex abusers', *Liverpool Daily Echo*, 3 May 2004; 'Tough sex laws protect children', *Evening Gazette*, 1 May 2004; and 'Tougher rape laws come into force', *The Times*, 1 May 2004. Also, misleadingly, during the Second Reading of the Sexual Offences Bill in the House of Commons, the Home Sectretary stated that: 'We are criminalising grooming' when referring to the proposed offence. Hansard, HC Deb. 15 July 2003: column 181.

[198] Applying an economic model to crime and the impact of criminalization, potential offenders are only likely to be deterred from breaking the law if, according to their calculations, the benefit they would receive from committing the offence is outweighed by the costs of being convicted, taking into account the probability that their crime will be detected. Ogus argues that, although not all potential offenders will make a subjective cost-benefit assessment in this way, many will do so instinctively. See Ogus 2006: 15. See also Becker 1976; and von Hirsch *et al.* 2000: 6.

[199] Ogus 2006: 104 and 106. See also von Hirsch *et al.* 2000: 8.

[200] Hansard, HL Deb. 22 July 1988: column 1669.

shaming effects of penal censure operate most readily when the legal prohibition bears a reasonable relation to widely held moral norms in the population.'[201]

However, even when potential offenders are directed to act in accordance with the law by their cost-benefit assessment, Robinson and Darley argue that they may still be unable to shape their conduct accordingly due to situational, social and/or chemical factors. One particular factor highlighted by the authors as an impediment to compliance is that prospective offenders often have personalities that involve a lack of self-control and acting on impulse.[202] Applying control theory to sexual offending, Simon and Zgoba argue that: 'Offenders molest children and rape women because they derive immediate sexual gratification from the acts, failing to consider the long-term consequences of their acts such as legal sanctions.'[203] I have already discussed Wortley and Smallbone's research in this area, which suggests that many child sex offenders abuse children because of an inability to exercise restraint.[204] Whilst this research may not be directly relevant to offences involving child pornography where the offender has not sexually abused a child, it could have real relevance to offenders who sexually abuse a child following a course of grooming. Ogus notes that the potential offender's subjective calculation of the likelihood of apprehension is in part influenced by whether the particular individual is risk adverse.[205] However, if it is indeed true that child sex offenders are governed by a lack of self-control, then even if the particular individual is risk adverse, this may not prevent him from creating child pornography involving the abuse of a child, or meeting a child he has groomed and committing a sexual offence.[206] He may perhaps only refrain from offending if he considers that there is a strong probability of apprehension.[207]

Besides increasing the amount of behaviour that is criminalized, another deterrence strategy is to increase the severity and certainty of punishment in order to achieve marginal deterrence. Thus, the idea is

201 Von Hirsch *et al.* 2000: 40.

202 Robinson and Darley 2004: 179–80.

203 Simon and Zgoba 2006: 69 and 88. I refer to the control model in Chapter 1, at 41. For a challenge to this, see Beauregard and Leclerc 2007: 117 and 126–7.

204 Wortley and Smallbone 2006. See also Summit and Kryso 1978.

205 Ogus 2006: 103–4.

206 To suggest that acts of grooming themselves occur due to a potential offender's lack of control is more problematic, since, as Craven *et al.* observe, 'sexual grooming is not an impulsive act' (2006: 290).

207 According to Beauregard and Leclerc's research, in assessing the risk of apprehension, sex offenders consider factors such as the presence or absence of a capable guardian, whether the environment is risky or favourable and whether the target is an easy one (2007: 127).

that introducing stricter penalties will make individuals less likely to offend because there is a link between making sanctions more severe and increasing deterrent effects. The government's expressed intention in increasing the sentences for the child pornography offences in 2000 was to make the punishment fit the crime.[208] Might such a legislative move also be likely to deter individuals from abusing and exploiting children for the purposes of child pornography? Whilst von Hirsch *et al.* consider that the criminal law does have deterrent effects, they are much more sceptical about marginal deterrent effects. What they do suggest is that large increases in punishment '*might* have some impact', although this is dependent on 'little-understood questions of potential offenders' thresholds'.[209] We should not assume, therefore, that the increase in the maximum sentences for the child pornography offences has, in and of itself, deterred would-be offenders or re-offending rates.[210]

There are thus reasons to challenge the view that the effect of increased criminalization is a positive one of deterrence. There are also strong reasons to argue that the consequences of this increased criminalization are negative, catching behaviour which is not harmful and unjustifiably restricting liberty. As I have noted, the introduction of the SOA has given rise to a blanket criminalization approach in terms of child pornography that potentially criminalizes 'normal' behaviour, an argument Spencer has raised regarding all of the child sex offences under the SOA.[211] The legislature has paid insufficient regard to the sexual liberties rights of sixteen- and seventeen-year-old teenagers, and the very limited marriage or enduring relationship exception does not adequately address this matter. There is a distinct possibility that this could give rise to a challenge to the current law under the Human Rights Act 1998, brought by a young couple where one or both partners is aged sixteen or seventeen. The strength of the desire to protect children to the greatest degree possible has, therefore, cost teenagers who have already reached the age of sexual consent their sexual liberty rights.[212] Waites is correct to argue that the SOA reforms have exacerbated 'unresolved

[208] See Chapter 4, at 169.

[209] The authors state that potential offenders have their own threshold levels, so that above and below a particular level of severity, changes to punishments imposed do not have an effect upon their behaviour. von Hirsch *et al.* 2000: 7–8 and 47.

[210] According to Beech *et al.*, social science evidence does not suggest that varying the severity of criminal penalties deters re-offending. Beech *et al.* 2008: 226. See also Jenkins 2001: 218.

[211] Spencer 2004: 353.

[212] See also Jenkins 2001: 220 (upon the same matter with respect to American law).

tensions and disputes over the correct relationship between "rights" and "protection"'.[213]

The extent to which child pornography offences impinge upon the sexual liberty rights of older teenagers depends greatly upon an appropriate exercise of prosecutorial discretion by the CPS. This, however, offers no guarantee that older teenagers will not be prosecuted. In respect of the offences against children under the SOA, Ashworth argues that reliance upon prosecutorial discretion to avoid the criminalization of older children's consensual sexual behaviour 'is unsatisfactory in general' and in Spencer's view, such an approach does not comply with the rule of law.[214]

In light of my concerns about ever-increasing criminalization, it seems apt here to reflect on what should be required before intended criminalization can be morally justified. According to Schonsheck:

> an essential task in justifying *any* criminal statute is an inquiry into the actual consequences of the enactment and enforcement of that statute … What 'side-effects' will result from criminalization – and will the 'costs' of these side-effects be so high that they exceed the expected 'benefits' of criminalization? … And as regards the behavior which constitutes a violation of the statute – does it pose so serious a threat to the social order that imprisonment – at the cost of the individual's liberty, and significant resources of the state – is warranted? Could the incidence of the behavior be reduced to an acceptable level by means less coercive and costly than a criminal statute? And the list goes on. In sum: No argument for morally justified criminalization is sound unless it takes full consideration of the realities of law enforcement.[215]

I would add a further requirement to Schonsheck's list in the context of the laws I have examined: an inquiry into establishing the consequences of criminalizing behaviour to avoid potential risks of harm. This has been the overarching justification for extending the criminal law on child pornography and creating the offence relating to grooming, but little attention has been paid to the effects of enacting and extending law on this basis.

Problematic legal constructs

The law surrounding child pornography is framed around the notion of indecency. I have already alluded to more general criticisms of the legal application of this construct, and similar concern was expressed

[213] Waites 2005: 207. [214] Ashworth 2006: 354 and 359; Spencer 2004: 354; and Husak 2008: 27.
[215] Schonsheck 1994: 11. See also Husak 2008: ch. 2.

about the uncertainty of the term by several MPs whilst the Protection of Children Bill was being debated in 1978.[216] Criminalization was the greatest priority for Whitehouse, the NVALA and the ABUSE campaign in the late 1970s. The legal presentation of child pornography as a matter of indecency is explicable, given that the PCB was introduced at a time when the legislative focus was centred on repressing written and visual depictions of obscenity and indecency. Those campaigning for the Bill were motivated in this, as in other endeavours, by what they perceived to be declining moral standards and moral corruption and the social and legal climates were conducive to their crusades to outlaw child pornography. Writing in 1981, McCarthy and Moodie commented:

> We have seen stricter enforcement of the laws governing obscenity, the Oz Trial being the most publicised example … There have been strong municipal incentives in the clean up of 'porn shops'; the use of conspiracy charges in sex cases, attempted Private Members' legislation on 'indecent display' and revival of the archaic blasphemy laws through Mary Whitehouse's successful prosecution of the editor of Gay News.[217]

Campaigners were no doubt assisted in promulgating the broader argument that the emergence of the growing problem of child pornography was just one effect of a decline in society's moral standards because of a failure on the part of the police to enforce obscenity laws. What Jenkins describes as 'pervasive police corruption' led to a number of officers from the Obscene Publications Squad going on trial in the 1970s.[218]

However, morality was not the only or primary concern of members of the legislature who supported a new law. Clearly, they were concerned about combating the exploitation of children through child pornography. The PCA is introduced as an Act 'to prevent the exploitation of children by making indecent photographs of them' and I have already discussed the significance attached to the way in which child pornography sexually exploits children by MPs in the 1978 Parliamentary debates. Notwithstanding this, since the main harm of child pornography was presented as the making, distribution or possession of an *indecent* photograph by the legislation, whether or not the person has committed an offence depends on reasonable people considering the image to be indecent. However, the question of whether, according to adult perceptions, the photograph is 'offending

[216] Hansard, HC Deb. 10 February 1978: columns 1850, 1859 and 1970.

[217] McCarthy and Moodie 1981: 49. [218] Jenkins 1992: 77.

against decency'[219] is not getting to the substantive harm, or wrong, of child pornography.[220] To centre upon indecency is to draw attention away from the harm that the child has suffered in order for an image to be created, harm by way of exploitation and, in some cases, sexual abuse. From the start, Parliament enacted legislation that was not directed to the very harm it was designed to target.

It could be contended that the harm of indecency in the context of indecent photographs of children is not the effect on the public, but the harm experienced by the child because of the nature of the material. However, indecency is primarily a moral concept of offence, as evidenced by the definition of indecency under the common law which refers to outrage and disgust.[221] In presenting the harm of child pornography within an adult discourse of morality, the law is failing to place the child's experience at the crux of the matter. Whilst Edwards argues that, once it has been decided that the image is indecent, the child's exploitation is a self-evident truth,[222] whether adults see the image as failing to meet common standards of propriety and offensive is irrelevant to the question of whether the child in the image has been exploited. This is, and should be, the only real issue. At least one member of the House of Lords appears to have had somewhat similar concerns during the PCB debates:

> We are attempting to use a court definition of 'indecency' to stop damage, psychological and otherwise, to children … However … there are pictures taken of children which undoubtedly may have done psychological harm and damage to them but which are in no sense of the word indecent … There are also pictures which may be thought to be indecent which probably do no psychological harm to the child at all.[223]

[219] The definition of indecent provided in *The Oxford Compact Dictionary and Thesaurus* 1997. Oxford University Press.

[220] See also Akdeniz 1996: 247–8; and Schalken 1988. 'Pornografiediscussie gaat over grenzen van staatsmacht' ('Pornography debate is about the limits of state power'), NRC Handelsblad – quoted and translated by Schuijer and Rossen 1992; and Williams 2003: 109.

[221] In *Knuller* v. *DPP* [1973] AC 435, Lord Reid outlined the test for indecency as being whether ordinary decent-minded people would be 'outraged or utterly disgusted' by the material (at 457). Gibbons comments that as a legal basis for regulation, indecency operates 'not because of the harm it tends to cause but on the basis of moral disapproval by the community at large'. Gibbons 1995: 87.

[222] Edwards 1996: 129.

[223] Hansard, HL Deb. 18 May 1978: column 560 (Lord Parker). Lord Parker sought to introduce an amendment which would have criminalized images that caused harm to the child. See also Hansard, HL Deb. 22 July 1988: column 1670 (Lord Houghton).

Perhaps the view Lord Parker and I share over-problematizes the indecency scaffolding that the PCB was secured by; child pornography was then, and is now, construed as being more than just an offence against morality, since the victims of the crime are children. In addition, it could be argued that in the late 1970s, an indecency law was the most apposite vehicle for criminalizing child pornography. Although feminist concerns regarding the harmful effects of pornography were emerging at this time, it was only in the early 1980s that real attention began to be paid to the exploitation of children through child pornography by feminist authors and activists.[224] However, now, in the wake of the gradual expansion of the law, the consequences of presenting the harms of child pornography within a framework of indecency are clearly apparent. For instance, because of the malleable nature of the social and legal construct of indecency, it has been possible for the law's grip to be extended to pseudo-images of child pornography that do not feature real children or the manipulation of a real child's image. A further problem is the possibility that images of naked children can potentially be construed as indecent simply on the basis of their content, a possibility that I have noted may not have been ruled out by the courts. As I will discuss in the next chapter, this gives rise to a dangerous presentation of children's naked bodies as sexualized.

The time is now overdue to move away from this moralistic, irrelevant presentation of harm, in order to ensure that the law is framed around what is really harmful about child pornography. As I have already intimated, this harm is that which is reflected in the introduction to the PCA: the exploitation of children. The legal framework of indecency should thus be cast aside and replaced with one of exploitation, as evidenced by the content of the photograph and, in some cases, the context in which the image was taken, and not adults' reactions to the photograph's content. To assist the jury in clarifying the nature of material that amounts to exploitative images of child pornography, the Sentencing Advisory Panel's league table, as adopted by the Court of Appeal in *Oliver*, could be a part of the statutory law. This should also prevent an over-broadening of the law. Much more needs to be addressed about the concept of exploitation and the matters of harm and appropriate criminalization,[225] however, and I develop my argument in this regard in the next chapter.

[224] See Jenkins 1992: 107–9; and Jenkins 1998: 126.

[225] e.g. as should become clear in the next chapter, applying the harm principle, I only advocate the criminalization of *harmful* exploitation.

A problematic legal construct also exists regarding grooming. Here, it is not so much the framework within which the s. 15 offence exists, but the legal presentation of the problem. The offence of meeting a child following a course of sexual grooming is directed at individuals who embark upon a particular course of action to groom a child for sexual abuse. I recognize that there are practical reasons as to why the offence is thus focused, namely that evidence is much easier to obtain when records of communications exist in e-mail messages or instant messages, for example.[226] However, the legislature needed to make it much more transparent that they were only tackling one smaller part of grooming, to ensure that society and law comprehend the range of grooming behaviour and methods that groomers employ. Instead, they have created a problematic generalized legal construct of stranger grooming through the use of modern technologies. The creation of the s. 15 offence could also have given groomers a sense of security, provided that they perfect their grooming technique so that evidence of any communications they have with the child is harder to come by. Grooming a child in an environment where the child feels comfortable and already knows the groomer is more conducive to the groomer's intention of avoiding apprehension. It avoids the need to utilize internet chat rooms, mobile phone text messages and other methods of communication that could leave an electronic trail of evidence. The existing research reveals that sexual abuse is already most likely to occur where the child knows the abuser. Thus, the potential danger of criminalizing behaviour related to grooming in situations that better reflect stranger grooming is that individuals intent upon sexually abusing a child simply ensure their grooming behaviour takes place in 'safer' situational contexts.[227]

As the argument in this chapter should have made abundantly clear, the matter of harm permeates the legal discourses surrounding child pornography and grooming. Harm and dominant constructions of harm thus form the framework for my analysis in the next chapter.

[226] See Select Committee on Home Affairs 2003: App. 7, para. 5 (Childnet International's memorandum).

[227] Research indicates, e.g. that child sex offenders will adapt their grooming strategies to avoid disclosure. See Conte *et al.* 1989. I will further explore the reasons why the legal construction of grooming is a cause for concern in the following chapter.

CHAPTER THREE

MATTERS OF HARM AND EXPLOITATION

The question of harm is fundamental to understanding and assessing the legal and societal response to child pornography and sexual grooming. At this point, it is thus unlikely to come as a surprise that I refer to John Stuart Mill's famous harm principle as providing an important rationalization for state interference with individual freedoms. Applying Mill's jurisprudence, it is only appropriate to criminalize behaviour related to child pornography and grooming and thereby restrict an individual's freedom when this behaviour inflicts harm upon others.[1] Mill's explication of the harm principle, and the development and refinements provided by Feinberg,[2] thus provide the 'conscientious legislator' with a morally defensible justification for criminalizing behaviour.[3]

There are numerous constructions of the harms of child pornography and grooming that have shaped the way in which society and law have responded to these phenomena. I will begin by examining the harms

[1] 'Whenever ... there is a definite damage, or a definite risk of damage, either to an individual or to the public, the case is taken out of the province of liberty, and placed in that of morality or law.' Mill 1993: 150.

[2] Discussed later, at 126–7. Feinberg also provides a full list of other 'liberty-limiting' principles (1984: 26–7). However, harm is my primary concern here. One point I do wish to make clear is that I see the offence principle as an inappropriate justification for the criminalization of child pornography. If we were to focus upon the evil of child pornography as being the wrong it causes to individuals who experience shock, or disgust or other forms of offence when they are presented with such material, we would seriously underplay the harm caused to the children involved. This is why I am so critical of the indecency framework surrounding the child pornography laws. On the offence principle, see Feinberg 1985.

[3] Von Hirsch 1996: 260.

caused by the creation and distribution of child pornography, before focusing at some length on the possession of child pornography. The latter warrants especial consideration because it is questionable whether such behaviour is, in itself, harmful. I then consider whether the legal prohibition upon pseudo-images is justified on the basis of harmful exploitation, and assess whether images of naked children are harmful. The discussion subsequently turns to grooming and the criminalization of behaviour where the wrong, or harm, goes beyond the act in question and I critique the common presentations of the harm of grooming. Finally, I present in detail my construction of the harm of child pornography and grooming as exploitation. Throughout the discussion in this chapter, I pay particular attention to different constructions of primary, direct, remote and potential harms and the question of whether criminalization of behaviour that is considered to cause these harms is legitimate.

THE HARMS OF CREATING AND DISTRIBUTING CHILD PORNOGRAPHY

Creating child pornography causes direct, primary harm to the child

As the sexual abuse and exploitation of children are the most direct and significant harms of the production of child pornography, the reader might expect more discussion of the harms of creating such material than I provide here. However, when child pornography depicts sexual abuse, or the child has been forced to pose sexually for a photograph, the abusive and exploitative harm caused by its creation is easy to establish; it is self-evident and overwhelmingly justifies the criminalization of the producer's behaviour. Indeed, the child's physical and sexual abuse is often the very subject matter of the material created. For Tate, 'child pornography is no more than the permanent recording of a child being sexually abused'.[4] In the Canadian Supreme Court case of *R.* v. *Sharpe*, it was stated: 'Child pornography … undermines children's right to life, liberty and security of the person … Their psychological and physical security is placed at risk by their use in pornographic representations.'[5] The very phenomenon of child pornography itself, then, often ensures the occasioning of direct

[4] Tate 1990:15 (although I do not consider Tate's explanation to be applicable to all forms of child pornography). See also Akdeniz 1997a: 227.

[5] [2001] SCC 2. Taken from the reasoning of L'Heureux-Dubé, Gonthier and Bastarache JJ, para. 189.

harm to the children involved in its production. Children are used in child pornography for adults' sexual gratification. In a society that recognizes the physical and psychological damage caused by child sexual abuse, it would be exceedingly difficult to argue that this harm is over-exaggerated and I would not wish to do so.

Creating and disseminating child pornography encourages the objectification of children as sexual objects

Besides the primary harm of exploitation and sexual abuse that the creation of child pornography causes, there is another way in which the harm principle could be applied to legitimate criminalizing both the creation and dissemination of such material. The argument here is concerned with the negative repercussions of allowing the creation and distribution of child pornography: the promotion of harmful attitudes towards children. This is based on the feminist precept that permitting the creation and dissemination of child pornography encourages an acceptance of the representations of children that child pornography conveys. Child pornography, in objectifying children as sexual objects or resources for unbridled exploitation, may promote the *reduction* of children to this status. If such objectification becomes reification, then the reduction of children to objects to satisfy adult sexual desires can only encourage those who commit actual child sexual abuse.[6] This may be taken further by reference to feminist arguments regarding the way in which adult pornography promotes female objectification and exploitation.[7] Kappeler argues that, through pornography, the pornographer 'is in direct communication with another subject, the spectator or reader'.[8] Thus, through the powerful medium of pornography, pornographers are able to propagate their own sexist, exploitative representations of women to a male audience.

When applied in the context of child pornography, Kappeler's theory would hold that the fantasies of the child pornographer, which include representations of children as exploitable sexual objects, are communicated to a receptive audience of those who have a sexual interest in children, representations that are willingly accepted by this audience. In fact, Kappeler's argument is more forceful when applied to the subject of child pornography. The contention that adult pornography causes

[6] For other arguments focusing upon the way that pornography objectifies women and children, see Demaré *et al.* 1993; and Mann 1997.

[7] Kappeler 1986. [8] Ibid.: 52.

the proliferation of certain representations of women in society seems to be predicated on an implicit assumption that adult pornography is predominantly consumed by a male audience that is particularly receptive to representations of women as exploitable sex objects. However, it may be possible to challenge this assumption; adult pornography does not arguably just attract a male audience willing to accept certain representations of women, it could also be attractive to a female audience that rejects any such implicit or explicit representations.[9] In contrast, child pornography seems to cater for one specific audience: those who fantasize about children as sexual objects. Thus, the representations within child pornography may be much more likely to be accepted and shared by the majority of its audience. The arguments raised by MacKinnon may also be more compelling when applied to child as opposed to adult pornography. MacKinnon argues that the common portrayal of women in adult pornography as the submissive, passive subject completely dominated by the male has a direct impact on the way in which men view women.[10] This argument can be challenged, however, as not all adult pornography does depict the woman as the submissive subject; in some cases, the woman is the dominant partner.[11] However, with regard to the content and themes of child pornography, and because of the completely unequal relationship of power between adult and child, the child features as a passive subject, exploited as a sexual object by the adult. Where the material features sexual activity between children without the involvement of an adult, the unequal relationship of power exists between the children and the adult producer of the material. Thus, child pornography can only promote a perception of children as being submissive objects who can be used for exploitation, despite the fact that they will always lack the capacity to consent to involvement in child pornography.[12]

If the creation and dissemination of child pornography does indeed cause the broader harm of objectifying children, then the criminalization of these behaviours can be further justified on the basis of the harm

[9] See, e.g. McElroy 1995; Rodgerson and Wilson 1991: 26–7, 56–9; and Carol and Pollard 1993.

[10] MacKinnon 1991.

[11] The fact that some adult pornography features women in the dominant role also challenges Kappeler's statement that: 'The fundamental structure of the transitive plot, which assigns her object status, remains the same. It is a paradigm of domination, or coercion and of the degradation of the other to object status.' (1986: 93.)

[12] Children's inability to consent to involvement in child pornography was noted by the Committee on Obscenity and Film Censorship 1979: para. 6.68.

principle. Mill refers to behaviour that is likely to cause harm, behaviour that poses a 'definite risk of damage'.[13] I have no hesitation in arguing that the objectification argument further bolsters the case for prohibiting the creation of child pornography, although it may be harder to justify the criminalization of distribution on this basis, because the distributor is committing a more remote harm.[14] Moreover, if we wish to exert cautiousness in the way in which we apply the harm principle to avoid distorting its scope, it is wiser to present the objectification argument as an additional justification for criminalizing the production of child pornography, alongside the most persuasive and clearly verifiable primary harms of sexual abuse and exploitation.

Disseminating child pornography exacerbates or underwrites the primary harm

There is an important difference between the creator who distributes the child pornography he has produced and the distributor who has not created the material he disseminates. There is little difficulty in defending the criminalization of the creator's subsequent act of distributing child pornography on the basis of the harm principle, because he is exacerbating the primary harm he has directly caused. His actions result in the child suffering further psychological harm if she is aware of the distribution, and also exploit her further for the benefit of himself and those to whom he distributes the image. In cases where the distributor is not the creator, his actions do not have as close a connection to the primary harm. However, he is only able to perpetrate his acts of distribution because of the creator's primary harm. Criminalization of the distributor's behaviour here is primarily justified on the basis of him underwriting and profiting from the primary harm of the creator.[15] Research suggests that the distributor profits from disseminating images in various ways: by gaining status, by receiving behaviour validation and, in some cases, by obtaining commercial profit.[16] Further, the distributor is

[13] Mill 1993: 150. See also Duff 2007: 125.

[14] Assuming the distributor is not the creator of the material. I will explore the concept of remote harm in the next section, and argue that it is necessary to establish a normative link between such harm and primary harm in order to justify the criminalization of possessing child pornography.

[15] See the discussion in the context of possession underwriting the primary harm later in this chapter, at 117–18.

[16] See Taylor and Quayle 2003: 78, 94, 132, 144 and 186; Quayle *et al.* 2006: 32 and 114; and Jenkins 2001: 94 and 106–8.

exploiting and taking unfair advantage of the children abused through their involvement in the creation of the images he is distributing.

THE HARMS OF POSSESSING CHILD PORNOGRAPHY

Applying an economic analysis to the criminal law, criminalizing the possession of child pornography could deter potential offenders from acquiring child pornography if, according to their cost-benefit assessment, the benefit they will obtain from possessing the material is outweighed by the costs of apprehension, taking into account the probability of detection.[17] If individuals have indeed been deterred from possessing child pornography since the introduction of the possession offence, it is still necessary to justify and rationalize this criminalization of behaviour on the basis of the harm principle. This is especially the case since, when the offence of possessing child pornography stands alone, the danger it represents is less obvious than the harm caused to children through their involvement in the production of child pornography. As Dubber comments in the context of possession offences generally: 'Liability for possession does not require having caused harm or, in fact, any result whatever. Possession thus is a *resultless* (*or harmless*) offense.'[18] However, as he goes on to note, although the legal definition of the offence of possession does not require harm, this does not lead to the conclusion that possession is, in fact, harmless. In order to ascertain whether the possession of child pornography causes harm, it is thus vital to identify and assess all of the potential harms that may arise from this activity. In particular, consideration must be paid to whether criminalizing possession can be legitimated on the basis that it is a remote harm normatively linked to a future or pre-existing primary harm.

Possessors of child pornography are actual or potential child sexual abusers

A common theme within the existing discourses surrounding child pornography is that such an activity represents a threat because it is invariably existing sexual abusers of children who possess and use child pornography as an incitement to commit child sexual abuse. It is also frequently argued that the possession and use of child pornography

[17] Assuming they are not prevented from acting upon this cost-benefit analysis by situational, social and/or chemical factors. See Chapter 2, at 96.

[18] Dubber 2005: 99.

present a real threat to children, because these are activities that incite individuals to become child sexual abusers. Authors such as Edwards and Tate argue that child pornography is both created and utilized by paedophiles.[19] Renvoize postulates that child abusers may actively seek and receive encouragement through their use of child pornography.[20]

Some authors have argued that child sex abusers use child pornography as a method of grooming children. For example, Lanning claims that when a child abuser approaches a child, it may be easier for him to persuade the child to take part in acts of sexual abuse if the child believes that other children also take part in such activities as a matter of course.[21] Lanning also believes that child pornography serves to reinforce the idea that the paedophile is not doing anything wrong and that there are other like-minded individuals who indulge in the same pastimes.[22] Potentially, then, the fact that child pornography is possessed and distributed is considered to be harmful to children due to the possibilities of such pornography fuelling the fantasies of child abusers and being adopted as both a seduction technique and a means of behaviour validation.

Proponents of the argument that the distribution and sharing of child pornography serves as a means of behaviour validation may find support from the insight offered by the international police investigation into the child pornography internet 'W0nderland Club'. A BBC *Panaroma* television programme shown in 2000 revealed that the sharing of child pornography effectively served as a means of behaviour validation for club members.[23] The evidence put forward by the police in the programme would seem to support the argument that child pornography can be used as a method of reassurance and confirmation that a paedophile's sexual fantasies are shared by others. However, this does not automatically signify that those club members who possessed child pornography actually shared the lifestyle of the actual abusers. Whilst club members may have shared the same sexual fantasies, they were not necessarily all incited to go out and live the same lifestyle as that experienced by members who were actual abusers of children, and to commit the same abuse.[24]

19 Edwards 2000: 13–14; and Tate 1990: 23–26.

20 Renvoize 1993: 121.

21 Lanning 1984: 86. See also Akdeniz 1996: 247; O'Connell 2003: 11; Taylor and Quayle 2003: 23; Kaufman *et al.* 2006: 121; and Marshall *et al.* 2006: 52.

22 Lanning 1984: 84–5; and see Tate 1990: 25–6.

23 *Panorama*, shown on BBC 1 on 13 February 2000.

24 Equally significant is the fact that some members of the club were *already* abusers of children; the sexual abuse of children was occurring without the existence of the behaviour-validating club. See 'How Wonderland spun its perverted web', *The Times*, 14 February 2001.

Certain research findings might appear to validate the argument that a relationship exists between the possession and use of child pornography and child sex abuse. For example, the findings from Marshall's research study involving fifty-one child sex abusers revealed that 67 per cent of the participants made use of 'hard core sexual stimuli'.[25] However, although such studies could reveal a correlative relationship, in that some child abusers do use child pornography, they may fail to demonstrate a clear *causal* relationship between the use of child pornography and the occurrence of child sex abuse. Certainly, it is possible that individuals use child pornography for sexual stimulation, yet have no inclination to actually go out and commit child sex abuse.

Other research studies have addressed the question of whether, apart from a correlative link between the possession of child pornography and the occurrence of child sex abuse, there also exists a causal link. Significantly, the findings of a study carried out by Elliott *et al.* indicated that 21 per cent of child sex abusers interviewed used pornography as a disinhibition method prior to committing abuse.[26] Similarly, Marshall's research indicates that just over one-third of the child sex abusers who participated in the study used 'hard core sexual stimuli' as an incitement to commit abuse.[27] However, these studies did not limit the categories of 'pornography' or 'hard core sexual stimuli' to child pornography. Indeed, Marshall notes that the child sex abusers who took part in his study did not make any greater use of child pornography than did other sexual offenders who participated, such as rapists.[28] What is more, Marshall himself comments that the focus on whether child sex abusers use 'hard core sexual stimuli' could cause abusers to make use of an opportunity for blaming their offences on external sources rather than their own internal selves.[29] Therefore, if we operate upon the assumption that a causal relationship exists between using child pornography and committing child sexual abuse, we may inadvertently provide child sex abusers with a convenient excuse for their behaviour.

A more recent Canadian study by Seto and Eke has revealed that only a low percentage of child pornography offenders committed a sexual

[25] Marshall 1988: 279. See also Edwards 2000.

[26] Elliott *et al.* 1995: 582. A further 14 per cent of those interviewed in the study stated that they used pornography to develop strategies to approach children (at 585). See also Craissati and McClurg 1996. 15 per cent of the eighty convicted perpetrators of child sexual abuse involved in their study stated that they used child pornography prior to committing abuse.

[27] Marshall 1988: 284. [28] Ibid.: 279. [29] Ibid.: 286. See also Howitt 1995b: 17.

offence involving contact with a child after they had been convicted for child pornography offences. In their study, 17 per cent of 201 offenders on the Ontario Sex Offender Registry offended again in some way during the follow-up period and only 4 per cent of this 17 per cent (actually only one offender) committed a sexual offence against a child.[30] The authors conclude that this 'finding does contradict the assumption that all child pornography offenders are at a very high risk to commit contact sexual offenses involving children'.[31] As some of the offenders had been convicted for possessing child pornography, it may have been expected that a much higher number would have gone on to commit an actual contact offence if a causal or correlative link did indeed exist. Furthermore, according to Wortley and Smallbone's research findings, only 10 per cent of the 169 convicted child sex offenders in their study admitted using child pornography.[32] If, as their research indicates, many child sex offenders do not have a strong interest in paedophilia,[33] the existence of a correlative or causal link between viewing child pornography and committing child sexual abuse is even more questionable.

The existence of a causal or correlative link would appear to be supported by those who enforce the law. Research undertaken by both Tate and Akdeniz involving members of the police forces in the UK and the United States serves as an indication that the general view amongst police forces is that possessors of child pornography are invariably actual or potential child sex abusers, and this is substantiated by two of the police officers I interviewed.[34] However, one police officer whom I interviewed expressed the view that there are people who use child pornography and never commit child sexual abuse. He had been involved in a research study on eighteen men who had downloaded child pornography. None of these men fell into the 'predatory' category and the vast majority had no previous convictions.[35]

It seems, therefore, that whilst the existence of a causal relationship between the possession of child pornography and the occurrence of child abuse is frequently espoused, the existence of such a relationship is far from certain.[36] However, the style of language adopted by Parliament and the judiciary in certain child pornography cases indicates that the existence of a causal relationship between the possession of child

[30] Seto and Eke 2005. [31] Ibid.: 208. [32] Wortley and Smallbone 2006: 12.

[33] See Chapter 1, at 40–41.

[34] Akdeniz 1997a: 228; and Tate 1990: 21–7. Interviews RX3 and RX4. [35] Interview RX1.

[36] 'Overall, there appears to be little support for the allegation of a direct causal link between viewing pornography and subsequent offending behaviour.' Taylor and Quayle 2003: 72.

pornography and the occurrence of child abuse is sometimes accepted in legal discourses. For example, that viewing child pornography can stimulate individuals and 'could lead to the commission of more serious offences', 'sometimes ... encourages them to other acts' and 'is often the first step on a ladder of crime that may end with tragic incidents' were used as justifications for increasing the sentence for possession by three MPs in 1994.[37] In the Canadian case of *R.* v. *Sharpe*, the Supreme Court held that the possession of child pornography posed a 'reasoned apprehension of harm'[38] because 'child pornography may change possessors' attitudes in ways that makes them more likely to sexually abuse children. People may come to see sexual relations with children as normal and even beneficial ... People who would not otherwise abuse children may consequently do so.'[39]

This may seem to reveal a judicial acceptance of the perceived threat to children presented by the possession of child pornography. However, the fact that judges consider the threat that the possessor represents to children when passing sentence evidences a judicial perception that, unless evidence exists to suggest the contrary, possessors are not actual abusers. In *R.* v. *Bowden*,[40] for instance, the defendant downloaded internet files containing indecent images of children, including a pseudo-photograph. The Court of Appeal subsequently dismissed Bowden's appeal against his conviction, but held that his sentence was wrong and excessive and reduced it to a twelve-month conditional discharge. It was stated that Bowden was at the lowest position on the scale in terms of committing an offence under the legislation. The Court of Appeal judges seemed to be looking for actual proof that Bowden posed a threat to children in order to justify the length of his sentence given by the lower court. Thus, they did not simply assume that Bowden, as a downloader of child pornography,[41] was also, necessarily, a child sex abuser.

This is the more common judicial perspective. However, the increase in the maximum sentence for the possession of such material and other judicial comment in child pornography cases evidences the fact that the threat presented to children by the possession of child pornography continues to be considered a very strong one. This is the case even though it

[37] Hansard, HC Standing Committee B: Criminal Justice and Public Order Bill, 15 February 1994: columns 748–9 and 751.

[38] [2001] SCC 2 at paras 88–9.

[39] [2001] SCC 2 at para. 87 (*per* McLachlin CJ).

[40] [2000] 2 WLR 1083.

[41] Bowden was held to have committed the offence of making an indecent image of a child under the PCA.

is not necessarily assumed in legal discourses that the possessor is, or will be incited to become, an abuser.[42] A further, powerful, non-causally-based argument to support this perception will now be discussed.

Possession encourages the market in child pornography: possession as a remote harm

As there is no clear proof that possessing child pornography incites the possessor to commit child sexual abuse, possessing child pornography does not in itself necessarily cause direct harm to children. However, it may do so indirectly by encouraging the occurrence of child sexual abuse that forms the content of child pornography.[43] The 'market reduction' argument proceeds along the following lines: if we allow individuals to possess child pornography, we are encouraging the market in child pornography, leading to producers of the material making more images to sell or exchange and thereby abusing more children. Thus, the criminalization of possessing child pornography should discourage producers from creating more material, since there will be fewer people willing to risk breaking the law and being caught in possession of such material; producers will have fewer people to sell their product to. This argument is applicable beyond the context of a commercial market in child pornography. As is the case with distributors, the existing research suggests that producers are not just, or primarily, incentivized to produce material for economic gain, but also for behaviour validation, or to acquire status as a producer of original material.[44] Again, if possession is unlawful, it will be harder to find others willing to take the risk of prosecution to provide this behaviour validation and bestow higher status upon the producer. The application of this argument is predicated upon a standard economic premise that rendering an activity unlawful and, therefore, increasing the costs to an individual who engages in it will normally lead to a reduction in demand for the product required for the individual to act in this way. Thus, in the context of possessing child pornography, the market reduction argument is focused on decreasing potential, future harm to children and can take on international dimensions when applied to the accessing of child pornography on the internet. I will first highlight the significance attached to the market reduction argument in legal discourses, before proceeding to explore the concept of possession

[42] As further evidenced in the Home Affairs Committee Report 1994: 126.

[43] See, e.g. Quayle *et al.* 2006: 61; and Taylor and Quayle 2003: 161.

[44] Indeed, Jenkins argues that it is non-economic motives which drive the majority of individuals who distribute child pornography on the internet (2001: 91).

as a remote harm and the circumstances in which criminalization of such harms can be legitimated.

The market reduction argument is regularly relied upon by the judiciary to legitimate the law which criminalizes the possession of child pornography and emphasize the gravity of the defendant's actions. In *Sharpe*, McLachlin CJ commented that:

> possession of child pornography contributes to the market for child pornography, a market which in turn drives production involving the exploitation of children ... Production of child pornography is fueled by the market for it, and the market in turn is fueled by those who seek to possess it. Criminalizing possession may reduce the market for child pornography and the abuse of children it often involves.[45]

Encouraging the market in child pornography appears to be the main 'harm' identified in *R.* v. *Royle*,[46] a case involving the downloading of images from the internet. When passing sentence, the Crown Court judge stated: 'The interest that the public have is that children are not subjected to the sort of pornographic treatment which they must, in order to create the[se] photographs.'[47] Thus, the judge considered that the fact that individuals wish to download and possess child pornography serves to encourage those who commit child sexual abuse. The same construction of the harm of possession is clearly apparent in the Court of Appeal judgment in *R.* v. *Artemiou*, in which it was stated that 'the practice of downloading indecent images of children of this kind perpetuates and encourages the exploitation of children for sexual purposes'.[48] Two further examples should suffice here to demonstrate the prominence of the market reduction argument in judicial discourses. In *R.* v. *Bishop*, Clarke J advised the defendant that 'the more people like you [who] are curious enough to want to access such images, the more there will be a market for them. The longer that market continues, the longer the cycle of abuse suffered by young children.'[49] Furthermore, in *R.* v. *Gardener*, Moses LJ opined that 'there is always indirect injury and damage to children by the exploitation of the children for the use of these photographs, for which anyone indulging in downloading or distribution must share a responsibility'.[50]

45 At para. 28. 46 [2007] EWCA Crim. 884. 47 Ibid., para. 5.

48 [2006] EWCA Crim. 3262, para. 4 (*per* Bean J). 49 [2005] EWCA Crim. 829, para. 8.

50 [2006] EWCA Crim. 2439, para. 4. See also *R.* v. *Earney* [2007] EWCA Crim. 1461, para. 4; *R.* v. *Hopkinson* [2001] 2 Cr. App. R. (S) 54, para. 12; *R.* v. *Grosvenor* [2003] EWCA Crim. 1627, para. 6; *R.* v. *Somerset* [2006] EWCA Crim. 2469, para. 7; *Osbourne* v. *Ohio* 495 US 103 (1990),

The market reduction argument has also been accepted and applied by Parliament. In 1988, when the proposed criminalization of possession was debated in the House of Lords, Earl Ferrers legitimated this proposal by stating that the market for child pornography should be reduced because individuals would not wish to face conviction and penalties and the consequent public shame.[51] When the proposed increase in the sentence for possession was considered during the Committee stage of the CJPO Bill in the House of Commons in 1994, three MPs provided the market reduction argument in support of the increase.[52] Perhaps because such claims derive from a standard economic argument, no research, evidence or proof was offered to substantiate them. Thus, that the possession of child pornography encourages the market in such material is a predicted, assumed harm, rather than a proven one.

It seems particularly apt to discuss the possession of child pornography as a remote harm in the context of the market reduction argument, and I will do so by drawing on the analyses of von Hirsch and Baker.[53] Baker defines a remote harm as follows:

> harm that occurs when X's innocuous conduct contributes to Y's decision to commit a harmful crime. X is only indirectly (remotely) connected to the direct (primary) harm, because the harm is contingent on Y making an independent criminal choice.[54]

This clearly applies to a situation where, due to his seeking of child pornography, an act which is harmless in itself, an individual encourages creators of such material to produce more of it. Criminalizing such a remote harm is more contentious than criminalizing the primary harm of creating child pornography because of the principle of fair imputation.

110; 'Judge speaks out against internet corruption', BBC News report, 14 September 1999, http://news.bbc.co.uk/hi/english/uk/wales/newsid_447000/447251.stm; and Akdeniz 2008: 29.

51 Hansard, HL Deb. 22 July 1988: column 1669. See also the Home Secretary's similar statements: Hansard, HC Deb. 18 January 1988: column 689.

52 Hansard, HC Standing Committee B: Criminal Justice and Public Order Bill, 15 February 1994: columns 748–50.

53 Von Hirsch 1996; and Baker 2007. For an alternative critique of the market reduction argument, see Kenney 2006: 52–3.

54 Baker 2007: 372. Von Hirsch provides a broader definition of remote harms (1996: 263–5). He refers to conduct: 'which has no ill consequences in itself, but which is thought to induce or lead to further acts (by the defendant or a third person) that create or risk harm' (264). Unlike Baker's definition, von Hirsch's could encompass the idea that possession encourages the possessor himself to commit child sexual abuse. However, I have chosen to keep my consideration of remote harm within the context of the most commonly accepted presentation of possession as causing indirect harm in legal discourses.

Von Hirsch comments: 'it is not always obvious how or why the actor should be held sufficiently accountable for the eventual harm that his current conduct can legitimately be deemed blameworthy. And if it is not blameworthy, how can the censure of criminal penalty be warranted?'[55] This is an acutely important question to ask regarding the possession of child pornography, considering the social stigma that is attached to a conviction for any behaviour related to child pornography.

In order to assess whether the market reduction argument provides a convincing defence of the legal prohibition upon the remote harm of possessing child pornography, I will adopt Baker's reasoning. First, I will consider the empirical evidence for the argument and then, secondly, assuming this evidence exists, I will look to the question of fair imputation. On the first matter, I can find no research which tests the market reduction argument in the context of possessing child pornography. As I have already noted, the acceptance of the argument's truth in legal discourses is not based on the presentation of empirical evidence. Rather, its validity is taken for granted because it is premised on a common-sense, economic assertion. To offer up a convincing case for criminalizing possession, then, the market reduction argument is in need of supporting empirical evidence, such as the definite existence of a commercial market in child pornography.

Whilst in the 1990s, authors such as Higonnet argued that child pornography was a 'marginal fringe phenomenon', most often 'home made and clandestinely circulated among a small group of people',[56] more recently, authors such as Jenkins and Taylor and Quayle have contended that the trade in internet child pornography has reached such levels that a commercial market does exist.[57] Even if there was no empirical evidence to support the existence of a large, commercially driven market for child pornography, the market-reduction argument could still be empirically tested if producers of child pornography are also motivated simply by the knowledge that others wish to view the material they produce. However, given the criminal nature of child pornography in many jurisdictions, obtaining clear evidence of producers being encouraged to create more material because of the existence of a market for their goods, commercial or otherwise, will not be easy. An interesting finding that does exist comes from a recent study which involved 122 internet-related cases of producing child pornography in America between 2000 and

[55] Von Hirsch 1996: 261. [56] Higonnet 1998: 179–80; and Kincaid 1998: 20.

[57] Jenkins 2001; and Taylor and Quayle 2003: 45–6.

2001. Only one-fifth of the offenders 'were clearly deeply involved in the Internet child pornography trade; they produced child pornography, distributed what they produced and possessed child pornography produced by others'.[58] This finding does not provide any powerful evidence to support the market-reduction argument.

However, let us assume that supporting empirical evidence can indeed be produced.[59] It is not only a question of establishing a factual link between the individual whose behaviour is remotely harmful and the subsequent primary harm that is committed by others, but also an imputational link. Otherwise, we would fail to recognize the individuality of actors as separate agents. As von Hirsch explains:

> Even if the prohibited conduct is done intentionally, and even if the conduct does empirically increase the risk of eventual bad consequences, it needs to be determined whether, and why, those consequences should be treated as the actor's responsibility in the imputational sense ...[60]

Baker convincingly argues that, if the possessor does encourage the market in child pornography, this is not enough to establish a normative link between his act of possession and the future wrongful harm, since: 'merely influencing another's behaviour is not sufficient for establishing a normative link'.[61] It would be unrealistic and inappropriate to criminalize behaviour purely because it can influence others to commit harmful behaviour. Consider potentially how much behaviour could be criminalized if this was the approach taken.

If we cannot find a normative link predicated upon the possessor's behaviour influencing others to commit harm, does a link between primary and remote harm exist elsewhere in the context of the possessor's actions? I share Baker's view that a normative link can be found on the basis of the possessor obtaining the proceeds of the primary wrong.[62] Individuals who possess child pornography are benefiting from and taking advantage of the actions of the producers of such material, who

[58] Wolak *et al.* 2005: 41.

[59] If such evidence can be produced, what von Hirsch refers to as the 'Standard Harms Analysis' would still require legislators to consider a number of factors before concluding that criminalization was appropriate. The following factors would be relevant: the severity and likelihood of harm, the social usefulness of the act and the gravity of the invasion of the actor's liberty that would occur if the behaviour was criminalized, and the interests that criminalization should not interfere with, such as privacy rights. See von Hirsch 1996: 261. The reasonableness of the actor's choice to accept the risk of harm can also be added to this list. See Feinberg 1984: 216.

[60] Von Hirsch 1996: 269 and see 266–7. See also Baker 2007: 371 and 373.

[61] Ibid.: 387.

[62] Baker 2007: 387–8.

cause the major, direct harm to the children involved. As knowledge of the nature of the material and the producer's use of children in order to create the images will inevitably be possessed by the individual who seeks out such material, it is fair to impute criminal liability to him. Criminalization of his actions as remotely harmful can thus be legitimated on the basis of the connection between his possession and the producer's creation of the image; the possessor underwrites the primary harm already committed.[63] There may also be cases of possession where the possessor has encouraged the producer to create child pornography in order that he can acquire more material for his collection. In my view, this encouragement can establish a normative link, *provided* the influence exerted by the possessor is intentional.[64] Here, the remote harm is connected to the subsequent primary harm rather than a harm that has already occurred.

Both of the above arguments offer a far more persuasive legitimation for criminalization of possession than does the market-reduction argument, since they do not require empirical proof of a large-scale market in child pornography and reflect the principle of fair imputation.

Possession exacerbates the primary harm and enables the continued exploitation of the child

Although the possession of child pornography is a more remote harm, it can be argued that it exacerbates the primary, pre-existing harm caused to children by their involvement in the creation of this material. The possession of child pornography could cause the child to suffer further harm because of her awareness that other individuals are deriving sexual pleasure from looking at indecent photographs of her. If correct, this serves to indicate that there is a causal link between the distribution and possession of child pornography and the occurrence of further psychological abuse to the child involved in the creation of the material in question. This was certainly the position taken by the Court of Appeal in *R. v. Beaney*. Keith J stated that children in indecent images are caused to suffer continued psychological harm as a result of the distribution of these images:

> If people like the applicant continue to download and view images of this kind … the offences which they commit can properly be said to

[63] 'By receiving a good that can only be produced through wrongful harm, you underwrite the wrongful harm.' Ibid.: 388.

[64] Baker 2007: 384.

> contribute to the psychological harm which the children in those images would suffer by virtue of the children's awareness that there were people out there getting a perverted thrill from watching them forced to pose and behave in this way.[65]

Significantly, in the aforementioned case of *R.* v. *Royle*, the defendant himself seemed persuaded by the exacerbation of primary harm argument. When appealing against the length of sentence he was given, the defendant expressed shame and remorse for the harm his actions of downloading the child pornography caused to the children in the images in question.[66] His subjective acceptance of this construction of the impact of his behaviour seems to have occurred prior to the intervention of the law, as he 'sought help' before he was arrested and had stopped downloading child pornography some two months earlier.[67] Thus, to adopt Berger and Luckmann's wording, Royle was 'resocialize[d] … into the objective reality of the symbolic universe'[68] of society, this accepted objective reality being that downloading child pornography causes further harm to the children in the images.

The exacerbation of harm position can be challenged where the child who was involved in the production of the child pornography remains unaware of her availability to others through the distribution of the material in question. Is it in any way possible for children to be psychologically harmed further if they are unaware that others are viewing the material of which they are the subjects? In my view, there is another construction of harm argument here, which does not necessarily require the child's knowledge of possession. The possessor exploits the child since, by possessing the image, he is taking unfair advantage of her and using her as a means to an end, whether or not the child is aware that the image is in the possession of others. As this is a more remote form of exploitation than the exploitation perpetrated by the creator of the image, the justification for criminalizing on the basis of such exploitation could be found because it underwrites the severe primary harm.

This position bears some similarity to an argument based on the possessor's 'visual abuse' of the child in the image. In his consideration of the American case of *New York* v. *Ferber*, Tien argues that, in the opinion of the court, the distribution of child pornography ensured that the child's abuse was relived through the eyes of visual abusers. Thus,

[65] At para. 9. The same line of argument has been influential upon the US Supreme Court. See *New York* v. *Ferber* 458 US 747 (1982), 759; and *Osbourne* v. *Ohio*, 111.

[66] Para. 10. [67] Para. 6. [68] Berger and Luckmann 1967: 114.

individuals who possess child pornography can recreate over and over again the infliction of previous harm to the child, and reproduce this harm through their own fantasies and imagination. In Tien's view, the judgment evidences the fact that: 'Child pornography focuses on the harm to children by being sexually used, including being viewed.'[69] Thus, proponents of this position would claim that the harm caused to children involved in the production of child pornography reoccurs over and over each time they are used as visual sexual objects by others. It can be contended that it is not the child who suffers the subsequent visual abuse; it is the image of child pornography that is distributed and possessed, not the child. As such, it is only the *visual representation* of the child that is used and abused by others. However, it remains the case that the actual child who appears in the child pornography is further exploited by the individuals who subsequently possess and use the image.[70]

Possession threatens society's shared morality

According to Devlin, immoral behaviour, even that which occurs in private, poses a threat to the moral fibre of society and, consequently, society itself.[71] Society thus has the right to take action through law to stamp out immoral behaviour in order to protect its very fibre.[72] Devlin's stance has been said to be one that is concerned with public, social harm (the moderate thesis) or with legal moralism (the extreme thesis).[73]

As applied to the act of possessing child pornography, Devlin's argument would suggest that such behaviour threatens public moral values which affirm the sacred, protected status of the child. At least some element of this argument is present in the Canadian Supreme Court's judgment in *Sharpe*, in which it was stated:

> The prohibition of the possession of child pornography is consistent with the democratic values which are essential in our community, and also with the … rights of children. It is legislation which promotes respect for the inherent dignity of children by curbing the existence of materials which degrade them. This in turn helps to protect children's equality and security rights. [74]

Therefore, the implication is that a failure to prohibit the act of possessing child pornography could place at stake the moral value in society

[69] Tien 1994: 131 and 133. *New York* v. *Ferber* 458 US 747 (1982).

[70] See Taylor and Quayle 2003: 31. [71] Devlin 1968. [72] Ibid.: 11.

[73] See Hart 1982: 48–52 and 55; and Harcourt 1999: 124.

[74] Taken from the reasoning of L'Heureux-Dubé, Gonthier and Bastarache JJ, para. 213.

which ascribes protective status to the child, and could fundamentally alter and corrupt the morality of those who come into contact with such material. The proposed criminalization of possession was justified in the House of Commons in 1988 because it 'will prevent adults from being enticed and corrupted to think about children in a sexual way'.[75] To avoid a corruption of morals, therefore, it is not only necessary to prevent individuals from disseminating child pornography, but also to stop individuals possessing it.

Williams considers the public morals thesis to be the main justification for the law's criminalization of possession. She critically analyses the arguments that possessing child pornography causes harm and concludes that, other than the primary harm caused to the children involved in the creation of child pornography, the risk of harm to children has not been proven. This leads her to argue that 'the reasoning for the law must fall back on the protection of sexual morality; the desire to prevent people obtaining sexual gratification, even if it does not interfere with the rights of children … merely because most people consider that viewing such images is abhorrent'.[76]

To support her case, Williams refers to the judgment of Woolf LCJ in *R.* v. *Smethurst*, in which he stated that offences under the PCA exist in order to protect public morals.[77] Woolf LCJ said much more than this, however, and it is clear that, in his view, the primary legitimation for the offences under the PCA and subsequent judicial interpretation of these offences was to protect children from exploitation. In finding that there was no contravention of Arts. 8 and 10 of the ECHR, he stated that 'the requirement to protect children justifies the terms of the offence … It is there for the prevention of crime, for the protection of morals, and in particular for the protection of children from being exploited which is undoubtedly a matter which is necessary in a democratic society.'[78] Thus, whilst I concur with Williams that the public morals argument is used in legal discourses,[79] it is only one of the justifications utilized by

[75] Hansard, HC Deb. 28 June 1988: column 305 (Geoffrey Dickens). See also Sentencing Advisory Panel 2002: para. 32.

[76] Williams 2004: 254. [77] Ibid.

[78] At 58. Earlier on the same page, Woolf LCJ also stated that: 'Unless there is a prohibition against the taking of indecent photographs, then there is no way in which children can be protected from being exploited.'

[79] For instance, when passing sentence in a Scottish child pornography case, Lord Turnbull stated that the court had to do what it could to express the 'total public abhorrence' of such cases. See 'Policeman jailed over child porn', BBC News report, 4 June 2008, http://news.bbc.co.uk/1/hi/scotland/glasgow_and_west/7435357.stm. See also Sentencing Advisory Panel 2002: para. 26.

the courts. In fact, as the earlier discussion should reveal, the judiciary much more commonly alludes to the market-reduction argument as one of the main justifications for prohibiting the possession of child pornography.

The problem with the public morals argument is that it is predicated on the wrong, moralized conception of harm and this kind of legal moralism makes it very difficult to adopt an objective, rational and proportionate response to the problem of child pornography. I should note here that, although I do not support the criminalization of possessing child pornography on public moral grounds, and I am critical of the presentation of child pornography within a moral discourse of indecency and corruption, it is inevitable that morality enters the debate at some point. This is unavoidable given the social moral condemnation of child pornography and related behaviour. When Devlin argues that the law treats as immoral 'what every right-minded person is presumed to consider immoral',[80] there is perhaps no better example than the subject of child pornography. Moreover, the harm principle is in itself a moral basis for criminalizing behaviour.[81] To reiterate, however, my objection lies in defining the harms of child pornography around moral constructions of harm.

Do these arguments legitimate criminalizing possession on the basis of harm?

If we consider that it is unnecessary to have definitive proof that possessing child pornography causes harm to children, but simply that it can be demonstrated that this conduct causes at least a potential risk of harm, then all of the arguments discussed here suffice. Dubber's critical analysis of possession offences leads him to conclude that: 'Possession is an incapacitationist tool for the elimination of threats. The all-important status that lies at the heart of the crime of possession thus is dangerousness.'[82] In the context of child pornography, it is hard to disagree. Indeed, the desire to protect children is such a powerful one that it would seem real proof of the harms claimed to be caused by possession has not been demanded in legal and societal discourses. However, because there is a lack of proof, the criminalization of possession and the infringement of individual liberty this causes remain less easily defensible than the criminalization of the creation and dissemination of child pornography.

[80] Devlin 1968: 15. Also note Devlin's disgust test, at 17: 'Immoral behaviour B should be made illegal if, when reasonable men in society S contemplate B calmly and dispassionately, they feel intolerance, indignation, and disgust.'

[81] See Hart 1982: x. [82] Dubber 2005: 113.

I have already noted that the harm principle can be applied to criminalize behaviour that creates a risk of harm. However, when we start along the path of criminalizing conduct that poses a risk of harm, as opposed to actual, proven harm, there are real dangers of an over-broad distortion of the principle. As highlighted by Persak:

> It is important to take notice of a major problem of the harm principle, namely its possible open-endedness ... This difficulty looms large if we extend the harm too much and put any kind of danger, risk, endangerment or remote harm on a par with the actual, direct harm as an equally valid reason for criminalisation.[83]

For Harcourt, arguments predicated upon harm have now become so easy to formulate that the harm principle has collapsed in upon itself.[84] I do not take so pessimistic a view, and would argue instead that the fact that harm and the risk of harm are so all-encompassing requires a thorough, careful analysis of harm claims. The application of the harm principle should serve to restrain state control over individual liberty, rather than restricting such liberty itself.[85] There is thus a real need for caution and, consequently, a powerful justification for criminalizing possession is required. In my view, it is possible to legitimate the legal prohibition placed on possession without a distortive expansion of the harm principle along the following lines: the possessor of child pornography directly harms the child in the image by exacerbating the primary harm (that is, causing further psychological suffering) if the child is aware that the image is possessed by others. Criminalization can also be legitimated because possession is a remote harm underwriting the primary harm. What is more, in cases where possessors intentionally encourage producers to create more material for them to acquire, possession is normatively linked to subsequent primary harm caused by the producers to children. Whilst the market-reduction argument appears to be the most commonly accepted presentation of the harm caused by possession, using it as a justification for criminalization on the basis of the harm principle is problematic. Even assuming it can be empirically proven, it is difficult to comply with the principle of fair imputation; a normative link does not exist between the act of possession and the future abuse and exploitation of children simply because the possessor may influence others to commit a more severe harm.

[83] Persak 2007: 44–5. [84] Harcourt 1999: 113 and 120. [85] Dan-Cohen 2002: 152–3.

Possession and viewing child pornography as therapy?

There is one other significant matter that I should consider before leaving the matter of possession and the question of harm. There is some research to suggest that viewing child pornography can have a therapeutic effect on individuals who have a sexual interest in children.[86] Taylor and Quayle's empirical research involving interviews with men convicted of possessing child pornography reveals that some of these men viewed child pornography to control their interests, as a form of escapism, to deal with their emotions and to prevent themselves from committing a sexual offence against a child. The authors found that considering the act of viewing of child pornography to be therapy:

> allows the respondent to present himself as someone who is 'ill' in some way and who has problems that are largely out of his control. It also allows for the respondent to appear to be behaving responsibly towards his problem by attempting both to explore and deal with it. This is used as a justification for accessing the images and becomes intertwined with ideas that it is also good for children, in that it prevents actual contact abuse.[87]

These findings are of particular interest, since they may indicate that, in some cases, depending on the impact viewing has on the individual, allowing the possession of child pornography could reduce the likelihood of children being harmed through sexual abuse. However, further research is required in this area in order to assess the positive and negative effects of perceiving the viewing of child pornography as therapy.

PSEUDO-IMAGES AND IMAGES OF NAKED CHILDREN: CRIMINALIZATION TAKEN TOO FAR?

Can criminalizing the creation, dissemination and possession of child pornography be justified when the material in question takes the form of a pseudo-photograph, generated on a computer without the involvement and abuse of a real child? Does criminalizing such material really reduce harm to children? These questions were addressed in the American case of *Ashcroft* v. *Free Speech Coalition*.[88] The Supreme Court

86 That using child pornography may have a cathartic effect was considered to be a 'significant factor to take into account' by Shaw J in *R.* v. *Sharpe* [1999] 169 DLR (4th) 536 (BCSC), at para. 48.

87 Taylor and Quayle 2003: 91 and 81.

88 535 US 234 (2002). See also *Free Speech Coalition* v. *Reno* 198 F.3d 1083, 1102 (CA9 1999).

affirmed the previous Court of Appeal's decision that statutory provisions which prohibited the creation and advertising of pseudo-photographs depicting children in sexual acts were unconstitutionally vague and overbroad, violating the right to freedom of speech guaranteed by the First Amendment. The Supreme Court rejected Congress's claims that such images represented a threat to children, emphasizing that they were not intrinsically related to child sexual abuse involving real children.[89]

It may be contended that, although a real child has not been abused to produce pseudo-images, criminalizing the creation, dissemination and possession of such images is still justified. The argument could be that such behaviour makes children more vulnerable to those who produce real child pornography by increasing the market for all indecent images of children, including real child pornography. According to Wasserman, 'the sale and possession of virtual child pornography would help maintain the child pornography market, which would leave open the financial conduit by which the creation of all child pornography is funded and would lead to an increased risk that real children would be violated'.[90] This claim can be linked with a 'slippery slope' argument, along the lines that if individuals are allowed to possess pseudo-images, this will encourage them to progress to seeking real images of child pornography.[91] Additionally, it could be argued that criminalizing pseudo-images reinforces the legal and societal stance that child sexual abuse in whatever form, real or fabricated, will not be tolerated.[92] If we do tolerate the creation, distribution and possession of such material, we may allow ourselves to become desensitized to images depicting the sexual abuse of children and would be encouraging the sexual objectification of children. Furthermore, in *Ashcroft* v. *Free Speech Coalition*, the government contended that pseudo-images should be prohibited because they can be used as part of the grooming process.[93] The difficulty with all of these claims, some of which have already been analysed above, is that they lack any real proof: we have no clear empirical evidence that allowing the creation and possession of pseudo-images encourages the market in child pornography, for instance.

[89] See Chapter 5, at 203. [90] Wasserman 1998: 270.

[91] See, e.g. Hansard, HC Standing Committee B: Criminal Justice and Public Order Bill, 15 February 1994: column 742 (Mike O'Brien).

[92] Consider, for instance, the justification given for criminalizing the possession of child pornography as a reinforcement of the laws prohibiting the creation of such material by McLachlin CJ in the Supreme Court case of *R.* v. *Sharpe*, para. 93.

[93] At 251. For discussion of such an argument, see Akdeniz 2008: 11 and 92.

None of these arguments, then, offers convincing, proven evidence for the criminalization of pseudo-images. To return again to the crucial question of harm: where no photograph of a real child is manipulated to produce a pseudo-image, its creation does not cause harm to an actual child. However, if an image of a real child has been manipulated to create the pseudo-image (a morphed pseudo-image), might she suffer harm as result?[94] Throughout this book, the construction of harm that I favour is that child pornography exploits children. Where a real child's image is used to create a pseudo-image, that child has been exploited through the misuse of her photographic image, whether or not she is aware of the pseudo-image.[95] However, this exploitation can only justify criminalization on the basis of the harm principle if it is *harmful* exploitation. My reasoning here is predicated upon Feinberg's account of harm and exploitation. Feinberg provides two meanings of harm: harm as a wrong and harm as a setback to interest. First, his normative presentation of harm is as follows: 'To say that A has harmed B … is to say much the same thing as that A has wronged B, or treated him unjustly. One person *wrongs* another when his indefensible (unjustifiable and inexcusable) conduct violates the other's right.'[96] In his second definition of harm as the setback of someone's interests, one individual harms another if his behaviour thwarts another's interest, leaving it 'in a worse condition than it would otherwise have been in had the invasion not occurred at all'.[97] Interests are explained as 'things in which one has a stake' and which are vital to an individual's wellbeing.[98] In Feinberg's view, it is only harms that fit into both categories, that is, setbacks of interest that amount to wrongs and wrongs that are also setbacks of interest, which can legitimate the legal prohibition of conduct.[99] Such harms are thus wrongful setbacks to interest.

Feinberg's analysis later turns to the specific matter of exploitation.[100] He sees that it is possible for morally repugnant exploitation to occur in a way that does not harm the exploitee's interests. He provides a number of possible presentations of exploitation in which B (the exploitee)

94 See Hansard, HC Standing Committee B: Criminal Justice and Public Order Bill, 15 February 1994: column 742 (Mike O'Brien).

95 I discuss the concept of exploitation in greater depth later in this chapter, at 139–47.

96 Feinberg 1984: 34. See also Uniacke 2004: 174.

97 Feinberg 1984: 34.

98 Ibid. See also Uniacke 2004: 174.

99 Ibid. I note that Feinberg's presentation of harm does not explain or justify the criminalization of conduct in every case. See, e.g. Duff, who discusses the criminalization of behaviour that does not cause a setback to interest in the context of the rape of an unconscious victim who remains completely unaware of the rape. Duff 2007: 128–9.

100 Feinberg 1988: chs. 31 and 32.

does or does not have her interests harmed by A (the exploiter), who may or may not profit, and where B either gives consent or does not consent to A's action.[101] For my purposes here, his most significant presentations of exploitation are: (1) where B did not consent to A's action, B's interests are harmed and A profits; and (2) where B did not consent to A's action, B's interests are not harmed and A profits. Examples of exploitation that fit into classification (1) are harmful instances of exploitation, the criminalization of which can be legitimated under the harm principle. Instances of exploitation that fall under (2) are non-harmful, since B's interests are not thwarted and 'the harm principle as a guide to the moral limits of the criminal law does not license liability for acts that tend to cause only nonharmful wrongs'.[102] I will now examine the question of whether, applying Feinberg's analysis, the creation of morphed pseudo-images can be seen as either harmful or non-harmful exploitation.

The creation of morphed pseudo-images as harmful exploitation

In legal discourses, it has been recognized that the creation of a pseudo-image through the manipulation of a real child's photograph negatively impacts on the child's interests. In *Ashcroft* v. *Free Speech Coalition*, Kennedy J noted that: 'Although morphed images may fall within the definition of virtual child pornography, they implicate the interests of real children and are in that sense closer to [images of real child pornography].'[103] How exactly can such images affect the real child's interests in a way that causes harm?

There are three possible ways in which the creation of a morphed pseudo-image could be construed as harmful exploitation in Feinberg's second sense of setting back interests. The first would be to argue that the manipulation of an image of a real child sets back the child's interests if the child becomes aware of the manipulated image and suffers psychological harm as a consequence.[104] In *R.* v. *H*,[105] for example, a school teacher manipulated photographs of school children by superimposing children's heads in these photographs onto bodies within child pornography images. When the pupils and their parents were informed of this by the police, a

[101] Ibid.: 215–16. [102] Feinberg 1984: 36. See also Wertheimer 1996: 28. [103] At 242.

[104] In 1994, the Home Affairs Committee placed much reliance upon police officers' views that children or their parents could suffer distress as a result of this awareness (Home Affairs Committee 1994: viii). See also Hansard, HC Standing Committee B: Criminal Justice and Public Order Bill, 15 February 1994: column 742 (Mike O'Brien); and Carr 2003: 4.

[105] [2005] EWCA Crim. 3037.

number of victim personal statements were made which indicated that more than one child had been significantly affected.[106] However, there are likely to be many cases in which the child whose image is manipulated never learns of the existence of the morphed pseudo-image, and it is difficult to argue here that, in addition to the child being wronged, her interests have been thwarted. If this is most often the case, as I suspect, then the creation of a pseudo-image through the manipulation of a child's photograph is not usually harmful exploitation. However, Feinberg states that: 'If the harm in question is very great, then a very small likelihood of its occurrence will do.'[107] What would need to be established, therefore, is that children who do become aware of their manipulated images suffer real psychological harm as a consequence, as opposed to mental distress.[108]

We could also argue, as a second alternative, that the child has an interest in not being defamed through her image,[109] which is set back if her image is manipulated and presented in a distorted, negative way. She suffers consequential harm because of this thwarting of her interest, even without her awareness of this manipulation. Feinberg does recognize that we can suffer harm through a setback to our interests of which we have no knowledge, since he states that his interest in a good reputation 'can be seriously harmed without my ever learning of it'.[110] He sees injury occurring in relation to this interest if those whose good opinions he values are presented with a 'libelous description' of him.[111] To equate a child's interest in not being defamed through her image with an interest in good reputation, it would have to be proven that the manipulation of her image is injurious in a similar sense. This could occur if the image is published, or if people who know the child are presented with the image or somehow stumble across it and have their perceptions of her altered by it.[112] We could then say that she is harmed, even without any knowledge of what has taken place. There must always be a risk, at least at some level, that the child and the morphed pseudo-image could be linked at some point in the future by someone she knows or later comes into contact with. Whilst it is unlikely that such an image would be published or

106 Ibid.: para. 7. 107 Feinberg 1984: 190.

108 For Feinberg's examination of how severe mental distress needs to be in order to amount to a harm to interest rather than just being a hurt, see ibid.: 48.

109 An interest in not being defamed through the publication of an image is recognized at law. See *Tolley* v. *JS Fry & Sons Ltd.* [1931] AC 333.

110 Feinberg 1984: 87. See also Wertheimer 1996: 25–6. 111 Feinberg, ibid.

112 In the law of defamation, it has been held that one can be defamed if others are made to avoid you, or somehow think less of you (*Youssoupoff* v. *Metro-Goldwyn Mayer* (1934) 50 TLR 581, 587). This is one possible reaction that may occur if those who know the child see the pseudo-image and think it to be real.

otherwise presented to those who know the child in the current climate of criminalization, there may be a greater chance of this occurring if the creation, distribution and possession of such images were lawful. Again, the likelihood of this harm occurring does not have to be great, provided the harm suffered by the child through the defamation of her image is severe.

The third way in which we could perceive the creator's action to be harmful exploitation is by arguing that the creation of pseudo-images sets back the child's interest in being recognized as an end in herself. However, if the Kantian maxim of treating people as ends in themselves could be construed as an interest, the setting back of which automatically causes harm with or without the exploitee's knowledge of the exploitation, then surely all forms of exploitation would be harmful *per se*? That Feinberg and others[113] explore the ways in which exploitation can and cannot be harmful reveals that the failure to recognize the exploitee as an end in herself is not enough in itself to establish a thwarting of interest and, thus, harm. Instead, this failure could be a wrong in Feinberg's normative sense of harm, or at least wrongful, as I will now proceed to argue. In my view, then, the first two of these three alternatives provide the strongest arguments that the creation of morphed pseudo-images is generally harmful exploitation on the basis of a setback to interests.

Finally, it is necessary to consider whether the creation of a pseudo-image through manipulating a real child's photograph is harmful in a normative sense. It could be contended that it is more defensible to argue that failing to recognize the child as an end in herself is always *wrongful* rather than always a *wrong*. Feinberg differentiates between wrongful behaviour and a wrong to a person constituting harm: 'exploitation is normally a way of using someone for one's own ends, which is somehow wrongful or blameworthy, whether it wrongs the other person or not'.[114] The implication of this statement is that although Feinberg sees exploitation as wrongful because of its nature, not all instances of exploitation necessarily wrong the exploited individual. I would disagree. Provided we can say that that we have a moral right not to be treated as a means, the exploiter's failure to respect the other individual as an end in herself does always amount to a wrong to that person.[115] Uniacke persuasively argues for the existence of such a right:

> Is there a right that we can plausibly be said to possess unconditionally … simply *qua* persons? Arguably the only such right is a right not to be

[113] Such as Wertheimer 1996. [114] Feinberg 1988: 177.

[115] For an analysis of exploitation on the basis of Kant's Categorical Imperative, see Wolff 1999: 112–14. See also Nielsen and Ware 1997: xiii; and Wood 1997: 15.

> treated merely as a means of promoting the welfare of others. Substantive rights implied by this more general right would include the right not to be … treated merely as an object.[116]

When, therefore, a child's image is manipulated in order to create a pseudo-image for the creator's own ends, the child's right not to be treated as a means to an end has been violated, and she has been wronged and thus harmed in the normative sense.

Is criminalizing pseudo-images justified on the basis of the harm principle?

The criminalization of morphed pseudo-images can be rationalized on the basis of the harm principle as harmful exploitation, following my analysis above.[117] However, I cannot see a legitimate basis for criminalizing pseudo-images that are wholly computer-generated, or created in some other way without the manipulation of a real child's image, through a reasoned application of the harm principle. There is a clear line between, on the one hand, real images that depict the actual sexual abuse of children or pseudo-images that harmfully exploit a real child and, on the other, completely fabricated images that do not cause harm to an actual child. As such, the creation of the latter amounts to a victimless crime. Higonnet argues that it is the boundary between real and fabricated images that should be reflected in law, if law aims to offer true protection to children, yet, at the same time, recognize freedom of expression.[118] Since the essence of my construct of harm is the exploitation of real children and, applying Feinberg's analysis, only exploitation that sets back interests and wrongs an individual meets the harm principle, I concur with Higonnet provided that the pseudo-image is not a morphed one. That is not to deny that other arguments justifying criminalization of *all* pseudo-images on the basis of possible, future harm to children, such as the market-reduction argument, can be raised. However, such arguments must be balanced against an overreaction that could make it very difficult to draw the line between what should and should not be prohibited.

It is vital to adopt a reasoned and proportioned approach. Otherwise, where is the line then drawn? Why should we not go the whole mile and

[116] Uniacke 2004: 180.

[117] In the event that it cannot be proven that the harms I have outlined are sufficiently severe, I consider whether it would be legitimate to criminalize such pseudo-images on an alternative basis later in this chapter, at 145–6.

[118] Higonnet 1998: 163.

also criminalize any drawings, cartoons or written material in which child sexual abuse features? In fact, this is exactly the matter that was considered by a recent Home Office public consultation following concern expressed by the police and child welfare organisations.[119] This takes us into the realm of prohibiting any material that might create a risk of harm; the existence of concrete harm becomes irrelevant. If we do not take a step back and evaluate carefully why such a broad-brush approach is being adopted and whether this approach can be rationalized on the basis of the harm principle, there is a real risk that this overreaction will continue. The effect of this overreaction is that behaviour is criminalized purely on the grounds of legal moralism rather than a real risk of harm.[120]

I should address one final point here. There is a practical concern that if we were to de-criminalize completely fabricated pseudo-images, this would make it harder for prosecutions to be brought in cases where it is difficult to tell if the particular pseudo-image has involved the manipulation of a real photograph.[121] Thus, there is a chance that harmful behaviour will slip through the net. There is a way around this, however. A defence could exist if the individual proves that the image was a fabricated one, the creation of which has not involved the manipulation of an image of a real child.[122] This would also comply with the harm principle since, in the absence of harm, criminalization would not be legitimate. I recognize that such an approach may be objected to on the basis that it could cause practical difficulties for the distributor or possessor who is not the creator of the image. In *Ashcroft* v. *Free Speech Coalition*, the Supreme Court considered that placing the burden on the defendant to prove the material is not unlawful 'raised serious constitutional difficulties', since it could be hard for the innocent possessor to prove the images are not real.[123] However, I believe this objection can be overridden; since possessors are prepared to take the risk that their behaviour underwrites a primary harm, they should also be prepared to face the possible negative consequences of their behaviour for themselves.

119 Home Office 2007a. See the final chapter, at 237–8.

120 See also on this general point, Duff 2007: 130.

121 An argument raised in Parliament when the CJPO Bill was at Committee stage. See the previous chapter, at 88, n. 172. See also 'Crackdown on computer porn', *The Guardian*, 26 November 1993; and O'Donnell and Milner 2007: 66.

122 For a similar suggestion, see Friel 1997: 258.

123 At 255–6.

Are photographs of naked or semi-naked children harmful?

Quayle *et al.* explore how abuse images (applying their terminology) victimize children. One level of victimization they discuss involves a child being photographed on a beach, or at a swimming pool, without her knowledge. Although not explicitly stated, given the setting of the scene, the reader can assume that the child is partially dressed or perhaps naked. The authors state that this type of image is commonly distributed on the internet and utilized for sexual purposes and, consequently, they argue that the image 'is clearly abusive, even if the particular child has no knowledge of the event, and cannot be identified'.[124] I would challenge the conclusion that the image is abusive. The fact that the child has not consented to the image being used in this way indicates that she has been wronged, but if she has no knowledge of this usage, where is the setback to her interests? The surreptitious taking of this image in a legitimate setting cannot be abusive to the child who has no knowledge of it. There is surely only a small risk of a setback to her interests in the future if she, or someone she knows, comes across the image and discovers how it has been used, assuming this knowledge causes her mental suffering. Furthermore, if Quayle *et al.*'s argument were to be accepted in legal discourses, any image of a naked child taken by parents in legitimate circumstances could be criminalized if it is later utilized for sexual purposes. Is it, then, appropriate for images of naked children to be captured by laws surrounding child pornography?

Higonnet is highly critical of the extension of American child pornography laws to photographs of naked children that do not depict any sexual activity.[125] In her view, extending the legal definition of child pornography to include images of children's bodies that do not depict sexual activity unjustifiably curtails freedom of expression and fails to provide an effective means of protecting children. The perceived 'harm' of such images lies in their potential to sexually stimulate the viewer. However, clearly, this is a separate matter from whether the child has been harmed through the creation of the image. For Higonnet, the real harm of child pornography is the harm caused to the children whose sexual abuse is depicted in images of child pornography. Her preferred approach is thus to move away from a legal prohibition upon images towards a 'law that targets actions'.[126] I agree that we should reassess a legal approach such as that in place in the US, which can criminalize

[124] Quayle *et al.* 2006: 49. [125] Higonnet 1998: 161–2.
[126] At 188. For an opposing argument, see Grasz and Pfaltzgraff 1998.

images of childhood nudity that do not involve sexual activity. Whilst case law indicates that such images would not be legally indecent in this jurisdiction, I have noted that uncertainty about this matter remains.[127]

In this jurisdiction, given the current climate of moral panic about any image of a child's body, allowing such images to be deemed indecent if the jury considers ordinary people would view them as such by applying recognized standards of propriety would be a potentially dangerous approach.[128] The response of some of the tabloid press to images of naked children included in an art gallery's photographic exhibition in 2001 evidences that there is a perception that even innocently taken images of naked children are sexualized and indecent.[129] As I will argue in the next chapter, this is a potentially damaging perception that can cause harm to children in terms of the way in which both they, and we, perceive their bodies. However, it is necessary to consider whether placing all images of childhood nudity that do not depict sexual activity outside the grasp of child pornography laws might fail to tackle harm suffered by children in certain cases. Would there be any other offence with which an individual who takes such a photograph and psychologically harms a child in so doing can be charged? Take, for example, a situation where an individual forces a child to pose naked for him in order that he can take a photograph of her to use for his own sexual gratification. He does not touch her in any way and does not act in any overtly sexual manner. However, the child suffers psychological harm as a result of this exploitative experience.[130] Focusing on the individual's actions as Higonnet advocates may well enable the criminal law to intervene in these circumstances, since these actions could amount to the crime of causing or inciting a child to engage in sexual activity under s. 10 of the Sexual Offences Act 2003. The child's act of posing for the photograph can fall under the definition of 'sexual activity' provided a reasonable person would consider that: (1) whatever its circumstances or any person's purpose in relation to it, it is because of its nature sexual; or (2) because of its nature it may be

[127] See the discussion of the judgments in *R.* v. *Carr* and *R.* v. *O'Carroll* in Chapter 2, 58–9 and Gillespie 2005.

[128] Moreover, 'if mere nudity constituted pornography then a lot of very famous photographs, sculptures and paintings could be also categorized as child pornography'. Edge and Baylis 2004: 82.

[129] See Chapter 4, at 186–8.

[130] It is only in such harmfully exploitative circumstances that I would concur with Grasz and Pfaltzgraff 1998: 626, that a child could suffer 'emotional and mental harm' by the creation of an image of herself nude.

sexual and because of its circumstances or the purpose of any person in relation to it (or both), it is sexual.[131]

There is also an alternative way in which the taking of this photograph could be criminalized without all photographs of children's naked bodies potentially being defined as indecent images of children. The jury could be directed to consider that, whilst such images should not generally be viewed as indecent, they could decide that the image is indecent by considering the context in which the photograph was taken, rather than the content of the image being the determinative factor.[132] Photographs of naked children that do not depict sexual activity or sexual posing would thus only be capable of falling under the legal definition of an indecent image if the surrounding circumstances in which they are taken warrant the construction and criminalization of the behaviour in question as taking an indecent image of a child. Significantly, altering the legal approach to the question of indecency in this way would not lend support to the conception that all images of naked children are in some way sexualized.

Such an approach to determining whether an image of a child is indecent has, however, been rejected by English courts. In *R.* v. *Graham-Kerr*, it was held that: 'the circumstances and the motivation of the taker may be relevant to the *mens rea* of the taker as to whether his taking was intentional or accidental ... but it is not relevant to whether or not the photograph is indecent'.[133] The Court of Appeal was not persuaded by the argument that the approach in cases of indecent assault – where the purpose and circumstances surrounding the assault are considered in order to ascertain whether the assault was indecent[134] – should be that applied in ascertaining whether a photograph of a child was indecent. In the later case of *R* v. *Smethurst*, the Court of Appeal reaffirmed that the question of whether a photograph is indecent is a matter for the jury to answer by considering the content of the image and applying recognized standards of propriety.[135] Ormerod argues that applying the approach taken in indecent assault cases would be problematic as 'it would be

131 S. 78 of the Sexual Offences Act 2003.

132 Such an approach has also been considered by Gillespie 2005: 31–3. *R.* v. *McKain* provides a good example of the relevance of context. Here, the appellant pressurized a fifteen-year-old boy to allow him to take photographs of him naked from the front and back. He also asked him to measure his penis with a tape measure. He persuaded him to agree to this by relying upon his knowledge of the boy's past behaviour, which his parents knew nothing about and would have disapproved of. The breach of trust he had committed – being a pastor at the church where the boy and his family were members – was also emphasized by the Court of Appeal judges.

133 At 1106, *per* Stocker LJ.

134 See *R.* v. *Court* [1989] AC 28.

135 Para. 21.

difficult to prove the motivations and circumstances of the images being created. It would be impossible to prove such matters where the prosecution was for possession/distribution by someone other than the creator.'[136] This would be less of a problem, however, if the *creation* of indecent images of naked children were the only behaviour criminalized.[137]

As I have already discussed, the moral framework of indecency is inappropriate in the context of child pornography given its failure to convey the nature of the harm caused to the child. Thus, although the approach outlined above would more appropriately define the scope of material that should be caught by the law, it is at best a case of trying to darn a sock that has too many holes. The braver step would be to dispose with the question of indecency altogether and replace it with the question of whether the child has been exploited. This exploitation would be evidenced in the case of a photograph of a naked child by the context surrounding the image's creation.

Such a revision of the indecency framework, or its replacement with a focus instead on harmful exploitation, would better address the issue of harm. Some images of naked children's bodies are harmful, but it is the circumstances in which the image is taken which harm the child. Children are not harmed by the creation of images of their naked bodies, unless such images are produced in such a way as to exploit them and set back their interests.[138] They may well be harmed, however, by damaging perceptions of childhood nudity[139] that are exacerbated by a legal approach that focuses on indecency.

THE HARMS OF SEXUAL GROOMING

Can criminalization of behaviour related to grooming be legitimated?

The obvious harm that grooming can lead to is child sexual abuse. As I have already noted, the criminalization of such behaviour provides an example of criminal law's intervention to prevent *potential* harm,

[136] Ormerod 2001: 658. See also *R.* v. *Graham-Kerr*, 1105–6, *per* Stocker LJ.

[137] See my later argument in this chapter, at 144.

[138] I am not arguing that the purpose for which an image of a naked child is viewed (where the individual views the image to obtain sexual gratification) should be the issue here. Whilst the context of use may be normatively harmful and exploitative, I do not see this context as being harmful to the child in the sense of thwarting her interests. To argue otherwise, it would be necessary to establish that children who become aware that an image of them naked is being used for sexual gratification suffer serious psychological harm.

[139] See Chapter 4, at 186–90.

which can be justifiable under the harm principle.[140] When faced with potential as opposed to actual harm, however, it is necessary to establish a strong causal link between the conduct in question and the harm to be avoided in order to prevent an over-broadening of the harm principle. As already discussed, the existing research demonstrates a clear causal link between grooming and child sexual abuse.[141]

When applying the harm principle to justify the criminalization ofbehaviour related to grooming, it is the ulterior harmful intent which provides the strongest connection between this conduct and any subsequent child sexual abuse.[142] As Horder notes in his analysis of crimes of ulterior intent, 'the normative significance of X's conduct changes dramatically when viewed in the light of his or her intent; whereupon the conduct becomes eligible for criminalization'.[143] The criminalization of behaviour related to grooming can be legitimated on the basis that we are essentially holding the groomer accountable for exploiting the child's naivety and vulnerability for his own calculated ends, for creating a real risk of future harm. Prohibiting this behaviour, which might in itself cause no harm to the child, can prevent the greater, ultimate harm of child sexual abuse.

It may not always be possible to establish that the groomer's exploitation of the child in itself sets back the child's interests. Initial acts of grooming may appear 'innocent' on the face of it, if, for example, they take the form of the giving of gifts.[144] However, this behaviour is perpetrated with the intention of facilitating the groomer's future harmful conduct that certainly will harm the child's interests, and this changes the character of the individual's conduct.[145] According to Horder: 'To engage in conduct with a (particular kind of) wrongful intention may make that conduct *ipso facto* unjustified. What then matters for criminalization is that one has actually changed the normative character of one's conduct, which affects one's normative position, in acting with the relevant intent.'[146]

[140] See, e.g. Mill 1993: 165. See also Feinberg 1985: 154. [141] See Chapter 1, at 32–9.

[142] Mill states in *On Liberty* that to legitimate the state's restriction of an individual's liberty: 'the conduct from which it is desired to deter him must be calculated to produce evil to some one [*sic*] else'. Mill 1993: 78.

[143] Horder 1996: 154.

[144] See, for instance, the discussion of *Re Attorney General's Reference (No. 41 of 2000)* in Chapter 2, at 76–7.

[145] Applying Horder's analysis, initial, seemingly innocent acts of grooming ('Doing something overtly innocent intending to commit a crime'), and acts of grooming that could amount to crimes in themselves ('Committing a lesser crime, intending to commit a greater one'), can be described as crimes of ulterior intent. Horder 1996: 156–7.

[146] Horder 1996: 168.

It would be inaccurate to classify grooming as a remote harm because it does not simply 'induce or lead to further acts',[147] as in the case of possessing child pornography. Rather, the individual sets out upon a course of grooming in order to facilitate his future sexual abuse of the child. It may, then, be easier to justify criminalization of the groomer's behaviour; his ulterior intention to commit future harm to the child whom he is grooming means that it is more straightforward to satisfy the principle of fair imputation than in the case of remote harms. The fault for the later primary harm to the child can be attributed to the groomer because there is a direct link between the grooming and any subsequent abuse that he perpetrates.[148]

What is also significant about some instances of grooming is that they may, in and of themselves, cause primary harm and thwart the child's interests. If, for example, the groomer threatens or blackmails the child, the child could experience psychological harm as a result. A case may be made that criminalization of this behaviour could be legitimated on the basis of the harm principle without any need to prove any ulterior intent. Yet, the fact that this ulterior intent exists exacerbates the wrongful nature of the individual's actions. Interestingly, for Horder, wrongdoing offers a better explanation for crimes of ulterior intent than harm. This is because the harm principle is generally applied by considering the harm that is done through the individual's actions. However, in the case of crimes of ulterior intent, harm is intended rather than committed[149] and it is the wrongful intention that offers the primary legitimization of criminalization. The fact remains, however, that the way in which the law presents and constructs the behaviour it criminalizes must also be appropriate. This was a matter I raised in the previous chapter and I now return to it, by considering whether social and legal constructions may increase the harms of grooming.

Do prevailing constructions of grooming exacerbate the threat of harm?

Situations which pose the greatest threat of grooming and the individuals who are most likely to be groomers are not being presented accurately by the law, the media and pressure groups.[150] Media coverage in

[147] Von Hirsch 1996: 264.

[148] Furthermore, certain grooming strategies can amount to crimes in themselves. Say, for instance, the groomer forces the child to look at images of child pornography. As discussed in Chapter 2, such behaviour would be caught by s. 12 of the SOA.

[149] Horder 1996: 156.

[150] See Chapter 2, at 90 and 102 and Chapter 4, at 170; and Kaufman *et al.* 2006: 116–17.

particular conveys the impression that grooming and meeting with children after communicating with them on the internet is a new form of harm in terms of child sexual abuse. However, according to Wolak *et al.*: 'Although a new medium for communication is involved, the non-forcible sex crimes that predominate offenses against youths online are not particularly new or uncommon.'[151] Moreover, the focus on stranger and online grooming tends to present public and virtual settings as places where children are at risk of harm, and directs attention away from the situational settings in which children are more likely to be groomed for sexual abuse:

> parks, public toilets, shopping malls, swimming pools and so forth … are typically associated with predatory offenders. They are the locations that many parents will regard as most dangerous and are the traditional focus of 'stranger danger' public education campaigns. In comparison to other locations, however, they are relatively infrequent places for locating children for sexual abuse.[152]

Prevailing social and legal constructions of grooming as being perpetrated most often by a stranger, online and through other communication technologies are thus inaccurate and problematic. It is the official and media representations that members of the public, without any direct experience of grooming and child pornography, are likely to accept as shorthand.[153] As a consequence, it is probable that children will be more vulnerable to other more common forms of grooming, because parents are less aware of the situations and circumstances in which children are most at risk.[154] As I have noted, the existing research reveals that groomers are looking for 'vulnerable' children.[155] For many children, vulnerability can be created and exploited as a consequence of their social situation. One police officer I interviewed commented that, in his experience: 'A lot of sex offenders have a knack of being able to attach themselves to vulnerable families, perhaps single parent families, looking for a bit of love … A lot of children in children's homes are vulnerable.'[156] This type of setting and context does not tend to be the one that prevailing popular constructions of grooming represent. Furthermore, if we fail to take into account the fact that grooming can occur in a multitude of settings, there is also a

[151] Wolak *et al.* 2008: 113. [152] Wortley and Smallbone 2006: 22.

[153] See my discussion of availability cascades in the next chapter.

[154] For a discussion of who poses the greatest threat to children, see Simon and Zgoba 2006: 76; and Chapter 1, at 36–7 and 44–5.

[155] See Chapter 1, at 34–5. [156] Interview RX4.

danger that we fail to recognize the harm caused to a child who has been groomed; some children who are groomed, especially young teenage girls, can be perceived as lesser victims. Another police officer stated that:

> young girls become a pseudo-victim because [the media] may well be suggesting that they might have been complicit or provocative. What does that do? It drives girls underground and doesn't provide them with the trust and confidence to report and so we don't get the true picture and that's why on many occasions when we investigate these offences, we find multiple victims who have been too frightened ... they've not reported the offences.[157]

There is a risk then, that popular constructions of grooming and of the 'archetypal' child victim are under-playing and increasing the harms of grooming. In the concluding chapter, I will discuss ways in which public awareness can be raised to reduce, rather than exacerbate, the harms of grooming. Now, however, I turn to my presentation of the harm of child pornography and grooming as exploitation.

CHILD PORNOGRAPHY AND SEXUAL GROOMING: CONSTRUCTING HARM AS EXPLOITATION

The term 'exploitation' is all too often bandied about without any real exploration of what the concept means, or how the author is using it.[158] Yet exploitation is also a constructed concept that could mean something very different to, on the one hand, an intellectual property lawyer and, on the other, a practitioner who works with sexually abused children. Exploitation is also a morally laden concept; a descriptive term applied to behaviour that we perceive to be wrongful. The concept of exploitation that I adopt revolves around one person's wrongful misuse of another, a situation or context in which an individual takes unfair advantage of someone else for his own ends.[159]

More specific definitions of sexual exploitation do exist. Whilst such definitions may be relevant and appropriate to child pornography and grooming, I would argue that their emphasis on *the sexual* is problematic. There are cogent reasons for moving away from the potentially dangerous morality discourse that highlights the sexual in the context of society's

[157] Interview RX2. [158] See also Wertheimer 1996: 5; and Wood 1997: 2.

[159] Wertheimer 1996: 16; Feinberg 1988: 177 and 179; Wolff 1999: 110–11; Wood 1997: 7; and Goodin 1987: 166, 171 and 182.

and law's response to child pornography and grooming, and children more broadly.[160] There is also a need to avoid the over-prioritization of sexual exploitation above other forms of harmful misuse of children.[161] It is thus a more universalized conception of exploitation that I advocate. Bearing in mind this note of caution, there are two definitions of sexual exploitation that include an element which I see as a common feature of exploitation in the contexts of child pornography and grooming. In 2003, the United Nations' Secretary-General defined sexual exploitation as 'any actual or attempted abuse of a position of vulnerability, differential power, or trust, for sexual purposes'.[162] According to Russell, the concept of sexual exploitation revolves around an imbalance of power and the abuse of this power by the stronger party in the relationship.[163] Thus, a further aspect of exploitation that I would extract from these constructions is the abuse of a position of vulnerability,[164] or differential power[165] and, in some cases, also an abuse of trust. One situation where the existence of a relationship of unequal power is arguably more questionable is where an individual possesses child pornography. However, although there is no actual relationship of differential power between the child and the individual who possesses the image in the physical sense, the individual has the power to use the child's image as he wants. The connection between the possessor and the child's image causes the child to be vulnerable to the possessor's exploitation (his taking unfair advantage of her); a virtual relationship of unequal power, which the child may remain unaware of, exists between them. Through the same reasoning, such a relationship also exists between the child and the individual who manipulates the child's image to create a pseudo-image.

Further light can be shed upon the nature of the child pornographer's or groomer's exploitation of a child by considering Wood's analysis of two senses of exploitation, which he refers to as 'benefit-exploitation' and, 'advantage-exploitation'.[166] Benefit-exploitation involves the exploiter's use of a characteristic or certain aspect of an individual for his benefit or own ends. Thus, the pornographer and groomer exploit the child's body for their benefit. However, it is also the case that the pornographer

160 See Chapter 4, at 189–91.

161 See the concluding Chapter 6, at 245.

162 See the UN Secretary-General's Bulletin *Special Measures for Protection from Sexual Exploitation and Sexual Abuse*. 2003. ST/SGB/2003/13.

163 See Russell 1984: 22.

164 Goodin goes so far as to argue that exploitation violates the moral norm and duty to protect the vulnerable. Goodin 1987: 187–8.

165 On the power imbalance, see ibid.: 167.

166 Wood 1997: 8.

and groomer advantage-exploit the child; that is, they make use of the child's vulnerability and taking advantage of this vulnerability enables them to benefit-exploit the child's body. On this account, the elements of advantage and benefit are crucial to our understanding of the dynamics of exploitation, and the unequal relationship of power assists the pornographer or groomer in undertaking exploitation in both of these senses.

In my view, the concept of exploitation better encompasses the harms of child pornography and grooming than focusing on sexual abuse. This is because not all behaviour related to child pornography involves sexual abuse. I am not, by any means, seeking to under-play the sexual abuse that does often form an essential and integral part of child pornography. What I am endeavouring to do is present the commonality underlying the harm of *all* behaviour related to child pornography, including distribution and possession. In the context of grooming, although a successful course of grooming may lead to sexual abuse, this is not always the result of the groomer's action,[167] and his grooming in itself is not sexual abuse until and unless it progresses to such. As I have argued, for the main harm of child pornography to be presented in legal and social discourses as exploitation, grooming too should primarily be seen as exploitation of children's trust and naivety. Wolff's analysis of exploitation as using someone else's vulnerability mirrors the exploitation that occurs in the grooming scenario: 'One's vulnerability is exploited if the person uses this weakness to obtain agreement to, or at least acquiescence in, a course of action that one would not have accepted had there not been this asymmetry in power.'[168] The groomer exploits the child's naivety, takes unfair advantage of the child and abuses his position of power and trust for his own purposes. The exploitative nature of grooming has been emphasized by Scotland's Commissioner for Children and Young People.[169] In a recent Scottish case involving grooming, in which a man communicated with a thirteen-year-old girl in an internet chatroom before meeting her and having sexual intercourse, Lord McPhail

[167] Goodin notes that an exploiter 'must succeed on two levels: exploiters must not only successfully seize advantages but also successfully transform them into real advantages'. Goodin 1987: 168. Thus, a groomer may fail in his endeavours because the child cannot be manipulated, or because his attempts to subsequently take advantage of the manipulated child fail.

[168] Wolff 1999: 111.

[169] When commenting upon the offence relating to sexual grooming under The Protection of Children and Prevention of Sexual Offences (Scotland) Act 2005. See also Home Office 2000: 95.

commented: 'This is a clear case of the callous, cynical and deliberate grooming and exploitation of a child by an adult male for sexual purposes.'[170]

The police officers involved in my study gave their views on the way in which grooming exploits children and highlighted similar matters to those I have discussed. For one, grooming deprives children of choice; groomers put children in a position they would not choose to be in.[171] Others saw groomers as abusing power, 'finding the vulnerabilities of the young person and taking advantage of these vulnerabilities',[172] although: 'There isn't a common vulnerability that groomers exploit. It really depends on what they discover about the child and can then use to their advantage.'[173] One officer stated that he tended to see the exploitation of 'young girls, thirteen, fourteen, fifteen years of age who don't know that they're being abused. That's the exploitation issue by giving them drink, drugs, money, whatever it may be. They are not aware that they're being abused.'[174] Significantly, the exploitation here has been so successful that the person being exploited does not realize she is a victim.

I have stated above that I advocate a more universalized concept of exploitation which does not over-emphasize the sexual and, for this reason, I contend that we should avoid presenting grooming as the manipulation and exploitation of children's sexual innocence. This is not least because such a presentation suggests that those children who are no longer sexually innocent cannot be groomed.[175] Furthermore, exploitation by way of grooming does not have to have a sexual element to it, although the subsequent harmful act must be characterized as such in order for behaviour to amount to grooming a child for sexual abuse.

Some readers may wonder why I have not chosen to highlight a lack of consent, or coerced consent, as a critical element of exploitation in the context of child pornography and grooming. This may have been anticipated, since I have differentiated between adult and child pornography on the basis of there always being a lack of valid consent on the part of the child in the case of child pornography, and I have stressed the fact that, during the grooming process, the child's consent is often obtained

170 See 'Man is jailed for sex grooming', BBC News report, 5 October 2007, http://news.bbc.co.uk/1/hi/england/shropshire/7282019.stm.

171 Interview RX1.

172 Interview RX6, also reflected in Interview RX5. Another officer expressed a similar view: 'They gain the child's trust and then abuse that trust. Successful groomers manipulate children by developing tactics so that they agree to do what they want them to do.' Interview RX7.

173 Interview RX8.

174 Interview RX3.

175 See the concluding Chapter 6, at 236.

through coercion or threats. However, constructing exploitation around the absence of consent could give rise to the implication that the adult's actions would not be exploitative if the child does, in fact, consent. This is problematic for two reasons. First, children cannot give legal consent to sexual acts that could form the content of the image of child pornography or the ultimate harm that grooming leads to. We are not faced with an autonomous actor capable of giving consent to the particular acts in question, and thus whether or not the child 'consents' should not affect the conclusion as to whether she has been exploited.[176] Secondly, consent can be a contentious matter in the context of an adult taking any kind of photograph of a child. In fact, the existence of a child's free consent to their image appearing in a photograph may always be questionable: 'Consent, both sexual and visual, always operates in terms of relationships of power.'[177] The validity of a child's consent could thus even be questioned where a parent simply takes a holiday snapshot for the family album.[178] Moreover, the argument that exploitation is not necessarily based on a lack of consent has been well presented elsewhere. According to Feinberg, Wertheimer and Wolff, there are instances of both non-consensual and consensual exploitation.[179] Thus, whilst a lack of consent may be indicative of exploitation, it is not an essential ingredient of the idea of exploitation that I employ.

Not all instances and forms of exploitation can be legitimately criminalized on the basis of the harm principle. The exploitation caused by behaviour related to real images of child pornography, morphed pseudo-images and grooming is harmful exploitation that justifies criminalization through the harm principle; the child is wronged, her interests are set back and the adult profits from his exploitation.[180] If a thwarting of interests cannot always be established in the case of the possession of child pornography (where the child has no knowledge of possession, for instance), the possessor's exploitation certainly underwrites the creator's primary harm and criminalization can be legitimated on this basis.

[176] I realize that there is an argument that in the case of older, mature children, a capacity to consent to sexual intercourse may exist. However, in law at least, such capacity would not be recognized below the age of sexual consent.

[177] Edge and Baylis 2004: 79.

[178] See also Higonnet 1998: 169. Issues of gender can also be relevant. Edge and Baylis (ibid.) discuss how, when private family images taken by mothers of their children enter the public arena, critics often present their arguments within a discourse of maternal irresponsibility. See also O'Riordan 2008.

[179] See Feinberg 1988: 178–9 and 201–2; Wertheimer 1996: ch. 8; and Wolff 1999: 113.

[180] See Feinberg 1988: 215–16 and 211.

In the case of grooming, the groomer intends that the child's interests are ultimately set back even if the grooming in itself does not have this effect. If it does not, the groomer's exploitation can still be harmful, if, for example, the child is threatened or blackmailed.

However, whilst all exploitation is a wrong in the sense that an individual is taken unfair advantage of, not all instances of exploitation are harms in the sense that they thwart the exploitee's interests.[181] Furthermore, a rational approach to the matter of exploitation must be taken. To avoid an over-broad distortion of the harm principle, it is necessary to draw the line at an appropriate point beyond which lesser, non-harmful and more remote forms of exploitation are not criminalized. Thus, to return to the possession of child pornography, for instance, if the possessor's exploitation is more remote, it is harder to legitimate criminalization when his exploitation is not normatively linked to a primary harm. This will occur when the child pornography he is in possession of is purely computer-generated without the use of a real child's image and, thus, in my view, such behaviour should not be prohibited by criminal law through an application of the harm principle. It is also illustrative to consider photographs of naked children here. The creator of such a photograph will have exploited and harmed the child if he has misused her or taken advantage of her for his own ends by forcing her to pose naked and to allow him to create the image. In such a scenario, we would have a set back to the child's interests that could defensibly be criminalized. Whether it is legitimate to prohibit the distribution and possession of a photograph of a naked child, however, is much more questionable. The distributor's and possessor's exploitation are again remote harms. If there is a normative link to primary harm (consider that the photograph of a naked child possessed by the individual may, in fact, have been taken legitimately), it is a less severe primary harm than that suffered by children who are sexually abused through the creation of child pornography.

As I am here concerned with the question of when the criminalization of exploitation can be rationalized, I will return to the matter of pseudo-images. My earlier argument that exploitation in cases where pseudo-images are created through the manipulation of a real photograph is harmful exploitation may not be accepted. Perhaps it could be contended that the existence of the pseudo-image will often not be known to the child or those whom she knows, and even if she or others she knows

[181] See Feinberg ibid.: 176.

come across the pseudo-image, the harm that she may suffer is not severe enough to justify the intervention of the criminal law. Furthermore, some might argue that although the child is wronged, even if she or others she knows come across the pseudo-image, her interests are not harmed in the sense I have claimed above. If this is the case, can we rationalize criminalization purely on the basis of exploitation, even though this exploitation is not harmful enough to justify criminalization under the harm principle? What we would be arguing, then, is that criminalization is warranted on the basis of the exploitation itself. Feinberg defines the 'exploitation principle' as follows:

> The principle that warrants the criminal prohibition of unjust gain (exploitation *per se*) even when it causes no unfair loss (harm) can be called 'the exploitation principle' and defined as the doctrine that it is always a good reason in support of a proposed criminal prohibition that it will prevent unjust gain, even when that wrongful gain is not accompanied by any unfair loss. That principle is clearly a form of pure legal moralism since its aim is to prevent a kind of non-grievance evil, and it makes no ultimate appeal to the prevention of derivative harms.[182]

In some, very limited, cases, Feinberg accepts that there is plausibility in justifying criminalization on the basis of exploitation.[183] However, he is very cautious about invoking the exploitation principle to legitimate legal intervention where the non-consenting exploitee's interests are not harmed, although the exploiter profits. This, as I have argued, can often be the nature of the exploitation that occurs in relation to pseudo-images if the child or someone she knows never comes across the manipulated image. Feinberg states that examples of this form of exploitation are difficult to find. The scenario he chooses to present is one in which a talented author makes huge profits from a book she has written about the inspirational life of a 'lonely hero' who has battled against adversity to achieve a laudable goal, and does not share any of her profit with the hero. In Feinberg's view: 'No wrong has been done the man, no promises broken, no harm inflicted. He has been left exactly as he was, no better, no worse … Any sensitive observer can feel the injustice in this, but the problem of designing a purely legal remedy defies solution.'[184]

Primarily, Feinberg does not see how this form of exploitation, or others in which the exploitee's interests are not harmed, can be resolved (either on the basis of criminal law or restitution) without practical

[182] Feinberg 1988: 213. [183] Ibid.: 214. [184] Ibid.: 218.

difficulties.[185] However, Feinberg's example of the author and lonely hero differs from our case in point, the creation of morphed pseudo-images, in an important way. There is nothing to suggest that the author has written anything but the truth about the lonely hero and, therefore, he has not been wronged in the Feinbergian sense.[186] In contrast, children whose photographs are used to create pseudo-images have indeed been wronged. The pseudo-image's creator has presented them in a manipulated, distorted and inaccurate way, violating their right not to be treated as a means, regardless of whether they are aware of the image's existence. In such a scenario, where we have exploitation that is normatively harmful but does not thwart interests, invoking the criminal law to punish this wrong seems less of an affront to liberty than in the case of exploitation that does not harm in the normative sense. Yet this is still a step removed from criminalizing exploitation which is harmful because it causes a setback to interests. I am reluctant to support criminalization on the basis outlined above; I have advocated caution in the way in which we apply the harm principle to avoid open-endedness, and I advocate the same for the principle of exploitation.[187]

Even if an approach based on the principle of exploitation alone were adopted, it would still be difficult to legitimate the criminalization of completely fabricated pseudo-images. I can only envisage two ways in which one could argue such images should be criminalized through employing the concept of exploitation. The first would be to claim that such images exploit all children through their objectification of children as sexual objects. The second would be to argue that they could be utilized as part of the grooming process, to exploit children in the future. However, again, I would argue that the legal construction of exploitation should be limited to the harmful exploitation of a real child (consider that my definition of exploitation requires the wrongful misuse of an actual person), not broadened out to future potential exploitation of unidentified children, or the exploitation of a fabricated child. Otherwise, this would result in rationalizing the criminalization of all non-photographic visual depictions and written material also.

A legal approach based on harmful exploitation such as I have suggested is not, in fact, far removed from the ideology that lies behind some of the offences that exist under the SOA relating to children and

185 Ibid.: 217–18.

186 Note Goodin's conflicting view that the act of exploiting an individual always amounts to a wrong because of its unfairness. Goodin 1987: 173, 174 and 182. See also above, at 129.

187 See also Feinberg 1985: 155.

vulnerable adults and an abuse of trust.[188] Much emphasis was placed on exploitation of children in *Setting the Boundaries*,[189] and I have noted how the exploitation of children was emphasized in the Parliamentary debates that preceded the PCA. The significant changes that would occur if the approach I advocate were taken relate to the child pornography laws. First, the indecency framework would be removed and the focus would instead be on whether the images exploit children. The content of the images would most often reveal this, although context may also be a relevant issue in some cases. For example, the creation of images of naked children would only be criminalized if there were evidence that the child was exploited to create the image, not on the basis of the images meeting the indecency test. Secondly, because my construction of harmful exploitation requires exploitation of real children, pseudo images that do not involve the manipulation of a real child's image would not be criminalized. This may seem a somewhat radical stance to take in the current protectionist social and legal climate and the emphasis attached to avoiding future, potential risks of harm. Two vital aspects of the social and political consciousness that have shaped this climate are the central concern of the next chapter.

[188] See ss. 16–19 and Sentencing Advisory Panel 2004.

[189] Home Office 2000: para. 7.6.

CHAPTER FOUR

MORAL PANICS AND THE IMPACT OF THE CONSTRUCTION OF CHILDHOOD INNOCENCE

This chapter explores in depth the question of how much of the social reality around us is socially constructed and defined. I examine whether a moral panic and availability cascades have impacted on societal and legal responses to the phenomena of child pornography and stranger grooming, and the effect of constructions of childhood innocence upon adults and children.

MORAL PANICS AND AVAILABILITY CASCADES

Initially in this section, I briefly analyse the origins of moral panics and availability cascades and relevant academic theory. I then proceed to investigate the question of whether the threats that child pornography and stranger grooming represent may have been blown out of proportion due to the existence of a moral panic about these phenomena and the effects of an availability cascade in our society. In particular, I assess the way in which the media, the public, the police, the judiciary and politicians have responded to this and related phenomena.

Origins of moral panics and availability cascades

> Reality is socially defined. But the definitions are always embodied, that is, concrete individuals and groups of individuals serve as the definers of reality.[1]

[1] Berger and Luckmann 1967: 116.

Goode and Ben-Yehuda outline five crucial ingredients for a moral panic: (1) an increased level of concern regarding the behaviour in question; (2) amplified hostility towards the individuals who engage in this behaviour; (3) widespread consensus that the behaviour poses a real threat; (4) a disproportionality between the perceived threat that the behaviour represents and the threat it actually and objectively poses; and, finally, (5) volatility – the moral panic begins and ends fairly suddenly.[2] Thompson has since argued that the two characteristics that most theorists consider to be essential are increased concern and hostility.[3]

Stanley Cohen's contribution to the moral panic literature is both foundational and crucial, and is thus vital reading for the author who aims to seriously engage with a conceptual analysis of the moral panic.[4] Cohen provides a rich empirical case study of the societal reaction to a specific youth culture in the 1960s – the Mods and Rockers. He analyses the presentation of and reaction to disturbances at seaside resorts involving the Mods and Rockers, focusing on media coverage and the responses of politicians, the police and the public. His work highlights what have become integral aspects of moral panic theory – the spreading and reinforcement of hostility through media reporting, the development of public consensus in response to this reporting and official reaction from the police and law-makers. Cohen's broader analysis of the moral panic phenomenon has been regularly updated with each new edition of his work.[5]

The concept of the moral panic is an example of sociological criticism that has taken hold not only within the academic arena,[6] but also in the mainstream social and political consciousness. Somewhat ironically, the media itself has enthusiastically embraced the idea of the moral panic.[7] In sociological circles, moral panic analysis may have, to some degree, become less fashionable than other more recently introduced theories.[8] However, despite the prominent place these later theories now have in sociological research, moral panic criticism can still play an important

[2] Goode and Ben-Yehuda 1994: 33–41. These ingredients appear to have been accepted by Cohen. See Cohen 2007: xxii.

[3] Thompson 1998: 9.

[4] Whilst Jock Young first utilized the term 'moral panic' (Young 1971), it was Cohen who subjected the concept to detailed academic analysis (Cohen 1972).

[5] The most recent edition being the third: Cohen 2007.

[6] See, e.g. Best 1990; Critcher 2002; Critcher 2003; Hall *et al.* 1978; and Jenkins 1992.

[7] See Cohen 2007: 1; and Thompson 1998: 2–5.

[8] Such as risk society theory, Beck 1992. See also Cavanagh 2007. For a post-modernist critique of moral panic theory, see McRobbie 1994: ch. 11.

role in drawing attention to the way in which our understandings of phenomena are shaped by important players in the debate. It is when attention is only paid to the media and it is assumed that members of the public simply passively accept the media's portrayal of events that the application of moral panic theory is arguably more problematic.[9]

Given the context of this work, it is significant to note that earlier historical examples exist of moral panics surrounding children and perceived threats to their innocence. Smart argues that the provisions of the Criminal Law Amendment Act 1885, which increased the age of sexual consent from thirteen to sixteen and imposed penalties for procuring children, were the result of a moral panic about children being sold into prostitution.[10] She refers to a newspaper column in which a journalist for the *Pall Mall Gazette* wrote about how he had been able to buy a child from her own mother with the professed purpose of using her as a prostitute, a practice which was apparently commonplace.[11] As a further example, Piper perceives the threat posed to the family by children working in factories and mines in the newly industrialized society in the early and middle nineteenth century to be the moral panic of its day.[12] By taking children away from the protection of their parents, she argues that the new workplaces were an easily identifiable evil that was portrayed by campaigners of the time as the primary cause of the corruption of children.

A more recent theory to appear within the legal literature fits neatly alongside moral panic theory, and an application of both as methods of analysis may reveal more about how common perceptions of child pornography and grooming evolve. According to Kuran and Sunstein, representations of a particular phenomenon or event become more plausible the more frequently they appear in public discourses and the more the main players and voices of authority adopt them. If we ourselves have no direct experience of the phenomenon in question, and are unable to easily obtain the relevant information through our own research, it is through the dominant representations in public discourses that we construct our personal risk judgements. In fact, Kuran and Sunstein argue that: 'Most risk judgments rest on little, if any, personal investigation; they depend largely, if not wholly, on trust placed in the judgments of selected others.'[13] This is their theory of availability cascades. An 'availability

[9] Meyer 2007: 10; and Watney 1993: 43.
[10] Smart 1989: 51.
[11] See also Walkowitz 1992: ch. 3; and Gorham 1978.
[12] Piper 1999: 36–7.
[13] Kuran and Sunstein 1999: 717.

cascade is a self-reinforcing process of collective belief formation by which an expressed perception triggers a chain reaction that gives the perception increasing plausibility through its rising availability in public discourse'.[14] Availability cascades can become so powerful that even those who have played a role in initiating them either for their own ends or for more altruistic purposes can come to believe their own claims regarding the risks of a phenomenon; they themselves are also caught up in the chain reaction.[15]

The case for a moral panic regarding child pornography and stranger grooming

I am applying moral panic analysis here to develop my argument that there is a high and disproportionate level of concern in society about the behaviour of those who have involvement with child pornography, or strangers who sexually groom children. This, in turn, causes the level of hostility towards these individuals to rise as it becomes considered that they pose a significant threat to society. I intend to highlight the role that the media, politicians, the judiciary, the police and pressure groups play in defining, and at the same time blurring, the social reality of child pornography and grooming. In examining the reactions of these various main players, I seek to avoid presenting a 'totalistic media-led explanation' of society's and law's responses to both phenomena.[16] Rather, I aim to explore the way in which all of these reactions have contributed to current prevalent perceptions.

I should note that I have chosen to focus on stranger grooming rather than grooming generally, because it is this specific form of grooming that most commonly attracts media coverage and has caught the attention of the legislature. Moreover, as I will discuss, it is much harder to quantify the occurrence of child sexual abuse and grooming that occurs in the home, which would make the application of moral panic analysis more problematic.

The moral panic analysis I employ takes something of a middle ground between a grassroots model and an interest-group model.[17] Under the former, the object of the study is a widespread, shared reaction by the general public to a phenomenon constructed as evil and the response of the media, politicians and the legislature is an articulation of this concern. In Goode and Ben-Yehuda's words: 'Politicians and the media cannot

[14] Ibid.: 683. [15] Ibid.: 733. [16] See Meyer 2007: 10.
[17] Goode and Ben-Yehuda 1994: ch. 9.

fabricate concern where none existed initially … the public's fears may be mistaken or exaggerated, but they are real, they do not need to be "engineered" or "orchestrated" by powerful agencies, institutions, bodies or classes'.[18] Under the latter model, it is a group or groups who bring a matter to the forefront of the public's attention because they have a vested interest in highlighting the issue as one of great importance.[19] Although Critcher considers the media's response to be the most significant,[20] Goode and Ben-Yehuda emphasize that it 'seems highly likely … that moral panics are not explicable by means of a single model'.[21] In the context of child pornography and grooming, it should become apparent that, although the media, interest groups and politicians have played a prominent role in shaping the response to the phenomena, so too has the public exerted pressure upon the legislature to react to the perceived level of threat.

Cohen's analysis of more recent potential and actual moral panics seems particularly apt to my subject. In his introduction to the third edition of his work, he asserts that three of the crucial ingredients for the construction of a moral panic are the existence of a suitable enemy lacking in power and thus unable to challenge ascribed folk devil status, a suitable victim with whom members of society can identify and a consensus that the behaviour in question is or could become an integral part of society.[22] The enemy that child pornography and stranger grooming present is not new. He is the pre-existing folk devil: the paedophile and child sexual abuser. The suitable victim is, of course, the child, perhaps *the* most suitable victim that society can be presented with and thus the construction of a moral panic is all the more likely, given the protectionist stance taken towards children and the societal concern about their welfare.[23] Therefore, the public concern that Goode and Ben-Yehuda observe is so vital to the generation of a moral panic already exists.[24] Finally, there is a consensus that child pornography and stranger grooming are related to child sexual abuse, a recognized societal problem that it is generally considered action must be taken against wherever possible to prevent the problem from becoming even more prevalent. This is neatly encapsulated by the words of an MP during the debates of the Protection of Children Bill in Parliament: 'I do not believe that the protection of children is confined to one sphere. We wish to attack the separate facets of the problem with all the powers we can muster.'[25]

[18] Ibid.: 127–34 and 141. [19] Ibid.: 138–41. [20] Critcher 2003: 138–9.
[21] Goode and Ben-Yehuda 1994: 134. [22] Cohen 2007: xi.
[23] See also Critcher 2003: 130 and 154. [24] Goode and Ben-Yehuda 1994: 26.
[25] Hansard, HC Deb. 10 February 1978: column 1874 (David Young).

The initial matter I will consider here is the moral content of the reaction, the vital component that loads the gun and triggers a moral panic.[26] Unsurprisingly, it is easy to find examples of the moral content of the social and legal discourses surrounding child pornography and stranger grooming. Moral justifications for the introduction of the Protection of Children Bill in Parliament in 1978 abounded. MP Anthony Grant described child pornography as a 'filthy trade that … goes well beyond anything that can conceivably be tolerated in what is called a civilised society', an 'evil cancer that is affecting our whole society'.[27] According to Jill Knight, 'permissiveness to pervert and destroy our children is a permissiveness that neither Parliament nor the people will tolerate'.[28] Neville Sandelson expressed his view that everyone in Parliament felt '(m)oral indignation at obvious social evil and personal wickedness'.[29] Such morality-based legitimations were echoed down the line when subsequent bills were being debated. During the second reading of the CJPO in the House of Commons, Michael Shersby issued this warning to those involved in the child pornography trade: 'Child pornographers … should take note that, this evening, the House is determined that their disgusting and corrupting behaviour should no longer be tolerated.'[30]

The strong moralistic societal reaction to child pornography and grooming also permeates through to the judiciary. The judiciary's authoritative role means that their reaction can play a significant part in shaping the societal response to child pornography and stranger grooming.[31] When the courts are presented with behaviour related to child pornography or grooming, a discourse of morality prevails. The moral character of the judiciary's chosen language in delivering their judgments and passing sentences in child pornography cases can hardly go unnoticed. The same can be said for the courts' perpetuation of common-sense assumptions about the immoral characters of those who

[26] Goode and Ben-Yehuda 1994: 142.

[27] 10 February 1978: columns 1879 and 1881.

[28] Ibid.: column 1902.

[29] Ibid.: column 1906. Other examples of clear moral undertones to MPs' support for the bill can be found in columns 1869 and 1912.

[30] Hansard, HC Deb. HC 11 January 1994: column 77. See also column 1843 (Brynmor John). Perhaps the most morally charged wording came in 1978 from the Countess of Loudoun in the House of Lords, when she argued that, without legislation criminalizing child pornography, this jurisdiction was partially responsible for the situation in America: 'Can we continue to allow the distribution of "kiddy" porn … because the anguish and the slaughter of innocents takes place in another country, when our money is still the driving force behind it?' Hansard, HL Deb. 5 May 1978: column 562.

[31] In Cohen's view, a moral panic is better maintained when voices of authority become involved. Cohen 2007: xvii. See also Critcher 2006: 74.

groom children or possess child pornography and the immoral nature of the material in question. For instance, in the case of *R. v. Fellows and Arnold*, Evans LJ referred to the 'perverted tastes' of collecting and viewing indecent photographs of children, and noted the 'public revulsion against paedophilia in all its forms'.[32] When passing sentence in a case of possession and distribution, the judge referred to the images as 'disgusting and degrading material of real children'.[33] Similarly, in a case involving the possession and creation of child pornography heard at Bristol Crown Court in which the defendant was Gadd, alias rock star Gary Glitter, Butterfield J commented that 'the potential corrupting effect of such filthy and revolting material is obvious'.[34] The implication, then, is that Butterfield J considered that viewing such material would have a direct and corrosive impact on the morality of its audience. As a final example, passing sentence in a recent case involving online grooming, a crown court judge told the defendant that: 'The good work of the police nipped your perverted desires in the bud'.[35] Thus, the judiciary may be seen to be responding to those individuals who have committed offences relating to child pornography and grooming in a way that indicates the existence of judicial opinion that this activity constitutes immoral behaviour which represents a clear, significant threat to our society.

A multitude of examples also exist of the utilization of morally charged wording by the media and pressure groups.[36] Both child pornography and grooming provide examples of a morality discourse that is plain for all to see. Nothing hides the moralistic judgements cast upon those who partake in these activities. Bergmann argues that: 'Morality is such

[32] [1997] 2 All ER 548, 559.

[33] See 'Teacher jailed for web grooming', BBC News report, 11 April 2007, http://news.bbc.co.uk/1/hi/england/manchester/6546081.stm.

[34] See 'Glitter gets four months', *The Guardian*, 13 November 1999.

[35] See 'Man jailed for internet grooming', BBC News report, 20 May 2008, http://news.bbc.co.uk/1/hi/england/devon/7410599.stm.

[36] See, for instance: 'Stop sordid grooming of region's children for sex', *Lancashire Telegraph*, 11 July 2006; 'Even sickos would be "disgusted" as Hamptons man sentenced for child porn', *New York Daily News*, 27 June 2008; 'Consumers of evil also should be rooted out, carefully, and either punished for funding this abusive trade or treated for their addiction … There is no need to magnify this evil by burning down the whole house of the Internet in order to get to these vermin. But the merchants of pain who first victimize countless children in making their pornography, then ruin the lives of their own paying customers, deserve no quarter' (from 'Editorial: Target child porn', *Buffalo News*, 12 July 2008); 'Across the Web, the evil of child pornography spreads like a toxin' (from 'Group out front of online child pornography battle', *NetworkWorld News*, 18 June 2008); and 'Charity urges online child porn crackdown', ITN News report, http://itn.co.uk/news/c89155b124bbf02c515349f91a865744.html.

a common and intrinsic quality of everyday social interaction that it is usually invisible to us, like glasses that provide a sharp sight of the area beyond although they themselves remain unseen.'[37] Whilst this may often be true, the morality discourse upon child pornography and grooming is in fact highly visible and its presence does not come as a shock; it is expected because we are so imbued by it.

The next matter to be addressed is the societal perception of the threat that child pornography and grooming represent. If there is evidence to suggest that societal views upon the dangers posed by both phenomena have become distorted, leading to an undue exaggeration of a perceived threat, then there may be grounds to argue that there is currently a moral panic in our society. In order to consider whether a moral panic does in fact exist, it is necessary to consider the assessments of the dangers child pornography and stranger grooming represent. Such assessments, made by the media, politicians, the judiciary, law enforcement agencies and the public, are all likely to have had an impact on the current societal stance taken.

Child pornography

The media's sensationalist coverage of child pornography undoubtedly plays a significant role in influencing the level of concern that is attached to this phenomenon. When reporting on cases involving child pornography, newspapers tend to use headlines which include emotive, deliberately shocking language such as 'Tide of Computer Porn No One can Stop'.[38] Such language over-emphasizes the level of danger that child pornography represents and is undoubtedly capable of provoking and – over time – reinforcing strong public reaction.

Early media coverage of child pornography in the form of reports of an influx in child pornography originating from outside the United Kingdom was most vociferous in 1977 and 1978 due, in large part, to Mary Whitehouse and the National Viewers' and Listeners' Association's ABUSE campaign.[39] Such coverage sat well with other media reports published at this time concerning PIE (Paedophile Information Exchange), an organization which had been founded in October 1974.[40] Riding on the shirt tails of the sexual liberation movement, PIE campaigned for a

[37] Bergmann 1998: 280.

[38] Headline from *The People*, 19 February 1995. See also the examples provided in the introduction, n. 73.

[39] See the NVALA Archives, Boxes 19, 114, and 115; and Jenkins 1992: 73.

[40] Jenkins 1992: 76; and NVALA Archives, Box 116.

reduction in the age of sexual consent, arguing for a right to have sex with children on the basis that children were sexual beings whose sexual liberty should be respected.[41] Extensive press coverage of the threat of child pornography enabled Whitehouse to gain public backing for her cause.[42] Whitehouse actively endeavoured to achieve an impression of strong public support for a law criminalizing child pornography by writing a letter to the editors of a large number of regional newspapers between October 1977 and early 1978. She stated in the letter that: 'experience teaches that public "shock" is very short lived, and it is essential therefore that the deep concern which all must feel at this new manifestation of commercialised degradation be effectively channelled so that the Government will be forced to introduce the necessary legislation to deal with it'. She also warned that 'more than 200,000 children (in the US) are being used by the pornographers'.[43] Extracts from this letter were then published in the newspapers. She asked the editors to ensure that, through their columns, all readers were aware of the NVALA's ABUSE petition, which called for action to protect children from pornography.[44] She then sent a second letter to provincial newspapers in January 1978, urging readers to write to their MPs and ask them to be present at the PCB's second reading, in which she again referred to the 'horrific' situation in America.[45] The NVALA was subsequently able to offer the positive replies from MPs to the letters that the newspapers' readers sent as proof that there was Parliamentary backing for the campaign.[46] As the voice of the ABUSE campaign, Whitehouse was able to utilize press coverage to remind Parliament of the public support for the PCB. In an article in the *Sunday Mirror* in December 1977, she was

[41] PIE was disbanded in 1984. Three individuals who were members of PIE were convicted of child pornography offences in 2006 and 2007. See 'Paedophile leader jailed indefinitely', *The Times*, 13 August 2007.

[42] Examples of press coverage at the time include the following newspaper headlines: 'Britain faces child porn boom', *Evening Standard*, 10 February 1978; 'Don't let this evil trade spread here', *Daily Mail*, 8 February 1978; 'Why the law doesn't tackle this evil trade', *Lancashire Evening Post*, 12 January 1978; 'Stop these evil men', *Evening News*, 10 February 1978; 'Home Office accused of indifference to Child Porn Bill', *Daily Telegraph*, 11 February 1978; 'Stamp it out, this abominable evil of using children for pornography', *The Times*, 24 November 1977; and 'End this abuse of the innocent', *Daily Express*, 19 November 1977. All of these newspaper articles are held in the NVALA Archives, Box 114.

[43] A copy of this letter is held in the NVALA Archives, Box 115.

[44] Whitehouse received a large number of letters from the public supporting the ABUSE campaign and petition. See NVALA Archives, Box 19.

[45] Letter dated 8 January 1978, NVALA Archives, Box 115.

[46] McCarthy and Moodie 1981: 58. For a critical examination of the tactics used to compel members of the public to 'bombard' their MPs, see HL Deb. 5 May 1978: column 553.

quoted as stating: 'I would say that any MP who voted against this Bill would lose his seat at the next election.'[47]

There is clear evidence that the passing of the Protection of Children Act 1978 and its rapid progression through Parliament was a reaction to the strong public feeling that the ABUSE campaign engendered. During the second reading of the PCB in the House of Commons, MPs justified the need for the proposed legislation with phrases such as: 'immense public pressure', receipt of 'masses of letters', 'responding to public opinion', 'many members of the public have called urgently for this measure', 'sense of public outrage' and 'reflects a widespread public concern … I can recall only one previous occasion on which I have had as many letters and petitions on a social issue'.[48] Only one member of the House of Commons, Emlyn Hooson, voiced unease about the fact that the PCB would be an example of reactive legislation,[49] but his caution fell by the wayside when two other MPs made it clear that this was not a matter for concern, but positive evidence that Parliament was taking due account of public opinion.[50] This suggests that Parliament was influenced by a grass-roots moral panic model, with the public demanding that the law reflect its perception of the problem of child pornography. However, in the House of Commons debates, Townsend was applauded for getting the press and media on his side in order to promote the Bill and gain public support.[51] Speaking in the debates in the House of Lords, Lord Redesdale considered both Parliament and Mary Whitehouse to be 'the initiators' of the campaign against child pornography.[52] In fact, Whitehouse continued to take her cause to the Home Office and Prime Minister throughout the Parliamentary debates.[53] She generated publicity for the London press conference at which she had arranged for Densen-Gerber to speak by issuing a NVALA press release and

47 NVALA Archives, Box 115. In a letter to Whitehouse dated 6 January 1978, Cyril Townsend thanks her for all of the NVALA's campaigning to draw MPs' attention to the PCB and then states: 'From a number of colleagues whom I have met recently it is clear that the lobbying is becoming effective.' NVALA Archives, Box 19.

48 Hansard, HC Deb. 10 February 1978: columns 1858, 1871, 1889, 1893 and 1906. See also columns 1873 and 1914.

49 Ibid.: column 1858.

50 Ibid.: columns 1877 (Audrey Wise) and 1889 (Robert Hicks).

51 Ibid.: column 1922.

52 Hansard, HL Deb. 18 May 1978: column 547. See also column 549 (Lord Bishop of Guildford).

53 In a telegram to the Prime Minister dated 15 April 1978, Whitehouse informed him that: '99.96% of those asked to sign the 1½ million strong ABUSE petition did so. This means that practically the whole country demands action to protect children from pornography.' (NVALA Archives, Box 19.) See also NVALA Archives, Box 115 for a further letter Whitehouse sent to the Prime Minister in May 1978.

sending it to national newspapers, religious magazines and periodicals, BBC Television, Thames Television, ITV, Capital Radio and the Press Association. She also sent a number of personal letters to MPs asking them to meet with Densen-Gerber. She kept in regular correspondence with Townsend as the Bill progressed through Parliament.[54] The success of the ABUSE campaign and Townsend's PCB does seem indicative of an interest group moral panic model, a successful orchestration of public feeling and reaction to child pornography through the utilization of the media. However, whilst it is clear that the media's coverage of the ABUSE campaign had a real impact on the public's reaction to child pornography, it is difficult to gauge how much of the public response was purely a consequence of this publicity.[55] It thus seems most appropriate to apply a combination of the grass roots and interest group moral panic models; the input of the public,[56] the NVALA, Mary Whitehouse, politicians and the media were all vital in shaping societal and legal responses to child pornography at this time.

A crucial question for moral panic analysis is whether the legislative reaction to the problem of child pornography was disproportionate. It is thus significant that there is a real likelihood of a discrepancy between the assumed and actual prevalence of child pornography during the 1978 Parliamentary debates. As discussed in Chapter 2, the ABUSE campaign provided much of the impetus for legislation and the evidence gathered as part of this campaign was referred to in the Parliamentary debates. However, most of Whitehouse's evidence derived from American press reports[57] and from American activist Judianne Densen-Gerber in particular. Densen-Gerber, a psychiatrist and lawyer, had become well known for founding Odyssey House, a community facility for drug treatment in New York in 1966. Having read a journalist's work on children's involvement in a commercial sex industry, Densen-Gerber launched a campaign

[54] NVALA Archives, Box 115; letters sent between Whitehouse and Townsend, NVALA Archives, Box 115.

[55] There was already much social concern, for example, about organized child sex rings (see Jenkins 1992: 81–2), which may evidence that a public concern about child sex abuse preexisted the ABUSE campaign.

[56] The public reaction to child pornography continues to be strong. For example, O'Brien refers to a 2005 Mori survey which revealed that the vast majority of those surveyed would support the blocking of access to child pornography websites and the tracking of visitors to such sites. See O'Brien 2006: 268–9. See also 'Child porn site blocks supported', BBC News report, 17 March 2005, http://news.bbc.co.uk/1/hi/technology/4354065.stm.

[57] For instance, Baroness Faithfull referred to a *Chicago Times* report that child pornography had grown into an organized multi-million dollar industry during the Parliamentary debates. Hansard, HL Deb. 5 May 1978: column 539.

against child pornography that ultimately led to the passing of federal legislation, the Protection of Children Against Sexual Exploitation Act 1978.[58] Jenkins explains how the statistics offered up by Densen-Gerber and other American activists to the media were 'derived from guesses or vague estimates'.[59] For instance, he notes that Densen-Gerber based her statement that 600,000 American children were involved in child pornography from journalist Robin Lloyd's claim that 300,000 boys were taking part in a commercial sex industry. She simply assumed that a similar number of girls were also involved and so multiplied the figure by two.[60] This is abundantly clear from Densen-Gerber's response to a question posed when she was giving evidence to the House of Representatives Committee on the Judiciary in 1977. When asked how many children she thought were involved in the pornography industry in America, she replied: 'we have close to one million children sexually and commercially exploited … That figure is based pretty much on the work of Robin Lloyd in which he counted 300,000 boys … Because we are probably as much heterosexual as homosexual so I matched Lloyd's figure for boys – equally 600,000 children.'[61]

When giving her evidence, Densen-Gerber also made a number of statements causally linking the use of child pornography with subsequent child sexual abuse, without offering any substantiation.[62] Densen-Gerber was the 'expert' whom Whitehouse presented to MPs and the British media to support her campaign against the international commercial child pornography industry, which, she claimed, was threatening Britain. The evidence relied on by Whitehouse that did come from within the UK was primarily predicated on a 1977 *Tonight* BBC documentary and tabloid press investigations.[63] McCarthy and Moodie argue

[58] See further Jenkins 1998: 122–4. See also Ennew 1986: 4–5; and Densen-Gerber 1977. For an illuminating analysis of the moral panic reaction to child pornography in the US in the 1970s and 1980s, see Jenkins 1998: 121–5 and 145–54.

[59] Jenkins 1998: 147.

[60] Ibid. See also Densen-Gerber and Hutchinson 1978, in which child pornography is presented as a 'billion-dollar industry' (p. 324), with little substantive evidence being provided in support.

[61] Densen-Gerber, Judianne, 1977. 'Selections from Official Report to Committee by Judianne Densen-Gerber', 23 May 1977: 8–9. Held in the NVALA Archives, Box 115.

[62] Consider, e.g. the following: 'The people who support and buy this kind of material are strengthening their pedophiliac fantasies. Now, when fantasies are stimulated people go home and act out. For example there is no doubt that incest is on the rise.' Ibid.: 4.

[63] Following the broadcast of the *Tonight* programme, Whitehouse sent a telegram to the Home Office (dated 9 November 1977) stating: 'BBC 1 "Tonight" programme last night fully established and exposed existence of child pornography in Britain and inadequacy of existing law.' (NVALA Archives, Box 115).

that this evidences 'that she acted, at least initially, from fear of what might or could happen and not from substantive evidence that child pornography was already a problem in the UK', and it was for this reason that she failed to convince the Home Office and government of her case and thus had to turn to the Opposition for backing.[64] Whitehouse also tried to obtain evidence that British children were being used in child pornography created in America, but Densen-Gerber was unable to provide any such evidence.[65] Townsend later made clear how much his own investigation into child pornography was informed by the newspaper reports and investigations and the BBC documentary.[66] Clearly, this was all the research upon child pornography in Britain that was available.

MPs supporting the PCB frequently relied on statistics, figures and evidence either without providing a source for the information, or where the source they relied on was questionable. Following his investigation, Townsend stated: 'It was impossible to prove beyond a shadow of a doubt that the photographing of children for pornographic purposes was on the increase in Britain, for this was an activity which had one foot in the criminal underworld. But the majority of people consulted *believed* that it was increasing.'[67] Sir Michael Havers commented that child pornography 'is a problem which we find is *probably* arising in this country, from the evidence that we have been able to see and which has been gathered by various quarters, including chief constables here'.[68] Jill Knight provided startling figures to support her claim that child pornography was a very big business, stating that she understood it brought in '£588 million a year in the United States' and '£24 million a year' in Britain. However, she cited no source for these figures, or for the other 'ample evidence' she was relying on to show that commercial child pornography had 'mushroomed' in the last two years.[69] By the time the debate moved to the House of Lords, for the majority of the Lords who participated, either the reliability of this evidence had been assumed or 'probably'

[64] McCarthy and Moodie 1981: 49. This was carried through to the Parliamentary debates. See, e.g. Hansard, HL Deb. 5 May 1978: column 538. Interestingly, in a letter addressed to a member of the clergy dated 12 October 1977, Whitehouse states that the 'number of children directly used in this industry are very small at the moment'. However, she then refers to the situation in America as illustrating the threat of what could happen in Britain (NVALA Archives, Box 115).

[65] Letter to Mary Whitehouse from Densen-Gerber, dated 16 August 1978. Held in the NVALA Archives, Box 115.

[66] Townsend 1979: 3. [67] Ibid. (my emphasis).

[68] Hansard, HC Deb. 10 February 1978: column 1893 (my emphasis).

[69] Ibid.: column 1901.

was good enough.[70] However, as I have discussed in Chapter 2, Home Office research referred to in the House of Commons' debates provided a convincing challenge to the 'evidence' relied on by proponents of the PCB. In the House of Lords, the Minister of State reiterated the Home Office's conclusion that there was no evidence of a child pornography problem in Britain and stated that neither Customs and Excise nor the Metropolitan Police were of the impression that the amount of child pornography in circulation had increased recently.[71]

Besides the Home Secretary's and Minister of State's cautious reaction to the PCB and their questioning approach to the evidence relied on by its supporters, there were only two other voices of reason in Parliament. The most forceful of these belonged to Lord Houghton, who made his views patently clear during the second reading of the PCB in the House of Lords:

> This is what I would describe as a buffalo Bill. It is a stampede. This is not legislation, this is a rush … What is the evidence upon which these proposals rest? Has the evidence been produced? Has it been examined? Can evidence be distinguished from propaganda and from pressure? If I may say so, hysteria is no condition in which to legislate.[72]

Lord Houghton proceeded to highlight the 'aggressive pressure' placed upon MPs as a consequence of press coverage and to criticize the rapid progress of the Bill through Parliament without amendment or debate. Once again, he articulated the view that Parliament was dealing with a 'bad' Bill 'surrounded by unhealthy attitudes' when the PCB was read for the third time. He informed the Lords present that he had spent some time in America looking for 'that load of child pornography that, we were told, would swamp this country', but could only conclude from his inquiries that the threat was very exaggerated.[73] Although not a dissenter, Lord Wigoder also expressed doubts about the conditions in which the proposed legislation was introduced, commenting: 'I see nothing in the Bill to warrant the slightly off-putting wave of hysterical enthusiasm with which it

[70] Baroness Faithfull stated as established fact the Chief Constable of Greater Manchester Police's estimate that 5 per cent of the pornography seized in Greater Manchester was child pornography (Hansard, HL Deb. 5 May 1978: column 539). Lord Redesdale was satisfied that a probable increase in the problem existed (column 547).

[71] Hansard, HL Deb. 5 May 1978: columns 574–7. See also Hansard, HL Deb. 20 June 1978: columns 1065–6.

[72] Hansard, HL Deb. 5 May 1978: columns 553 and 558.

[73] Hansard, HL Deb. 20 June 1978: columns 1058 and 1060.

has been greeted outside your Lordships' House.'[74] However, despite his reservations about the social and Parliamentary reaction to the PCB, his questioning of estimations about the extent of the problem and the fact that he was keen to see the bill amended, Lord Wigoder still welcomed it for plugging a gap in the existing law.[75]

If there were any other would-be dissenters, perhaps they were silenced by predictions of the dire consequences that would materialize if legislative action were not taken. Alluding to the recent criminalization of child pornography in America, Baroness Faithfull warned that as a result of the American market no longer being available, 'it is reasonable to suppose that the British merchants of child pornographic magazines will seek to develop their own lucrative markets in this country using British children even more extensively than has been done in the past'.[76] This caution was then repeated by a number of other supporters of the PCB.[77] Following the enactment of the PCA, Townsend reiterated the potential danger that his Bill had avoided.[78] According to Cohen's analysis, such claims that strong measures are immediately necessary to prevent the problem getting worse are indicative of a moral panic reaction.[79]

In the beginning at least, the lack of clear evidence of a real existing problem regarding child pornography did have an impact on the government's position. When initially approached by Whitehouse in September 1977, the government remained unconvinced of the necessity for a new law to bring the problem of child pornography under control. The Home Secretary's reluctance to press ahead with new legislation is demonstrated in a letter he wrote to Margaret Thatcher, Leader of the Opposition:

> I feel some reluctance ... to rush into legislation which may prove to be unnecessary or ill-aimed ... we do need first to establish how far a substantial problem exists ... contrary to statements in the press, child pornography is not widely or indeed easily obtainable and the

[74] Hansard, HL Deb. 5 May 1978: column 541. [75] Ibid.: column 541–4.

[76] Ibid.: column 538.

[77] Ibid., columns 539, 546, 560 and 565. Similarly, in 1993, when announcing the government's intention to criminalize pseudo-images, Michael Howard stated: 'It is vital to take tough measures at the outset if we are to succeed in stamping out this vile trade.' See 'Crackdown on computer porn', *The Guardian*, 26 November 1993. In 1994, the Minister of State informed the House of Commons Standing Committee that the government was taking action to avoid pseudo-photographs becoming a serious problem. MP Mike O'Brien predicted that the pseudo-image was 'the early version of what will become all too soon – almost certainly this year – films consisting of many sequences of pseudo-photographs'. Hansard, HC Standing Committee B: Criminal Justice and Public Order Bill, 15 February 1994: columns 735, 740 and 745.

[78] Townsend 1979: 4. [79] Cohen 2007: 67.

> effectiveness of the present law and its enforcement is undoubtedly an important factor in restricting its availability. In these circumstances it does not seem to me that there is an immediate need for the law to be strengthened.[80]

Once the ABUSE campaign succeeded in bringing the matter to the attention of Parliament and Townsend had introduced the PCB, however, the government was swayed by the tide of public opinion. The decision was made that the PCB would not be opposed, despite the Home Secretary's questioning of the evidence submitted by Townsend during the PCB's second reading in the House of Commons.[81] Following concern that the PCB's progress would be delayed because it was one of many other Bills awaiting detailed examination by a Common's Committee, the decision was taken (without any ministerial dissent) that the Bill should be brought back to the floor of the House for its Committee sittings.[82] Townsend later criticized the Home Secretary for 'allowing the Home Office to get so out of touch not only with the views of MPs from all Parties, but also with the man in the street and the policeman on the spot'.[83] MPs who did object to the PCB were maligned. Labour MP Ian Mikardo's objection to the PCB being given an undebated third reading led to him being described as 'that nasty little man' in the press and an influx of letters from members of the public protesting about his actions to MPs, the NVALA and the newspapers.[84] In the wake of this reaction, Labour Whips and the Prime Minister intervened to ensure that the PCB was given the necessary time it needed in Parliament to be passed. In the House of Lords, the only real opposition came in the form of Lord Houghton's aforementioned concerns that, due to public pressure and hysteria, the PCB was rushed through its Parliamentary stages and inadequately debated. Baroness Elliot's response to his lack of support for the PCB was to insinuate that Lord Houghton was more concerned about protecting animals than children.[85] Perhaps he should not have been surprised then, that other Parliamentary Members who had criticized the Bill did not voice their concerns during the debates.[86]

The remarkable journey of the PCB through both Houses of Parliament is assessed by McCarthy and Moodie:

[80] Townsend 1979: 6. [81] See Chapter 2, at 85.

[82] 'Speed up of Child Porn Bill', *Daily Telegraph*, 11 March 1978; and Letter to Whitehouse from Townsend, dated 14 March 1978, NVALA Archives, Box 115.

[83] Townsend 1979: 6. [84] McCarthy and Moodie 1981: 59.

[85] Hansard, HL Deb. 5 May 1978: columns 558–9.

[86] Hansard, HL Deb. 20 June 1978: column 1060.

> Despite Lord Houghton's critique, the Lords, too, succumbed to the pressure which the campaign had generated. He objected to the Bill being given a third reading but received no support; no tellers were appointed for the 'Not Contents', so the Bill was passed without a vote. It was returned to the Commons, where it was passed without discussion … In no [other] case was a bill bulldozed through Parliament in the sort of atmosphere in which the Child Protection Bill was … Fact was largely eschewed in favour of emotive supposition, the actual was ignored in favour of the potential and the remotely possible was selectively interpreted as imminently probable.[87]

Whilst the PCB was debated, albeit hurriedly, the clause under the Criminal Justice Bill (CJB) which became the provision criminalizing the possession of child pornography under the CJA 1988 received what can only be described as a minimal amount of Parliamentary attention and critique. This lack of detailed Parliamentary scrutiny was mainly the result of the clause being introduced at a later stage by an amendment in Committee. By and large, criticism of this was left to one, now familiar, Parliamentary voice: Lord Houghton. His troubled opinion was that 'we are doing something which is a kind of appendage to this Bill which raises issues regarding separate laws of their own which should be dealt with in the proper context … we are not even allowed a Committee stage to deal with amendments of this importance'.[88] Concern was also raised by Lord Monson, who was uncomfortable with pressing ahead with criminalization without clear evidence to indicate that banning possession would decrease rather than increase the risks to children. His fear was that if those who wish to look at child pornography to satisfy their sexual fantasies were prevented from so doing, this might be more likely to result in them committing child sexual abuse. Lord Monson's question as to whether the government had 'thought through the matter thoroughly and dispassionately' following consultation with psychiatrists and other experts rather than introducing the possession clause 'as the result of a perfectly understandable gut reaction against this mainly disgusting material' remained unanswered.[89]

It is possible to see a parallel with the control culture surrounding the Mods and Rockers in the moves to criminalize possession during this time. In his analysis, Cohen argues that: 'Any changes or proposed changes were … legitimated' by invoking 'exaggeration and negative

[87] McCarthy and Moodie 1981: 60–1. [88] Hansard, HL Deb. 22 July 1988: column 1672.
[89] Hansard, HL Deb. 22 July 1988: column 1673.

symbolization'.[90] This can be linked with Best's argument that new claims can be more readily accepted if claim-makers enlarge the sphere in which the existing problem resides.[91] In the context of possession, MPs were able to latch on to the now firmly entrenched protectionist discourse and child pornography threat. The proposed criminalization of possession was justified by arguing that it would reduce the production of child pornography and enable the prosecution of individuals posing a threat to children who currently escape the clutches of the law. According to the Home Secretary in 1987: 'The police are concerned that some paedophiles have … formed closed cells in which they circulate their filth. These cells are hard to penetrate and it is often difficult to establish that the material involved was intended for further distribution. Possession is, on the other hand, simple to establish.'[92] Once exaggeration and negative symbolization has taken hold and the sphere within which the problem exists has grown, it becomes possible to blur the distinction between harmful and less harmful examples of the phenomenon. For instance, it is interesting that in the explanatory notes accompanying the Criminal Justice and Court Services Act 2000 (CJCSA), the increase in penalties for child pornography is justified by reference to the actual abuse of children and yet also by using the fact that prosecutions have risen since pseudo-images were criminalized:

> The government is concerned that the level of penalties available for those exploiting children through the production of child pornography should reflect the fact that its production involves actual abuse of children. The number of offences committed under the Protection of Children Act 1978 and Section 160 of the Criminal Justice Act 1988 has increased significantly since the concept of pseudo-images … was added to the legislation …[93]

That the government sought to rationalize the increase in penalties by drawing attention to the sexual abuse of real children, but was then also able to bolster this by referring to an increase in child pornography offences which do not involve the abuse of real children, further reinforces the idea of a belief system taking hold. Through this belief

[90] In other words, the power of a 'belief system' takes hold. Cohen 2007: 67–8.

[91] Best 1990: 65–6.

[92] 'Labour backs Hurd on child pornography', *The Times*, 17 October 1987. Later, in the House of Commons' debates, the Home Secretary informed the House: 'We are persuaded that it would be justified to criminalise simple possession in the hope of stamping out this degrading trade.' Hansard, HC Deb. 18 January 1988: column 689.

[93] *Explanatory Notes to Criminal Justice and Court Services Act 2000*: para. 19.

system, the criminalization of behaviour and material that would not have been considered acceptable or necessary when the problem of child pornography was first identified and tackled is validated. Once the belief system has a powerful grip, it is also possible to legitimate proposals for criminalizing less harmful behaviour by presenting the matter as the next, growing danger which must be addressed within the context of the accepted wider problem. For instance, when pseudo-images were the issue before Parliament, MPs referred to a 'serious growth in pseudo-photographs of children', the 'new growth area' and a 'dangerous area of pornography'.[94] That a Detective Inspector had dealt with one case in which child pornography took the form of pseudo-images that were exported and then re-imported back into the UK was considered to suffice as evidence of the way in which child pornography producers were moving down this path.[95]

The significant part played by pressure groups in ensuring legislative action has been taken against child pornography cannot go unnoticed. Jenkins highlights the influential and authoritative role played by pressure groups such as the NSPCC in the child protection movement generally.[96] More specifically, he refers to influential claims made by pressure groups such as Childwatch and ChildLine between 1989 and 1992, which 'reinvigorated the campaign against child pornography'.[97] Increasing pressure from child protection lobby groups ensured that the maximum sentence that can be imposed on an individual convicted of one of the offences under the PCA was raised from three to ten years by the CJCSA.[98] The tabloid press in particular tends to make reference to experts from pressure groups to lend credence to continued claims that judicial sentencing in child pornography cases is lenient and 'pathetic'.[99]

[94] Hansard, HC Standing Committee B: Criminal Justice and Public Order Bill, 15 February 1994: columns 735, 740 and 743.

[95] Ibid.: column 743. [96] Jenkins 1992: 197. [97] Ibid.: 96–7.

[98] For example, strong criticisms of the sentences that were imposed upon members of an internet child pornography ring by a Crown Court judge before the maximum sentence for possessing child pornography was increased were expressed by the director of the charity *Kidscope*, and a coalition of several children's charities in a newspaper article written shortly after. See 'Crackdown demanded on internet child porn – charities in call for tougher jail sentences', *The Journal*, 13 January 2000; and 'Outrage at "lenient" jail terms for internet child porn gang', *The Times*, 14 February 2001.

[99] See, for instance, 'It's a sick joke; anger at short jail terms for net child porn ring', *The Mirror*, 14 February 2001; 'Giving a green light to perverts', *Bath Chronicle*, 8 March 2001; 'Outrage at ruling on "victimless" child porn, *Sunday Times*, 18 March 2001; '80 child porn pictures… but perv is freed', *The Mirror*, 31 January 2003; 'Outrage as Langham is freed early after child porn shame', *Daily Mail*, 15 November 2007; and 'Anger as child porn man, 45, is spared jail', *Coventry Evening Telegraph*, 2 May 2007.

A presentation of child pornography posing a strong and growing danger is promoted by the police. Police experts have consistently made demands for a hard-line reaction to the problem and to those involved and the media accepts the authority of such demands.[100] As noted in Chapter 2, the intervention of the Chief Constable of the Greater Manchester Police was particularly influential upon the Parliamentary debates on the PCB, and he also ensured that his understanding of the scale of the problem was made clear to the press.[101] Townsend acknowledges the impact that the Chief Constable's intervention had in Parliament: 'This professional and authoritative view of an outstanding police officer clearly made a deep impression on the House of Commons.'[102] As discussed in Chapter 2, the government received pressure from the police to introduce the possession offence in 1988[103] and, in 1994, it was the evidence of the Metropolitan Police that the Minister of State referred to when suggesting that pseudo-images 'could be the new growth area' if the legislature did not act.[104] In 1990, the Head of Scotland Yard's Child Pornography Squad added his powerful voice to concerns that Britain would see a huge increase in imported child pornography following the lifting of customs barriers within the European Union in 1992.[105] Members of the police and probation service have called for an extension to the sentences imposed on those convicted of the child pornography offences,[106] and for wider powers and more resources to track down child pornography offences on the internet. Such calls resulted in the passing of the Regulation of Investigatory Powers Act 2000, 'to give police and other law enforcement agencies the powers they need to intercept and decrypt communications between child pornographers'.[107] Furthermore, the fact that the police consider

[100] See also, generally, Jenkins 1992: 200 and 214. For notable exceptions to a hard-line police reaction, see 'Watching child porn "need not mean prison". Some paedophiles should be urged to seek treatment, says police chief', *Daily Telegraph*, 2 June 2007; and 'Police call for probe into net link to abuse', *Bath Chronicle*, 17 February 2001.

[101] McCarthy and Moodie 1981: 53.

[102] Townsend 1979: 4.

[103] See the discussion at 86.

[104] Hansard, HC Standing Committee B: Criminal Justice and Public Order Bill, 15 February 1994: column 735.

[105] 'NSPCC says ritual child abuse rife', *The Times*, 13 March 1990. Concerns about importation were also circulating when the earlier legislative decision to criminalize possession was taken. See Jenkins 1992: 95 and 97.

[106] 'Lenient sentencing fuels net child porn: epidemic takes hold across Britain', *The Observer*, 7 January 2001.

[107] See 'Full text of Jack Straw's speech', *The Guardian*, 20 May 2001, available at http://politics.guardian.co.uk/print/0,3858,4189352–107748,00.html. See also 'Internet porn: police call for new agency', BBC News report, 4 March 2005, http://news.bbc.co.uk/1/hi/programmes/

tackling child pornography to be a priority is evidenced by the existence of specialist units, such as Scotland Yard's Paedophile Unit, which tracks down those who possess and distribute child pornography, and Greater Manchester Police's Abusive Images Investigation Unit.

Stranger grooming

That the media focuses on stranger grooming, and online grooming in particular, is abundantly clear from the examples of headlines already given in this book.[108] As Wolak *et al.* note, 'Media stories about "online predators" who use the Internet to gain access to young victims have become the staple of news reports since the late 1990s'.[109] It is important to note that the media's extensive coverage of paedophilia *generally* has clearly evoked a powerful public reaction. Child abuse experts have commented that nearly all media coverage of paedophilia is sensationalist and counter-productive.[110] The *News of the World's* 'Naming and Shaming' campaign to 'out' convicted child abusers in the wake of the tragic death of the school girl Sarah Payne serves as evidence that the media's focus on paedophilia struck a responsive chord with some members of the public.[111] Further media coverage of Sarah's murder and the consequential focus on paedophilia led to the occurrence of vigilante action against the individuals named by the newspaper as convicted child abusers. In Portsmouth, a number of residents from the Paulsgrove estate committed escalating acts of violence, vandalism and intimidation in the name of protecting children. Such a public response does appear to indicate the existence of a phenomenon that, following Cohen and Young, at least resembles moral panic.[112]

breakfast/4317219.stm; and 'Child porn fight "lacks funding"', BBC News report, 2 November 2004, http://news.bbc.co.uk/1/hi/technology/3972763.stm.

108 See some of the examples given in Chapter 2, n. 197 and in the Introduction, n. 73.

109 Wolak *et al.* 2008: 111.

110 See 'Experts slate child abuse "hypocrisy"', *The Guardian*, 30 July 2001.

111 Just before The *News of the World* launched its 'Naming and Shaming' campaign, a MORI poll found that 58 per cent of the 1,004 members of the public who participated agreed that convicted paedophiles should be publicly named. 76 per cent agreed that local people should be told if a convicted paedophile lived in their neighbourhood. See www.ipsos-mori.com/content/naming-shaming-poll.ashx.

112 See Victor 1998: 543; and Critcher 2002. For an example of an instance of a mob attacking a man's home having mistakenly believed him to be a paedophile named in the *News of the World's* campaign, see 'To name and shame', BBC News report, 24 July 2000, http://news.bbc.co.uk/1/hi/uk/848759.stm. For an analysis of the moral panic surrounding paedophilia in the UK, see Critcher 2003: ch. 7.

In the introduction, I highlighted the Labour Party's focus on child pornography in its 2001 Manifesto. The possible dangers posed by grooming were stressed in the same Manifesto:

> Our criminal laws already cover some paedophile activity over the internet. For example it is illegal to produce or distribute indecent images of children over the net, or to ask children to perform indecent acts over the net. But there is one key area which has not yet been addressed – the non-sexual approaches which paedophiles make to children over the net as a way of 'grooming' children for an eventual sexual assault. Such approaches often take the form of apparently 'harmless' e-mail messages and so are difficult to tackle using the criminal law.[113]

This was followed by an emphasis on the need to protect children from acts of grooming initiated by sexual abusers in order to provide the opportunity for subsequent sexual abuse in *Protecting the Public*.[114] The disparity between the perceived and actual prevalence of different types of grooming is reinforced by the way in which the government has chosen to pay particular attention to stranger grooming.[115] Convincing the public to accept these representations regarding the prevalence of stranger grooming advanced the government's agenda; its creation of legislation to deal with these problems (namely the SOA) was then more likely to be perceived as a suitable response to the societal demand to offer better protection to children from abuse.[116] Whilst the s. 15 offence was being shaped, the need to respond to public demand was also a concern for MPs. For example, in presenting ten years as the appropriate maximum sentence, Conservative MP Dominic Grieve argued that a lesser sentence could lead to a situation where: 'The public will consider that we have provided them with insufficient protection … I fear that there will be more than one or two examples of judges saying, "This is all that I can do".'[117]

When earlier proposals had been made to revise the law to criminalize grooming, just as in the case of child pornography, figures highlighting the problem of online grooming were given in the House of Commons debates without further substantive detail. MP Jackie Ballard referred to an American survey which 'said that approximately one in five young people aged between 10 and 17 had received an unwanted sexual

[113] See 'Full text of Jack Straw's speech', *The Guardian*, 20 May 2001, available at http://politics.guardian.co.uk/print/0,3858,4189352–107748,00.html.

[114] Home Office 2002: para. 54.

[115] The opposition too has focused upon stranger online grooming. See n. 76 in the Introduction.

[116] See Cohen 2007: 161.

[117] Hansard, House of Commons Standing Committee B, 16 September 2003: column 199.

solicitation or approach on the internet'.[118] Within just a few columns of Hansard, those figures are then inaccurately presented in a way that suggests they apply to all children who use the internet. MP Paul Burstow informed the House that: 'There is a loophole that paedophiles are using, and abusing children as a result. One in five children is contacted in chat rooms by paedophiles.'[119]

Much has been done to keep stranger online grooming at the forefront of public consciousness. In 2004, the government launched a radio, cinema and online advertising campaign on the dangers of online grooming.[120] There is also a Directgov web page[121] which provides advice to parents about how to ensure their children use the internet safely to avoid grooming. In addition, the Child Exploitation and Online Protection (CEOP) Centre provides an education programme website, *thinkuknow*,[122] which includes advice regarding the use of internet chatrooms, social networking and instant messaging. Pressure groups and children's charities also focus on online, stranger grooming. For example, Baranardo's has an internet safety web page resource.[123] Childnet International played a key role in the creation of the s. 15 offence, working with an MP to raise Parliamentary questions, recommending that the government review the law to ensure that those involved in online grooming could be prosecuted and proposing a grooming offence to the Home Office.[124] Their *Chatdanger* website highlights the 'potential dangers' of interactive online services.[125] This concentration on online grooming appears to have had an impact on the public. In a Mori Poll conducted in 2006, 1,001 participants were asked whether they had worried about protecting children from contact with paedophiles in internet chatrooms in the last two to three weeks. Of those questioned, 44 per cent of participants had worried about this 'a great deal' and 20 per cent had worried 'a fair amount'.[126]

118 Hansard, HC Deb. 14 March 2001: column 1083. Ballard would seem to have been referring to the survey completed by Finkelhor *et al.* (see Chapter 1, at 51), but provided no detail about, e.g. the number of participants involved.

119 Hansard, HC Deb. 14 March 2001: columns 1085 and 1086.

120 See Home Office press release, 'Protecting Children Online When They are Most at Risk', http://press.homeoffice.gov.uk/press-releases/Protecting_Children_Online_When_?version=1.

121 See *Keeping Children Safe Online*, www.direct.gov.uk/en/Parents/Yourchildshealthandsafety/Internetsafety/DG_071138.

122 www.thinkuknow.co.uk/.

123 www.barnardos.org.uk/resources/resources_internet_safety.htm.

124 See Gardner 2003: 4.

125 www.chatdanger.com/.

126 Britain Today Poll, results available at www.ipsos-mori.com/content/britain-today.ashx.

There was a particular emphasis on stranger grooming, in the work of the police officers I interviewed, whether this was online grooming or 'on street grooming'.[127] However, this is unsurprising, given the difficulty of finding grooming and evidence of this when it occurs in the intrafamilial setting. According to one officer, in the case of online grooming:

> footprints are left ... Although the groomers are and can be very proficient on the internet, it's difficult not to leave the footprint of contact. And so provided you've got the appropriate skills by way of the High Tech Crime Unit who interrogate and examine computers ... that should provide you with a significant evidence chain to allow you at the very least to identify and apprehend the individual in question. [However in intrafamilial abuse] you've got that physical control that is difficult to get to the bottom of and more difficult to prove when all you've got is the word of the victim.[128]

Furthermore, when the grooming has taken place in the intrafamilial setting, it is highly likely that abuse will already have occurred in the cases which are brought to the attention of the police.[129]

It thus seems clear that the public are presented with constructions of stranger grooming and child pornography that stress their dangers and may overemphasize their prevalence. I will now discuss the impact that this has on public discourses surrounding the phenomena.

Availability cascades: shaping the public discourse

For social construction theory, language is crucial, since it 'objectivates ... shared experiences and makes them available to all within the linguistic community, thus becoming both the basis and the instrument of the collective stock of knowledge'.[130] Therefore, language, the choice of words and the framing of the risks of child pornography and grooming determine the way in which these risks are constructed. Applying availability cascades theory, the language adopted by voices of authority plays a major role in shaping the public discourse upon child pornography and grooming. The experiences of the judiciary, police, child protection experts and Members of Parliament regarding child

[127] Which one officer described as being the situation where individuals look for children to groom in public places where they know they are likely to find them (Interview RX4).

[128] Interview RX2.

[129] One police officer commented that his force's 'Child Abuse Unit don't do anything around preventative work. That's not their fault, I'm not sure that they can do an awful lot about it.' (Interview RX3.)

[130] Berger and Luckmann 1967: 68.

pornography and grooming and the individuals involved forms the basis of the stock of knowledge shared by the community. These are trusted voices, either because of their direct knowledge and experience of the phenomena or, as in the case of Members of Parliament, because they have the means to gather research and evidence to support the claims they make. Examples of the language used by these voices of authority and their framing of the dangers of child pornography and grooming appear throughout this chapter.[131] What I wish to emphasize here is the manner in which the voices of authority frequently present warnings of the menace of possessing child pornography. Thus, for instance, a police expert tells us that: 'Wherever you find child pornography, you are likely to find paedophiles quite capable of attacking or abusing children.'[132] A BBC News report from 2004 quotes John Carr, internet adviser for the NCH Charity: 'over one in three people found in possession of child pornography, according to a very large American survey, will in fact be involved in hands-on abuse'.[133] No further information is provided about this survey. It appears that the author of the news report expects the reader to make the assumption that because this information has come from an expert, it must be correct and does not need further substantiation. Furthermore, when it comes to the official political presentation of the risks of child pornography and grooming, because of the language of fear and risk discourses, the government is highly unlikely to advise that it is best to wait for clear empirical evidence regarding the dangers of the phenomena.[134] Instead, the government promotes the perception that it is responding to current and future menaces of both phenomena now, rather than taking the risk of appearing soft on these issues.[135] Thus, the language of danger and risk is supported.

As is apparent from the words of the police officer and child protection expert cited above, an important filter that the official language goes through is the media.[136] Thus, the public stock of knowledge may be the

[131] See also Chapter 2, at 82–91.

[132] 'Yard officers seek more help to fight child pornography', *The Times*, 4 April 1988.

[133] See the BBC News report referred to in Chapter 1, n. 70 (also referred to by O'Brien 2006: 268). Consider also the following example, again from John Carr: 'the types of image a person is found in possession of are not necessarily any kind of guide at all to the danger they might represent to children in the future'. 'Call for child porn court review', BBC News report, 8 December 2004, http://news.bbc.co.uk/1/hi/uk/4077689.stm.

[134] See Kuran and Sunstein 1999: 701; and Beck 1992: 34 and 62.

[135] As evidenced by the quotations from government ministers prior to the introduction of proposals for new laws on child pornography in the 1980s and 1990s, provided in Chapter 2.

[136] Kuran and Sunstein 1999: 719; and Best 1990: 88 and 108.

result of the media's selected language from judges, police, Members of Parliament and child protection experts. Since many members of the public will not have any direct experience of crime related to child pornography or grooming, the official presentation of these phenomena, as sifted through the media's lens, can become the dominant accepted social construction.[137]

It is therefore revealing that the police officers I interviewed considered the way in which the media often report cases of grooming to be problematic. The media's tendency to dramatize was a particular concern: 'a lot of the time it's sensationalism rather than [a] common sense approach';[138] 'It's very emotive. I think that's to the detriment of progress really';[139] whilst 'they're in the business of raising awareness and increasing education, they're [also] in the business of selling papers'.[140] This latter officer emphasized the importance of the media reporting cases in a responsible manner.[141] Another discussed his experience of the way in which journalists had distorted the information he had provided: 'You can give information to the media and then discover that it has been presented in a very different way when it appears in print in the newspaper. They emphasize what they think will sell the story and underplay what can often be very important aspects.'[142]

I have explored the dangers of the impact of availability cascades in relation to accepted constructions of grooming in Chapter 3. These accepted constructions cause parents and children to be ignorant of the greater risk of grooming occurring other than though the internet. Moreover, as Kuran and Sunstein argue, although we have a tendency to underestimate the risks of a certain event occurring that is reported infrequently by the media, when it comes to events that are commonly reported as taking place, we can 'grossly overestimate' their prevalence.[143] In the context of child sexual abuse more generally, this can lead to overreaction and fear: 'if you ask people about their violent fury toward paedophiles, they tell you to look at the figures. "Child abuse is everywhere!" We know more about the prevalence of paedophiles than we

137 Surette and Otto 2001: 147. 138 Interview RX3. 139 Interview RX1.

140 Interview RX2.

141 Three other officers made very similar comments: Interviews RX4, RX6 and RX8.

142 Interview RX7. Another officer substantiated this: 'we've had some really poor reporting [from a national broadsheet newspaper] that was a mile off. It was really unhelpful for the parents. It was presented as though police and social workers didn't find [the abuse] soon enough, whereas everyone had done their absolute level best to save this girl from some horrendous abuse.' (Interview RX5).

143 Kuran and Sunstein 1999: 707.

used to, and have been told that they remain a menace for life. Alarming uses of the Internet are well reported, and newspapers have done their bit to expose paedophile rings.'[144]

In order to define the perceptions of child pornography and stranger grooming as a panic, and to describe as distorted the representations of these phenomena the public has come to accept as shorthand, it must be proven that these perceptions are based on an inaccurate estimation of the risks of child pornography and stranger grooming. This is the matter to which I now turn.

How much of the reaction is disproportionate?

As a starting point, I should reiterate here that I am not questioning the argument that the creation of child pornography is a harm in itself, if a real child is involved in its creation, and that society should react to this harm in an appropriate way. However, I have, for example, challenged the argument that a completely fabricated pseudo-image causes harm. The main thrust of my moral panic argument is thus based on the assessment of the extent of harm of child pornography and stranger grooming. Waddington critiques moral panic theory on the basis that, conceptually, it lacks any criteria of proportionality which can be used to ascertain whether the reaction to the phenomenon in question is defensible.[145] Goode and Ben-Yehuda also recognize the significance of disproportionality, although their argument does not dispute the validity of the moral panic concept:

> The concept of moral panic *rests* on disproportionality. If we cannot determine disproportionality, we cannot conclude that a given episode of fear or concern represents a case of moral panic … we can only know disproportionality by assessing threat from existing empirical research.[146]

A persuasive argument that the situation definitely represents a moral panic can only be made when and if there is clear empirical proof that the level of threat which child pornography and stranger grooming represent is much less in reality. However, there is no existing empirical research that establishes the true prevalence of child pornography and grooming and it is unlikely that such research ever will exist; there is no real likelihood of all child pornography being discovered and all instances of grooming being reported. This may seem to suggest that

[144] 'The real truth about paedophiles and us', *The Guardian*, 9 January 1998.
[145] Waddington 1986: 255–7. [146] Goode and Ben-Yehuda 1994: 38.

a moral panic analysis of the response to the phenomena is doomed to fail. However, as Goode and Ben-Yehuda note, we can in fact never be completely certain about the knowledge we possess about the material world.[147] More recently, Critcher has argued that: 'It is the distortion of the nature of the issue, rather than its disproportionality, which is important.'[148] If this distortion exists, there is surely room to argue, at the very least, that the situation is indicative of a moral panic.

Moral panic analysis can certainly offer evidence to suggest distortion. Goode and Ben-Yehuda refer to the following as two indicators of disproportionality: that figures are exaggerated, and that the attention paid to the behaviour in question is 'vastly greater' than to other conditions or behaviour, when the damage engendered by the other conditions is no less than the behaviour in question.[149] These indicators can surely also evidence distortion. The first indicator is present when we consider, for instance, the estimations given as to the amount of child pornography in the country during the House of Commons' debates in 1978 and the figures relied on from Densen-Gerber. Further given the findings of the existing research, the media and legislature's portrayal of the prevalence of stranger grooming cannot be accurate since there is a much lower incidence of stranger sexual abuse than there is familial or acquaintance sexual abuse.[150] Turning to the second indicator, despite what the existing research indicates about the prevalence of child sexual abuse in the home, this subject does not attract the same media attention as child pornography or stranger grooming. This is no doubt because it lacks the sensational aspects that the media can emphasize to generate moral reaction.[151]

Thus, I recognize that I cannot prove that the assessment of these harms by the media, politicians and campaigners is undoubtedly inaccurate and disproportionate to the actual harm.[152] However, I have raised questions about the perceived extent of this harm due to the reliance on exaggerated, unsubstantiated figures, the media's sensationalist presentation of the problem and the overemphasis on stranger grooming in comparison to grooming in other contexts.

[147] Ibid. [148] Critcher 2003: 111. [149] Goode and Ben-Yehuda 1994: 43–4.

[150] See the references in Chapter 1, nn. 9–11. [151] See Thompson 1998: 108.

[152] There is one particular area in which recent research suggests that it would be difficult to find evidence of disproportionality: the trading and accessing of child pornography upon the internet. See Jenkins 2001. Moreover, it is very hard to gather empirical evidence of the prevalence of child pornography on the internet in order to test moral panic theory, because surveillance of users' activities is difficult. See Taylor and Quayle 2006: 172–3; and O'Donnell and Milner 2007: 50–1.

The question of volatility

It seems almost inevitable that a moral panic reaction to child pornography and stranger grooming will endure for a lengthy period because of the subject at risk or, to use Cohen's phraseology, the suitability of victim.[153] Whilst it is recognized that some panics will be around longer than others,[154] the attribution of a moral panic to the response to child pornography, which has had a more lasting duration, seems to be at odds with analysis that emphasizes volatility as an essential aspect of the phenomenon. In applying moral panic analysis to the reaction to paedophilia, Critcher observes that an initial difficulty encountered is the fact that the panic has been prolonged since it first emanated in the 1970s. In his view: 'Paedophilia is a recurrent, serial panic. A permanent focus of news and policy-making, it is likely to be reactivated at any time.'[155] The same can certainly be said for child pornography, although not so much for grooming given its more recent appearance as a matter of great concern in its own right. However, the more enduring panic surrounding child pornography does not necessarily represent a problem, since this response has become more intense during certain specific periods of time. According to Goode and Ben-Yehuda: 'The fact that certain concerns are long-lasting does not mean that they are not panics … since the intensity of these concerns … waxes and wanes over time.'[156] The concern surrounding child pornography gained intensity in the late 1970s due to morality campaigns. This intensity was later renewed in the late 1980s, in the wake of police and interest group pressure to criminalize possession. The representation of a new threat in the form of modern technologies fuelled concern again in the early 1990s.[157] It is possible to see the enactment of legislation at the end of each of these periods as the conclusion to that particular instance of intensity. For Critcher: 'What the law represents … is a symbolic resolution of the moral panic.'[158] That

[153] Cohen 2007: 1. [154] Ibid. [155] Citcher 2003: 110. See also Meyer 2007: 10.

[156] Goode and Ben-Yehuda 1994: 41 and 103. Critcher suggests that intensity may in fact be a better descriptor than volatility. Critcher 2003: 139 and 151. See also Watney 1993: 41–2.

[157] 'Changes in the law are … needed to keep up with new technology. Computer pornography poses a particular threat. The [CJPO] Bill … will … ensure that there is no legal loophole for paedophiles who create indecent images of children through the use of computers.' Michael Howard, Hansard, HC Deb. 11 January 1994: column 30. Concern about modern technologies made the concern regarding grooming more intense in the early 2000s: 'The Internet has opened up new possibilities for children both for learning and leisure. However, we need to ensure that we tackle those who want to use it to take advantage of the innocence of children.' Hansard, HL Deb. 13 February 2003: column 773 (Lord Falconer).

[158] Critcher 2003: 141.

each instance of legal reform has only provided temporary resolution suggests the presence of a moral panic that is never dormant, a panic that is ready to become active again whenever a new threat related to child pornography appears on the horizon.

The consequences of the moral panic

If indeed we are witnessing a moral panic about child pornography and stranger grooming, I have already noted that this moral panic could be perceived to be one small part of a much larger moral panic about sex abusers in general.[159] Although this wider moral panic may have encouraged vigilante-type behaviour in some factions of our society, it has also led to some positive initiatives which have served to control the activities of child sex abusers once detected, such as, for example, the Sex Offenders' Register and Multi-Agency Public Protection Panels.[160] However, the fact remains that the probable existence of a moral panic could colour our perceptions of the actual threat represented by child pornography and stranger grooming. It is necessary to stand back and objectively assess the real dangers of both phenomena in order to *avoid* moral-panic-induced counter-productive reactions. As will become apparent from the discussion in the next part of this chapter, however, it is difficult to do this when there is so much of a societal and legal focus on safeguarding childhood innocence from any threat.

As a final point here, my argument that evidence exists which is indicative of a moral panic about child pornography and grooming does not lead to the conclusion that they are not real phenomena.[161] Cohen states that: 'Calling something a "moral panic" does not imply that this something does not exist or happened at all and that reaction is based on fantasy, hysteria, delusion and illusion or being duped by the powerful.'[162] What I have sought to demonstrate, however, is that an examination of the responses of the media, the public, law enforcement agencies, the judiciary and politicians and the existence of an availability cascade certainly suggests that a moral panic currently exists concerning child pornography and stranger grooming in our society.

159 See Critcher 2003: ch. 7.

160 See Pt. 2 of the SOA. Multi-Agency Public Protection Panels make arrangements for risk assessment and management of the most dangerous offenders on release from prison. See http://noms.justice.gov.uk/protecting-the-public/supervision/mappa/.

161 See also Adler 2001a: 934–5 and the criticism of moral panic theory raised by Meyer 2007: 10.

162 Cohen 2007: viii.

THE CONSTRUCTION OF INNOCENCE: PROTECTING OR ENDANGERING CHILDREN?

> Innocence and its corruption are, of course, adult terms for the description of childhood rather than anything intrinsic to the state of childhood itself ...[163]

It is undoubtedly the subject at risk that makes society so susceptible to a moral panic reaction regarding child pornography and stranger grooming. One of the most enduring and prevalent constructions of the child and childhood is that of innocence. To begin with, I examine the history behind this construct and parallels between its application during the Victorian era and today. I then argue that the contemporary application of, and over-reliance on, the construct in social and legal contexts has led to the 'innocent child' becoming a social and legal entity. I unmask the functions of this construct and contend that the pervasive presence of the innocent child in social and legal discourses, including those surrounding child pornography and grooming, impacts on children's lived experience negatively and actually makes children more vulnerable to sexual abuse.

The historical construct of childhood innocence

Different and contrasting constructions of children have co-existed through history,[164] and the Christian religion has had a significant impact on the way in which children are regarded. The fourth century saw Saint Augustine of Hippo's teachings on original sin, the idea that Adam and Eve's fall from grace meant that all humankind became sinful.[165] Thus, according to Augustine's doctrine of original sin, children are sinful when born and will go to hell if they are not baptized and thereby cleansed of this sin. Augustine's reasoning was influential on Western Christian theology and the Catholic Church in particular. However, this is not the only construction of the child promulgated by the Christian religion. In fact, Archard observes the confused visions of childhood that have originated from Christianity. On the one hand, the child is presented as being nearest to God, as being born innocent, but gradually being corrupted by human society the older she grows. This is juxtaposed against the Calvinist revival of Augustine's conception of the child as being born with original sin, in urgent need of being cleansed of her corruption by being taught the correct moral path.[166]

[163] Mitchell 2001: 115. [164] Gittins 1998: 149; and Cox 1996. [165] Parker 1989: 53.
[166] Archard 1993: 37–8.

Aries's historical analysis of childhood reveals that childhood itself, the idea of a period in time during earlier life that is of a significantly different nature from adulthood, did not exist in medieval society. However, from the fourteenth century onwards, a distinct period of childhood was recognized and assigned special characteristics.[167] Childhood innocence did not appear to be the vision held by society at the start of the seventeenth century. Aries discusses adults' encouragement of what would now be considered indecent behaviour towards the young Louis XIII on the part of his elders.[168] At the start of the eighteenth century, however, Hendrick argues that childhood's meaning was 'ambiguous'.[169] The publication of Rousseau's *Émile* in 1762 introduced a significantly different alternative construction of childhood as naturally innocent. In Rousseau's view, the child is 'a moral innocent, close to Nature and deserving a freedom to express itself, who is standardly corrupted by social convention'.[170] Human beings are originally and naturally innocent. It is human society that corrupts.[171] Rousseau's presentation of childhood is thus the antecedent of Victorian and more modern constructions of childhood innocence.

The nineteenth century witnessed the promulgation of significant constructions of the ideal child. Hendrick has examined how the labelling of working-class children as delinquents in the middle of the nineteenth century served to promote the accepted middle-class construction of children as helpless and dependent beings. Rebellious, self-dependent working-class children were the 'other', the direct consequence of a parental failure to protect, who had to be suppressed and brought back under control.[172] The vision of the ideal child was that of a dependent being in need of love, moral guidance and protection. However, it was the ideal of childhood innocence that came into its own in the Victorian era. There was a definite Christian element to this notion of innocence. For example, Piper refers to an 1886 NSPCC tract which stated that children, in their purity and innocence, were nearest to God.[173]

Once childhood innocence was all the rage, it did not take long before this construct became an object for exploitation. Innocence was recognized as an exploitable commodity for advertising, the use of Millais's *Bubbles* to promote Pears soap being perhaps the most famous example.[174] More importantly, emphasizing innocence was a ploy that could be relied on when it was considered necessary to draw attention

167 Aries 1962: 128–9. 168 Ibid.: 100–2. 169 Hendrick 1990: 35.
170 Archard 1993: 22. 171 Rousseau 1979. See also Gittins 1998: 148–9; and James *et al.* 1998: 13.
172 Hendrick 1990: 42–5. 173 Piper 1999: 47. 174 Holland 2006: 12.

to the inhumanities suffered by poorer children.[175] One effect of this exploitation of constructed innocence was the increase in the age of sexual consent from thirteen to sixteen by the Criminal Law Amendment Act 1885 in the wake of a campaign against the prostitution and ruin of young girls.[176] According to Smart, the legislature's intention 'was to maintain the ideals of purity and innocence in childhood, yet the defiled and "knowing" child became an anathema and an embarrassment'.[177] 'Fallen' or 'knowing' girls who did not meet the constructed ideal of purity were treated harshly, confined in industrial schools or reformatories lest they contaminate their innocent peers.[178] The increase in the age of sexual consent primarily protected working-class girls who were considered to be at the greatest danger of abuse from men.

There is a clear parallel here between the impact of this accentuation of innocence on children in Victorian times and the modern day. Whilst this emphasis on innocence in Victorian England restored working-class children to the vision of childhood that society supported, it failed to recognize and give due account to these children's lived experience of childhood. For with reference to the campaign against prostitution, Waites comments: 'Such imagery did not reflect young working-class women's sexual attitudes and knowledge, and ignored the opportunities offered to them by prostitution to combat poverty and dismal employment prospects'.[179]

Childhood innocence as a contemporary construct

That the law prioritizes children's welfare and safety is undoubtedly a consequence of legal and social constructs and a morality discourse surrounding the child, which centre on vulnerability and, significantly, innocence. The construction of childhood innocence is as enduring today as it was in Victorian times and it continues to serve the same important purpose. Referring to children's innocence bolsters laws and other measures designed to protect them. Piper observes that 'the public image of the child, which has served to both encourage and to justify social policy, is of an "unsexualised" person who is vulnerable, weak and innocent ... The more clearly the child is constructed as innocent, weak and dependent, the more powerful the image as a force to legitimate protective action.'[180] As should be evidenced from the earlier

[175] Archard 1993: 39. [176] Waites 2005: 73; and Walkowitz 1992: 82, 94 and 103.
[177] Smart 1989: 51. [178] Ibid.: 51–2; and Waites 2005: 73. [179] Waites 2005: 73.
[180] Piper 2000: 27 and 32. See also Meyer 2007: 3.

discussion in this chapter, the PCB was legitimated and speedily passed by relying on the image of innocent, vulnerable children who needed protection from impending danger. Innocence is a particularly powerful construct when employed in social campaigns against sexual abuse and exploitation. For instance, the *Innocence and Integrity* campaign calls for children's protection from internet pornography,[181] *Innocence Atlanta* is a campaign against child sexual exploitation and slavery,[182] while *Stolen Innocence* is a Canadian national education campaign against the commercial sexual exploitation of children.[183] In 1999, UNESCO launched its *Innocence in Danger* campaign, drawing public attention to child trafficking and sexual abuse.[184]

As noted by Young and others, innocence is one of the most dominant ideologies of childhood used in the media, advertising and films.[185] Indeed, innocence has become an essential, taken-for-granted representation of childhood, to such an extent that those children whose characters serve to challenge conceptions of childhood innocence are considered to be monsters, nefarious beings who have merely taken on the *semblance* of children. In discussing the media discourses surrounding the murder of Jamie Bulger,[186] for example, Young maintains that his child murderers, Thompson and Venables, 'are portrayed as aberrations of childhood, approximations of what a child might be, or fraudulent impostors. Thompson and Venables appear to be children but are not: they are more like evil adults or monsters in disguise.'[187] Similarly, Holland argues that, through their murder, Thompson and Venables breathed life into the much older construction of childhood as evil.[188] It is interesting to note that, for Gittins, children who kill cause adults to recognize that a universal child is a fiction and childhood is a social construction. Yet, she argues, this recognition is then replaced by a more tolerable conclusion that such children are essentially non-children.[189] I suggest that this conclusion, itself a social construction, enables children like Thompson, Venables and Mary Bell[190] to be categorized as the 'other'. This ensures that the much more comfortable,

[181] See www.innocenceandintegrity.com/mainpage.html.

[182] See www.innocenceatlanta.org/about.

[183] See www.swc-cfc.gc.ca/pubs/b5_factsheets/b5_factsheets_6_e.html.

[184] See www.innocenceindanger.org/index.php?id=212&L=1. [185] Young 1996: 115.

[186] For coverage of the case by *The Guardian*, see www.guardian.co.uk/uk/bulger.

[187] Young 1996. [188] Holland 2006: 119. See also Jenks 1996: 129.

[189] Gittins 1998: 39.

[190] For the BBC's coverage of the Mary Bell case in 1968, see http://news.bbc.co.uk/onthisday/hi/dates/stories/december/17/newsid_3261000/3261087.stm.

reassuring conception of childhood innocence remains unthreatened and unchallenged.[191]

A primary component of our construction of childhood innocence is a lack of knowledge about sex. Indeed, it is children's 'sexual innocence' that differentiates them most from adults.[192] The construct of innocence operates here to keep children unknowing and to reassure adults that sexuality remains in the domain of adulthood. Knowledge of and contact with sex thus corrupts the child and expunges her innocence forever.[193] This emphasis on sex debauching a child's innocence is also evident in the language employed by the legislature[194] and academic authors. For instance, Quayle *et al.* refer to the corruption of children caused by child pornography.[195] Such a presentation of harm can mask the reality of the exploitation that has occurred. As Jackson and Scott observe, child sexual abuse is 'frequently constructed as a despoliation of innocence rather than an abuse of power'.[196]

Alongside the innocent child, social discourses are also pervaded by the appearance of the sexualized child in the media and fashion advertising. In 2002, the Archbishop of Canterbury, Rowan Williams, presented his view of a society that treats its children as consumers, as economic and erotic subjects.[197] Just as I will shortly argue that innocence is a dangerous construct, so too is that of the sexualized child. Higonnet argues that: 'To the extent that the sexualization of the child is an objectification of the child, it is a strategy of a consumer culture that leaves children vulnerable, and which … is exploitative.'[198] According to a recent report by the American Psychological Association, the way in which the media sexualizes girls is having a harmful effect on their self-image and healthy development.[199] The conflicting constructs of innocence and the sexualized child in social discourses can only promote confusion and offer a disturbing presentation of childhood.

In legal discourses surrounding child pornography, deference to a conception of childhood innocence as sacred and deserving of protection is clearly evident. In explicating the purpose of its report on computer pornography and the possible dangers to children that internet child pornography presents, the Home Affairs Committee stated in 1994 that

191 See also Jenks 1996: 129. 192 Jackson 1982: 28. 193 Piper 2000: 32.

194 See, e.g. Hansard, HL Deb. 5 May 1978: columns 545 (Lord Wigoder) and 562 (Countess of Loudoun).

195 Quayle *et al.* 2006: 35. 196 Jackson and Scott 1999: 104.

197 'The loss of childhood: why we must preserve innocence', *The Times*, 23 July 2002.

198 Najafi 2002: 10. See also Adler 2001b: 254. 199 American Psychological Association 2007.

a primary concern was the 'threat to the innocence and decency of our children posed by computer pornography'.[200] When presenting the PCB to the House of Commons, Cyril Townsend emphasized that: 'Above all, we have a duty to protect innocent children.'[201] The main harm of child pornography was presented by MP Michael Alison as 'the absolute loss of the child – and its innocence and integrity – used in the photograph'.[202] In the House of Lords debates at the time, the Lord Bishop of Guildford stated that 'children should have time to enjoy childhood, and thus to acquire that inner treasure of spontaneity, innocence and modesty of which the pornographers, by their actions, rob them'.[203] Similarly, in the recent case of *R.* v. *Earney*, the judge who passed sentence commented that: 'It is tragic to see children robbed of their innocence in this graphic way.'[204] This equation of the loss of innocence with the loss of the child only underlines how essential the construction of innocence is to the very concept of the child.

The desire to protect children becomes even more compelling when their innocence is set against constructions of the possessor of child pornography as immoral and depraved. The following statement from a judge when sentencing in a possession case is not unusual: 'The effect on *innocent* children whose bodies have been abused to satisfy the *perverted* taste of men like you can hardly be imagined.'[205] The characters of the child victim and the individual who possesses child pornography are thus presented in legal discourses as being at two polarized extremes. On the one hand, the child is pure and chaste, on the other, the possessor of child pornography is depraved and perverted. The breadth of the chasm between innocence and depravity serves to justify the legal prohibition on any activity which draws the innocent child and the corrupt possessor of child pornography together, even if the child's presence is in the form of a visual representation only. Grooming and child sexual abuse

200 Home Affairs Committee 1994: xv. See also Home Office 2002: para. 54.

201 Hansard, HL Deb. 10 February 1978: column 1827.

202 Ibid.: column 1854. Other examples of the significance attached to childhood innocence can be found at column 1857 (Arthur Bottomley) and column 1870 (Sir Thomas Williams). At the trial of university lecturer Anthony Atkins (see *Atkins* v. *DPP*), Atkins argued that he was conducting an ethnographical study examining the development of sexual identity in childhood. The stipendiary magistrate stated: 'If the extension of human knowledge has to pay the price of stealing the innocence of just one child, it is a prize too far.' See 'Academic fined over child porn', *The Guardian*, 28 May 1999.

203 Hansard, HL Deb. 5 May 1978: columns 551–2.

204 At para. 4.

205 See 'Glitter gets four months', *The Guardian*, 13 November 1999 (my emphasis). More broadly, Critcher observes that 'The paedophile discourse is primarily a discourse of evil.' (2003: 114).

are exemplars of the battle between corruption and innocence, and good and evil,[206] a battle often depicted in the press.[207] There is a significant effect of emphasizing the chasm between innocence versus depravity and the notion of fighting evil in order to protect the good of childhood innocence: claims that the rights of adults involved with child pornography and grooming can be overridden become more acceptable.[208]

For several crucial reasons, reliance on popular constructions of children as innocent in legal and social discourses surrounding child pornography and grooming is problematic. What is more, the emphasis placed on innocence to legitimate measures taken to protect children may ironically cause more harm than good. First, innocence is a contrived, false and unrealistic representation of the reality of childhood. If children truly are innocent, then how can this be reconciled with evidence cited by James *et al.* that 'by far the majority of the physical, sexual and emotional abuse that any child is likely to receive will be from other children'?[209] When it comes to sex, children are not as innocent as adults might like to believe and the vulnerability they possess, constructed or real, is more likely the result of other factors such as immaturity and impulsiveness.[210]

Secondly, the prevalence and acceptance of the innocence construct makes it that much harder for discourses that promote children's autonomy, sexual independence and liberty to gain credence, since: 'The images of children which sustain a discourse of rights are those of "knowing" and, in some measure at least, autonomous people with a sufficient level of understanding to exercise rights. Such images are threatening to adults and particularly so when they include the possibility of sexual independence.'[211] It is, therefore, much harder for children to be permitted sexual liberty rights, as the extension of the child pornography offences to sixteen- and seventeen-year-olds reveals. This blinkered vision approach to innocence has a negative impact on any child who is sexually aware and, perhaps, experienced, because the 'knowing' child is perceived as a lesser victim, lacking the vital aspect of childhood that society sees as deserving of protection.[212] The 'knowing' child must thus be presented as the 'other', a non-child, or society runs the risk that

[206] Kitzinger 1997: 168; and Meyer 2007: 70.

[207] See, for instance, 'Neighbour shock at perv', *The Sun*, 22 June 2006, in which a photograph of the face of a convicted child sex offender is given the caption 'Face of evil …' and a photograph of children playing near his home is captioned 'Innocent …'

[208] See Kincaid 1998: 11–12 and the discussion of individual rights in the next chapter.

[209] James *et al.* 1998: 52. [210] See, e.g. Wolak *et al.* 2008: 116. [211] Piper 2000: 39.

[212] Kitzinger 1997: 168–9; and Piper 2000: 32.

the justification for protectionist legal intervention in children's lives becomes more contentious.[213] A child who has been corrupted through sex becomes 'disqualified' from being a child.[214] There is, therefore, a parallel with 'fallen' or 'knowing' girls in Victorian England.

A further consequence of the representation of childhood innocence is that children are not given the knowledge they need to make informed choices and decisions about sexual matters. Archard argues that: 'A premature education in the facts of life is viewed with suspicion [since] it might corrupt children with an inappropriate "adult" knowledge ... talk of innocence serves ideologically to hinder the empowerment of children through awareness and knowledge. For such knowledge is maligned as preternatural and improper.'[215]

Society and law are thus forcing children to conform to an adult notion of childhood that is false and restrictive of their liberties and their access to knowledge. However, could this straight-jacket approach be justified because a symbolic universe in which the notion of innocence prevails protects the children who exist within it? Whilst it is true that the focus on childhood innocence may have ensured the enactment of legislation that aims to protect children, the very idea of childhood innocence could itself be arousing to child sex abusers. As Kitzinger comments:

> Innocence is a powerful and emotive symbol, but to use it to provoke public revulsion against sexual abuse is counterproductive. For a start the notion of childhood innocence is itself a source of titillation for abusers ... In a society where innocence is a fetish ... focusing on children's presumed innocence only reinforces men's desire for them as sexual objects.[216]

Kitzinger's argument receives reinforcement from the findings of Howitt's research study, involving a group of paedophiliac sex offenders. Howitt questioned the participants regarding their use and experience of pornography. Perhaps the most significant finding which emerged from the study was that, whilst on the whole, child pornography did not play a part in the offenders' fantasies and sexual activities, some of the offenders were aroused by non-pornographic imagery of children. Material such as children's clothes catalogues, Walt Disney videos and television advertisements showing naked babies or toddlers in nappies were some

[213] See also King and Piper 1995: 64. [214] Gittens 1998: 9.
[215] Archard 1993: 40. See also Ennew 1986: 36; and Gittins 1998: 158 and 172.
[216] Kitzinger 1998: 79–80. See also Adler 2001a: 944–5; and Kitzinger 1997: 168.

of the types of non-pornographic imagery referred to by offenders.[217] In our focus on childhood innocence and the sexualization of this innocence, therefore, we may be promoting an ideology of childhood which *encourages* child sexual abuse.[218] Our construction and objectification of children as innocent may cause us to *reduce* them simply to objects of innocence, the one aspect of childhood that may be of the greatest attraction to the child sexual abuser.[219]

Certain attitudes to childhood innocence as represented by non-pornographic images of naked children may further encourage constructions of children as sexually arousing, particularly given the response to such images from some elements of the media. In March 2001, for example, the editor of the *News of the World* tabloid newspaper launched a scathing attack on a London gallery exhibition including work by Tierney Gearon. The photographs in question featured Gearon's naked children standing on a beach, urinating in the snow and wearing pig and adult facemasks. Whilst the government's Culture Secretary warned against censorship of the exhibition and legal experts pointed to the fact that the children were in natural rather than indecent poses, the police and some of the tabloid press took an alternative view, believing that the photographs were indecent and an encouragement to paedophiles.[220] Choosing some of Gearon's photographs in support of her claim that the exhibition was both perverted and revolting, the *News of the World's* editor censored the photographs so that the children's genital areas were concealed. However, as Gearon herself has commented, in printing the photographs outside of the intended context of the exhibition, and in raising the question of whether pictures of *innocent* naked children can ever be viewed without an element of perversion, the photographs have actually been made to look pornographic: 'the accusers have polluted my images … The pictures looked dirty for the first time.'[221]

[217] Howitt 1995a: 175. See also Ennew 1986: 116–35; Jenkins 2001: 81; and Taylor and Quayle 2003: 156.

[218] See also Adler 2001b: 259; and Higonnet 1998: 191.

[219] See Higonnet 1998: 194, and Jacobson and Mazur 1995.

[220] See 'Legally indecent?', *The Times*, 13 March 2001 and 'Police obscenity squad raid Saatchi Gallery', *The Guardian*, 10 March 2001.

[221] 'There's nothing seedy about these pictures of my kids. They are not "child porn". They are wholesome', *The Independent*, 13 March 2001. See also 'No charges over Saatchi photos', *The Guardian*, 16 March 2001. On the subject of the sexualization of images of children, see 'Little girls lost', *The Observer*, 31 August 1997. If Gearon's photographs raise questions about the boundaries between adult and child life, they do not do so in any sexual way. See Martin Maloney's interpretation of her work in Saatchi Gallery 2001: iii.

The kind of response to the exhibition epitomized by the *News of the World* would appear to stem from an acceptance of the idea that child nudity becomes sexualized when captured on camera. This is reflected in the response of 67 per cent of *The Mirror* newspaper readers who participated in a phone poll vote and considered that the images should be banned.[222] Although the Crown Prosecution Service decided not to bring a prosecution against either the gallery or Gearon for showing indecent photographs of children, such responses to the exhibition reveal the sexualization of images of naked children, especially when they are placed in the public domain.[223]

In fact, the concern about presenting images of naked children in the public domain has progressed so far that, in 2007, the managers of the Baltic Centre for Contemporary Art in Gateshead alerted the police to an image that was included in a photographic exhibition for fear that it constituted an indecent photograph of a child. The image in question, *Klara and Edda Belly Dancing* by Nan Goldin, is part of the American artist's *Thanksgiving* installation, a series of images depicting her personal life, and is owned by Elton John. It features two young girls playfully dancing, one is semi-clothed, the other is naked, sitting down and bending backwards. Her legs are open and her genital area is exposed. Although the photograph has been exhibited on numerous other earlier occasions worldwide without concern, it was seized by the police from the same 2001 exhibition as the Gearon photographs. In 2001, the conclusion of the CPS was that the image was not indecent, the decision that was again reached some six years later following its removal from the Baltic Centre's exhibition.[224] If the Goldin photograph does cause some to feel uncomfortable, the only reason for this can be that one of the girls' genital areas is in plain sight, facing the camera; there is nothing provocative or sexual about the image.[225] However, this aspect of the photograph and the perception of this part of the girl's body as taboo was enough to eroticize the whole image and for the question of indecency to be raised.[226]

[222] 'The pics are okay … but I wouldn't put them on view; readers give verdict on nudes display', *The Mirror*, 17 March 2001.

[223] See also Edwards 1994: 42.

[224] 'Seized Elton artwork not indecent', BBC News report, 26 October 2007, http://news.bbc.co.uk/1/hi/england/tyne/7063564.stm.

[225] As is the case with the Gearon photographs. Gearon describes them as 'very unsensual, very unsexual'. *The Independent*, 13 March 2001, above, n. 221.

[226] For criticism of the reaction to the image, see 'The notional paedophile now dictates what we can look at', *The Guardian*, 4 October 2007; and 'Naked fear on display', *The Times*, 30 September 2007.

As noted by Toynbee, this idea that children's nudity becomes sexualized when presented in a photograph can only serve to promote the notion of child nudity as sexually arousing: 'Nude and rude adults can be thrusted obscenely everywhere, but children's bodies must be shrouded as if they were indeed sexual. This is the world upside down – the paedophile's view, not ours.'[227] A good example of such a perception can be found in the *Daily Mail's* reaction to Gearon's photographs. Honing in on the fact that the children were wearing pig and adult facemasks in some of the images, the writer of the editorial stated: 'What is at issue here isn't a celebration of childhood innocence ... Masks and relentless nudity appear to hint at child abuse rituals.' Readers were informed that the exhibition 'encourages all those paedophiles who have never accepted that their perversion is wrong to believe that their activities have the tacit sanction of the great and the good'.[228] Such an interpretation of the photographs is the dangerous consequence of a societal objectification of the child as innocent, and the consequent tainting of this symbol of childhood when child nudity is photographed.[229] There is a real danger that this perception may serve to reinforce the idea of childhood innocence and nakedness as both sexualized and titillating, potentially making children more vulnerable to sexual abuse.

Applying Foucault's work, discourses surrounding sexuality develop and shape what sexuality is.[230] If popular social discourses focus on the danger of seeing children's nude bodies in public because of the way in which such bodies could be viewed by those who have a sexual interest in

[227] 'The voyeurs have won', *The Guardian*, 13 March 2001. See also 'The myth of childhood innocence', *The Guardian*, 13 March 2001; 'Naked fear on display', ibid; and Adler 2001b: 256 and 2001a: 954–7.

[228] 'Encouraging evil', *Daily Mail*, 16 March 2001.

[229] A social climate in which any image of a naked child is viewed with suspicion can also have a dangerous impact upon parents. See Adler 2001a: 964–5. Danay refers to a Canadian case involving a father who was arrested in 2000 for making child pornography following the processing of his roll of film by a photography lab. The film included images of the man's four-year-old son playing without his pyjama bottoms on. Although the man was released on bail, it was a condition that he left the family home and, whilst the charges against him were subsequently dropped, a custody hearing was demanded. Both he and his wife were required to take parenting courses. (Danay 2005:173.) According to a CBC News report, the man had to spend all his savings in order to clear his name ('The Supreme Court and child porn', CBC News, 22 June 2004). In this jurisdiction, there was much publicity surrounding the seizure of family photographs of a child in the bath and the subsequent arrest of her mother (Julia Somerville) and her partner in 1995. They were both later released without charge. See 'Julia's pictures: could it happen to you?', *The Independent*, 6 November 1995; and 'No police action on Somerville photos', *The Guardian*, 6 December 1995.

[230] See generally, Foucault 1986.

children, this becomes the way in which children's bodies *are* perceived generally. The repression of childhood nudity encourages a perception that what is being hidden is something sexual and dirty; what we have constructed as childhood innocence becomes perverted.[231] In other words, this discourse frames the way in which we construe children's bodies, with the result that children's naked bodies become sexualized. In such a climate, it is imperative that legal discourses differentiate between images of child pornography and images of naked children.[232] Otherwise, judicial discourses will further reinforce and confirm the sexualization of childhood innocence apparent in social discourses.[233]

As social constructions of children's sexualized naked bodies take hold, it is even more disturbing that such constructions could also have a harmful effect on children themselves in terms of the way in which they perceive their bodies and their lived experiences of being children. Gittins observes that whether or not children are affected by adult constructs, and whether the idea of childhood innocence has any meaning for them, depends on the way in which they understand the adult world around them.[234] In my view, children have no choice but to understand, or at least accept, adults' sexualization of their naked bodies and the construction of childhood innocence as sexual, since these aspects of the adult world are invading their lives, their perceptions and their lived experiences of themselves within this world. This embedded social construction of the child has become one part of the reality that children are forced to live in.[235] Thus, not only are we infringing children's rights, particularly, their right not to be ashamed of their own bodies, but we are shaping and affecting their subjective experience of being a child. Nowhere is this more apparent than in journalist Cosmo Landesman's anecdotal discussion of the societal reaction to naked children in public, written in the wake of the controversy surrounding the Goldin photograph. He details the way in which other parents and children reacted disapprovingly and anxiously to the sight of his naked three-year-old son playing in a fountain in a public park. Upon seeing the naked boy run from the fountain to the play area, one

[231] See also Adler 2001b: 269–70.

[232] Unless an image of a naked child is taken in exploitative circumstances. See the previous chapter, at 133–5.

[233] For the problems currently presented by American and Canadian law in this regard, see Chapter 5.

[234] Gittins 1998: 162–3.

[235] See generally Hacking 1999: 203; James and James 2004: 13; and Jackson and Scott 1999: 91–2.

child remarked: 'That's disgusting!' As Landesman asks: 'If children can regard the nakedness of other children as "disgusting", what will they think about their own bodies?'[236]

The controversy surrounding the Gearon and Goldin photographs in England has recently been mirrored in Australia, with the removal of artist Bill Henson's photographs of naked twelve- and thirteen-year-old girls from a gallery in Sydney by police.[237] No charges were brought and the photographs were later put back on display. A few months later, *Art Monthly*, an Australian arts journal, published a front cover image of Polixeni Papapetrou's *Olympia as Lewis Carroll's Beatrice Hatch before White Cliffs*, a photograph of a naked six-year-old girl sitting on a rock. In the journal's editorial for this issue, it is stated that the photograph was chosen 'in the hope of restoring some dignity to the debate; to validate nudity and childhood as subjects for art; to surrender to the power of the imagination (in children and adults) and dialogue without crippling them through fear-mongering and repression'.[238] A public debate ensued, with child pornography campaigners objecting to the publication of the image. Australia's Prime Minister, Kevin Rudd, who had referred to the Henson images as 'absolutely revolting', gave his opinion that 'we are talking about the innocence of little children here. A little child cannot answer for themselves about whether they wish to be depicted in this way.'[239] However, the most important voice in the whole of the debate surrounding Papapetrou's photograph was the now eleven-year-old girl who was the subject of the image, Olympia, the artist's daughter: 'I was really, really offended by what Kevin Rudd said about this picture. It is one of my favourites – if not my favourite – photo my mum has ever taken of me.'[240] There is thus a real concern that her perception of her body, as represented in the photograph, will now be tainted by this very public reaction. Her lived experience has been invaded by a negative adult construction that her posing for this image, and the subsequent public presentation of this image, is harming her. In a social world in which children have so little control over the construction of their bodies that is accepted in public discourses, Olympia's positive construction

[236] 'Naked fear on display', above, n. 226. See also 'It's ridiculous that we treat child nudity as a problem', *The Independent*, 8 July 2008. And note Ennew's point that 'Cultural norms of shame are particularly easy to pass on to children through linguistic and bodily taboos.' Ennew 1986: 28.

[237] 'Police seize "child porn" art from Sydney gallery', *The Independent*, 24 May 2008.

[238] O'Riordan 2008.

[239] 'Art or abuse? Fury over image of naked girl', *The Independent*, 8 July 2008.

[240] Ibid.

of her own image becomes irrelevant. Therefore, as Loizidou argues in another context: 'The truth about children derives not from the child but rather from the interpreter of the child.'[241]

What I have sought to argue here is that whilst law and society attempt to protect children through deference to the ideal of childhood innocence, notions of innocence and purity may actually be those most attractive to the individuals from whom society is trying to protect children. Furthermore, current societal reactions to photographs depicting childhood nudity as sexual and children's naked bodies on display in public may cater for paedophiles and harm children by affecting the way in which they view their own bodies. In her analysis of the way in which advertising and media culture sexualizes the notion of childhood innocence in girls, Holland perceptively observes: 'It may be that a loss of innocence is the best protection against exploitation.'[242] This is all the more true in the context of the broader social construction of the child as innocent. Until we can let go of the illusion that we have fabricated of the pure child who must be protected from corruption at all costs and lift the taboo that we place upon the child's naked body, we will continue to fail in our endeavours to offer children a lived experience of childhood that is free, as far as possible, from harm and exploitation. Instead, we exacerbate children's vulnerability to sexual abuse, a vulnerability that society and law has seemingly, albeit unwittingly, played a large role in constructing.

[241] Loizidou 2000: 135–6.

[242] Holland 2006: 195.

CHAPTER FIVE

THE LAW ELSEWHERE AND QUESTIONS OF INDIVIDUAL RIGHTS

Many jurisdictions other than the UK have had to grapple with the problems of child pornography and sexual grooming. The initial discussion here is focused on the way in which Canadian and American jurisdictions have dealt with the phenomena. I have chosen to direct my comparative analysis on these jurisdictions for specific reasons. First, in both the United States and Canada, the criminalization of child pornography in particular has been examined through the critical lens of individual rights and freedoms to a greater degree than in this jurisdiction. This is no doubt due to the substantial, long-standing protection offered by the US constitution, and the longer history behind the Canadian Charter of Rights and Freedoms[1] when compared to the Human Rights Act 1998. There is a history of robust judicial protection of free speech in both jurisdictions.[2] Because of the powerful presence of the First Amendment, it is perhaps unsurprising that critical academic commentary and analysis on child pornography laws has been more prolific in the United States than in this jurisdiction.[3] However, it is interesting that, despite the limits placed upon state power by the First Amendment and the Canadian Charter of Rights and Freedoms, the

[1] Incorporated within the Constitutional Act 1982. See also Peysakhovich 2004: 817–19.

[2] See also Johnson 2006: 377.

[3] For example, the following are just some of the journal articles on the legal response to pseudo-images: Adelman 1996; Burke 1997; Duncan 2007; Kenney 2006; Liu 2007; Lodato 1998; and Wasserman 1998.

laws in both the United States and Canada still criminalize more material than English law.[4]

Secondly, unlike this jurisdiction, the legislation in both Canada and the United States defines child pornography. In my consideration of England's legal response to child pornography, I have been critical of the moralistic nature of the concept of indecency, and the potential danger of it being applied to and sexualizing images of naked children. However, as will become apparent, the statutory definitions of child pornography in Canada and the United States are equally problematic because of their focus on perceived sexual elements of images that do not depict actual sexual abuse. Moreover, morality pervades the way in which these national laws construct child pornography and the child.

I also undertake an analysis of the way in which grooming has been tackled in Canada and the United States, to reveal more about whether English law's construction of grooming reflects a common understanding of how law can best protect children from the threat created by such behaviour. I then turn to consider rights relating to privacy, freedom of expression and the right to a fair trial in the context of individuals suspected and convicted of offences related to child pornography and grooming and, generally, the impact that this has on their lives. A further focus here is the matter of fair labelling regarding individuals who download material from the internet and are convicted for the offence of making indecent images of children, and those individuals who create pseudo-images and have not directly harmed or exploited a child. Finally, my analysis centres on the way in which children's rights, especially rights to be protected from sexual exploitation, have increasingly come to the fore in the international arena, through treaties that numerous countries worldwide have committed themselves to.

THE CANADIAN AND US LAWS SURROUNDING CHILD PORNOGRAPHY

The law in Canada and the challenge brought under the Charter of Rights and Freedoms

> Noble and urgent motivations do not necessarily generate good law or good public policy. Our legislators have yielded too quickly to the

[4] As shall become apparent, Canadian law criminalizes written material and US federal law may catch innocuous images of children and prohibits obscene drawings and cartoons of the sexual abuse of children that depict minors engaged in sexually explicit conduct.

> temptation to adopt apparently simple solutions to a complex, disturbing and systemic social problem. In doing so, they have pushed back our traditional understandings of the appropriate limits on the use of the criminal law to suppress expressive material.[5]

In contrast to English law, the law in Canada is not framed around a moral discourse. However, the section of the Canadian Criminal Code that houses the child pornography offences appears as one of a number of provisions under the title 'Offences Tending to Corrupt Morals'. According to Persky and Dixon, this is the remaining vestige of the traditional English legal approach to materials of a sexually explicit nature in Canadian law.[6] After the Second World War, Canadian jurisprudence gradually turned away from this framework to a legal approach based on a more Millian and, subsequently, in the 1990s, feminist conception of harm.[7] However, in the context of child pornography law, morality has not left the picture altogether. In fact, as I will discuss, morality seems to have been an influential factor in shaping the definition of a child under the child pornography provisions.

Various offences relating to child pornography are listed under s. 163.1 of the Canadian Criminal Code, such as making, printing, selling, distributing, importing, publishing and making available such material.[8] It is also an offence to possess child pornography with a view to its distribution, publication or sale and simply to have such material in one's possession.[9] Additionally, knowingly accessing child pornography (causing child pornography to be viewed by, or transmitted to, oneself) is criminalized.[10] On the face of it, the inclusion of this offence would seem to indicate that Canadian law goes one step further than the law in this jurisdiction, which stops at possession. However, the broad judicial interpretation of 'making' child pornography under English law when it comes to downloading such material, or such material being saved in a computer's temporary cache, means that this is, in fact, not the case.

5 Ryder 2003: 102. 6 Persky and Dixon 2001: 64.

7 *R.* v. *Labaye* [2005] 3 SCR 728, in which it was emphasized that indecency revolves around the community standard of tolerance and the concept of harm rather than moral corruption; *R.* v. *Butler* [1992] 1 SCR 452.

8 S. 163.1(2) and (3). This section of the Criminal Code was enacted in 1993. It is interesting to note that, unlike in the US and the UK, there was no pressure group publicity or controversy that led to the enactment of the Canadian law on child pornography. See Persky and Dixon 2001: 46.

9 Criminal Code, s. 163.1(4).

10 S. 161.1(4.1) and (4.2). This could catch, e.g. the viewing of child pornography on the internet without downloading.

According to the Code, child pornography can be a photographic, film, video or other visual representation and can be in electronic format.[11] Thus, the emphasis is placed on the broader concept of a *visual representation*, rather than a photograph, as under English law. A visual representation constitutes child pornography if it shows a person who is or appears to be aged under eighteen, who is or is depicted as being engaged in explicit sexual activity.[12] This therefore includes pseudo-images. In addition, a visual representation can also be defined as child pornography when its 'dominant characteristic … is the depiction, for a sexual purpose, of a sexual organ or the anal region of a person under the age of eighteen years'.[13] Any written or visual material which advocates or counsels sexual activity with a person under the age of eighteen that would be a crime also constitutes child pornography.[14] Furthermore, written material or audio recordings which have as a dominant characteristic 'the description, for a sexual purpose, of sexual activity with a person under the age of eighteen years' that would be a crime are caught by the legal definition of child pornography.[15] Although I will analyse aspects of this definition later in this section, it should be clearly apparent at this point that it encompasses much more material than the legislation in this jurisdiction.[16]

The definition of a child as being under the age of eighteen and the fact that the age of consent to sexual activity in Canada is sixteen means that there is a clear parallel with English law. It is of interest to note that, until 2008, the age of consent to sexual activity in Canada was fourteen. There was thus even more of a marked disparity between the age at which two teenagers could engage in lawful, consensual sexual intercourse and the age at which they could lawfully record themselves engaging in such activity.[17]

My analysis will now focus on the impact of the child pornography provisions on constitutionally guaranteed rights and freedoms in Canada, specifically in the context of the possession offence. As I have already

[11] S. 163.1(1)(a). [12] S. 163.1(1)(a)(i). [13] S. 163.1(1)(a)(ii). [14] S. 163.1(1)(b).

[15] S. 163.1(1)(c) and (d).

[16] There is, however, a clear similarity in terms of the severity of the punishments imposed by the Canadian Criminal Code. An individual convicted of creating, publishing, importing, distributing, selling or possessing child pornography for the purpose of publication or distribution can be sentenced to a term of imprisonment of up to ten years (s. 163.1(2) and (3)). An individual who is convicted of the possession offence can face up to five years' imprisonment (s. 163.1(4)).

[17] The age of consent was raised by the Tackling Violent Crime Act, which was signed into law on 28 February 2008.

argued, it is harder to legitimate the offence of possession because the danger it represents to children is less evident than the harm caused by the production of child pornography. It is, therefore, in the context of private possession that the right to privacy and freedom of expression are especially pressing and, with this in mind, it is to the seminal case of *R. v. Sharpe* that I now turn. Robin Sharpe was charged under s. 163.1 of the Canadian Criminal Code with the offences of having in his possession child pornography for the purpose of distribution and sale, and of simply having child pornography in his possession.[18] Various items of child pornography had been discovered, including written text of a work entitled 'Kiddiekink Classics', photographs and other books, manuscripts and stories. Sharpe mounted a challenge against s. 163.1 of the Criminal Code, contending that it was unconstitutional. He argued that he had an expectation of privacy, which formed a part of the wider freedom of expression guarantee under s. 2 of the Canadian Charter of Rights and Freedoms. His right to privacy had been violated as a result of the Criminal Code's provisions relating to the mere possession of child pornography under s. 163.1(4). The Crown contended that the violation was justifiable under s. 1 of the Charter, which states that the guarantee of the rights and freedoms under the Charter is subject to reasonable limits as prescribed by the law and justifiable in a free and democratic society.

In the Supreme Court of Canada,[19] it was held that the possession provisions were constitutional, but, to ensure that the law could be defended as placing a reasonable limit on the right to freedom of expression, the majority read two exceptions into the Code's definition of child pornography. McLachlin CJ gave judgment[20] that the application of the provision should be excluded in cases where: (1) the material in question is expressive material, written, or other 'visual representations of thought' created by an individual alone, and kept exclusively for his own personal use; and (2) visual recordings of lawful activity created for and by an individual alone and kept by him purely for his own personal use.[21] She was especially concerned about adolescents' self-fulfilment and identity, stating that 'for young people grappling with issues of sexual identity and self-awareness, private expression of a sexual nature may be crucial to personal growth and sexual maturation'.[22] In McLachlin's view, without the exceptions she highlighted, the law trenched too much upon

[18] Under ss. 163.1(3) and 163.1(4). [19] *R. v. Sharpe* (2001) SCC 2.
[20] Iacobucci, Major, Binnie, Arbour and LeBel JJ concurring. [21] At para. 115.
[22] At para. 107.

freedom of expression and came dangerously close to criminalizing the expression of thought in words.[23]

Although acknowledging that the evidence put forward by the Crown regarding the possible relationship between the possession of child pornography and the occurrence of child sexual abuse was not conclusive, McLachlin CJ stated:

> While the scientific evidence is not strong, I am satisfied that the evidence in this case supports the existence of a connection here: exposure to child pornography *may* reduce paedophiles' defences and inhibitions against the sexual abuse of children. Banalizing the awful and numbing the conscience, exposure to child pornography *may* make the abnormal seem normal and the immoral seem acceptable. [24]

In relying on the state interest in protecting children, the majority thus held that the legislature had a pressing and substantial purpose for criminalizing the possession of child pornography. Although the minority agreed that the provisions were constitutional, they did not support the exceptions written in by the majority. In their view, possession of such material could still be harmful and was justifiably prohibited: 'Parliament also sought to prevent the harm which flows from the very existence of images and words which degrade and dehumanize children and to send the message that children are not appropriate sexual partners.' [25]

The court ordered Sharpe's retrial. When the case was returned to the British Columbia Supreme Court, Shaw J ruled that Sharpe's 'Kiddiekink Classics' did not counsel sexual activity with children and, as a consequence, Sharpe was not guilty of an offence in respect of these materials.[26] He was, however, found guilty of the possession offence in relation to some of the other materials and was subsequently sentenced to four months' house arrest.

Fundamentally different judgments to that of the Supreme Court were given earlier by the trial judge[27] and the British Columbia Court of Appeals.[28] In the British Columbia Supreme Court, Shaw J considered that the harm to children that child pornography represents could be dealt with sufficiently under the provisions prohibiting the production and dissemination of such material.[29] There were only limited benefits to criminalizing possession, and these were outweighed by the detrimental

[23] At para. 108. [24] At para. 88 (my emphasis).
[25] At para. 217 (*per* L'Heureux-Dubé, Gonthier and Bastarache).
[26] *R.* v. *Sharpe* [2002] BCSC 423. [27] *R.* v. *Sharpe* [1999] 169 DLR (4th) 536 (BCSC).
[28] *R.* v. *Sharpe* [1999] 175 DLR (4th) 1 (BCCA). [29] At para. 52.

effects of the prohibition.[30] He thus dismissed the two counts of simple possession, although he confirmed the counts of possession for the purposes of distribution or sale. In his view, the provision in this respect was a justified violation of freedom of expression, since: 'The dissemination of materials that counsel or advocate sexual abuse of children must pose some risk to children.'[31] The trial judge's decision generated a maelstrom of media criticism and political opposition.[32] In the Court of Appeals, by a two-to-one majority, the possession offence was also held to be unconstitutional. Southin JA found that the offence criminalized behaviour that was not proven to be harmful to children and was too great an infringement on freedom of expression.[33] Concurring, Rowles JA emphasized that the possession offence caught material that could be created without causing children harm, the recording of thoughts and works of the imagination and constituted 'an extreme invasion of the values of liberty, autonomy, and privacy'.[34] Dissenting, McEachern CJBC concluded that criminalization of possession was warranted to meet Parliament's objectives. In his view:

> Possession for purely innocent purposes cannot be assured by any legislation and it is impossible to know how much harm will be done to children by allegedly innocent possession. Future harm to children cannot be predicted with any degree of accuracy. Any real risk of harm to children is enough to tip the scales in favour of the legislation in the context of this case.[35]

Following the Court of Appeals' decision, the Canadian police were anxious to see the possession offence retained, citing an alternative justification for the existence of the offence to that given by the police in this jurisdiction.[36] According to an Ontario Provincial Police Inspector, the possession offence was 'the tool we use to enter into a house to gather evidence of the making, the distribution and the importation of child pornography and also to uncover evidence of sexual abuse of children'.[37]

[30] At para. 50. Shaw J explained these deleterious effects as follows: 'an individual's personal belongings are an expression of that person's essential self. Books, diaries, pictures, clothes and other belongings are personal and private expressions of their owner's beliefs, opinions, thoughts and conscience. The simple possession prohibition deals with a very intimate and private aspect of a person's life and, in my view, that fact should be given considerable weight. I find that the limited effectiveness of the prohibition is insufficient to warrant its highly invasive effects' (para 51).

[31] At para. 62. [32] See Persky and Dixon 2001: 117. [33] At para. 95.

[34] At paras 171 and 174. [35] At para. 291. [36] See Chapter 2 , at 86.

[37] See 'The Supreme Court and child porn', CBC News, 22 June 2004. The Canadian judiciary appear to have accepted this line of argument. See, e.g. *R. v. Meyer* (2004) CarswellSask 946, para. 31.

The final appeal judgment in *Sharpe* indicates that the Supreme Court adopted an analogous position to that taken by the English judiciary, considering that the mere possibility of harm being caused to children by the possession of child pornography is significant enough to justify legislative provisions that criminalize such activity. This is despite the fact that even the MPs involved in the drafting of the child pornography provisions considered them to be hastily drafted and over-broad and they were rushed through the necessary Parliamentary stages.[38]

In the wake of the *Sharpe* case, the government was quick to react. Following amendments to s. 163.1 that were presented in two unsuccessful Bills introduced and read in Parliament between 2002 and 2004, Bill C-2 was passed in July 2005.[39] As noted above, the definition of child pornography has now been extended to include 'any written material whose dominant characteristic is the description, for a sexual purpose, of sexual activity with a person under the age of eighteen years that would be an offence under this Act'.[40] Notably, since there is no exception where individuals have created the material themselves exclusively for their own personal use, this means that one of the exceptions read into the legislative provisions by the Supreme Court in *Sharpe* has effectively been removed.[41] The possession offence now suffers from the over-broadness that the majority in the Supreme Court sought to remedy.

The definition of child pornography under Canadian law: necessarily broad to prevent harm or harmful in itself?

In the Supreme Court judgment in *Sharpe*, McLachlin CJ elucidated the range of material caught by the Canadian legislation:

> Written material and visual representations advocating the commission of criminal offences against children [are] caught. Visual material depicting children engaged in explicit sexual activity is caught, as is material featuring as a dominant characteristic the sexual organ or anal region of a child for a sexual purpose. The reach of prosecution is further brought ... by extending it to the depiction of both real and imaginary persons.

38 Persky and Dixon 2001: ch. 2. See also 'The Supreme Court and child porn', ibid.

39 See Johnson 2006: 379–80.

40 S. 163.1(1)(c). The Bill has additionally replaced the artistic merit defence that previously existed under the Criminal Code with a narrower 'legitimate purpose' defence that also requires the defendant to prove that the material 'does not pose an undue risk of harm' to minors. S. 163.1(6)(a) and (b).

41 See also Danay 2005: 177–8.

> As a result, the law appears to catch a substantial amount of material that endangers the welfare of children.[42]

If the central concern remains the harm suffered by real children who are involved in child pornography, then the inclusion of all of this material is surely unnecessary. However, as is evident from McLachlin's final point, when harm is broadened to endangerment, to a risk of potential, future harm, then the grasp of the law becomes extremely broad and powerful. In fact, freedom of expression in this context appears to be a freedom to think thoughts alone; as soon as these thoughts are translated into words or a visual representation, then the individual leaves himself exposed to the criminal law. However, such an expansive infringement upon freedom of expression is hard to justify by arguing that, for example, the writer of material that discusses sexual acts with children may influence others to go out and commit offences against children. There is an insufficient normative link to criminalize such written material. Whilst the concern may also be that such written materials could be utilized as part of the grooming process, as Akdeniz argues, such grooming behaviour could be caught by the 'luring a child' provision under the Criminal Code.[43] The breadth of the Canadian definition of child pornography provides an example of the expansion and distortion of the harm principle that I warned against in the previous chapter. In Canada more so than this jurisdiction, the risk of harm has become a liberty-limiting principle.

Furthermore, the Canadian definition sexualizes images of children that show their genital areas. I have already noted that material can be defined as child pornography if its dominant characteristic 'is the depiction, *for a sexual purpose*, of a sexual organ or the anal region of a person under the age of eighteen years'.[44] In examining judicial interpretation of this provision, Danay discusses the British Columbia Supreme Court case of *R.* v. *Nedelec*,[45] which involved the possession of child pornography. One particular image which the defendant had acquired, seemingly taken without any sexual purpose in mind, featured a girl aged between three and four. She was sat opening Christmas presents on the floor, her nightgown up and around her waist, and her genital area in view. Shaw J judged that in light of the context of the defendant's collection of images of child pornography, he had kept this 'disturbing' image

[42] At para. 72.

[43] See Akdeniz 2008: 156–8 and my later discussion of this provision, at 212.

[44] My emphasis. [45] [2001] BCSC 1334.

for a sexual purpose.[46] In Danay's opinion, in concluding that: 'However innocently the picture was taken, the clear and prominent depiction of the little girl's genital area is startling',[47] Shaw J had taken on the gaze of the paedophile, viewing an innocently taken photograph as sexualized purely because the child's genital area just so happened to be in view.[48] This judicial approach to classifying images as child pornography is indeed troubling, since it raises the question of just how broad the definition of child pornography actually is by virtue of the judiciary's interpretation of the Canadian legislation. On the basis of such analysis, a family snapshot of a child in the bath or playing naked on the beach could potentially amount to child pornography, if the context in which it is possessed suggests a sexual purpose. The matter of harm, as a result, seems irrelevant.[49]

In the Supreme Court in *Sharpe*, McLachlin CJ interpreted 'for a sexual purpose' to mean: 'reasonably perceived as intended to cause sexual stimulation to some viewers'.[50] Thus, she construed the sexual purpose test as relating to the purpose for which the image was *taken*. However, she continued that whilst a family photograph of a naked child would not normally meet the test. 'Placing a photo in an album of sexual photos and adding a sexual caption could change its meaning such that its dominant characteristic or purpose becomes unmistakably sexual in the view of a reasonable objective observer.'[51] Thus, the judgment in *Sharpe* supports the analysis subsequently undertaken by Shaw J in *Nedelec*, namely, consideration of the purpose for which the image is *possessed*. Although I have argued that context is an important matter that the legal test of indecency under English law currently fails to take into account, it is the context in which the image of the naked child or the child's exposed genitalia is *taken* which I have contended is relevant to the question of whether the child has suffered harm.[52] Leaving innocuously taken images of naked children open to being defined as child pornography is a dangerous course to adopt. For, as Shaw's J opinion in *Nedelec* and my discussion in the previous chapter reveal, such images themselves come to be viewed as sexualized and disturbing.

Turning to the definition of the child in the child pornography provisions, in the British Columbia Court of Appeals, Southin JA was

[46] At para. 49. [47] Ibid. [48] Danay 2005: 158–9.

[49] 'The question of whether a photograph appeals to a pedophile often bears no relationship to the conditions under which it was produced or to the experience of the child subject.' Adler 2001a: 957. See also O'Donnell and Milner 2007: 229.

[50] At para. 51. [51] At para. 52. [52] See Chapter 3, at 133–5.

concerned about the difference between the legal age for sexual consent and the definition of a child under the child pornography provisions.[53] However, in the Supreme Court, Justice L'Heureux-Dubé justified the setting of the age of a child as under eighteen in the following way:

> Parliament had a strong basis for concluding that the age limit in the definition of child pornography should be set at 18 in order to protect children from the harm of being used in the production of child pornography. The provision recognizes … that whilst adolescents may be capable of consenting to sexual activity, their consent is vitiated in circumstances where there is a possibility that they may be exploited.[54]

In her view, then, the possibility that exploitation may occur suffices to legitimate Parliament's imposition of a blanket criminalization upon the visual representation, written or drawn depiction, or recording of older adolescents engaging in sexual activity. The implication must be that exploitation automatically becomes a possibility whenever a sixteen- or seventeen-year-old's sexual activity is depicted, recorded or visually represented. But this is surely not the case, and as I argued in the context of English law, this legal position fails to take into account the sexual liberty rights of teenagers of these ages. Critical of the dissenting Supreme Court judges' attitudes towards adolescent sexuality in *Sharpe*, Persky and Dixon reason that:

> The only way to make sense of the insistence on retaining an under-eighteen definition of 'child' is to speculate that what's at play here is the importation of a particular moral view into what ought to be a matter of judging harm … But since the law emphatically claims to be not about morality, but about the prevention of harm to children, such reasoning, however reflective of societal confusion, seems disconnected from the legislative aims.[55]

Yet, as the legislature has gone further in expanding the definition of child pornography since Persky and Dixon raised this critique, the legislative aims themselves, and the impact a morality discourse has on these aims, must also now be questioned.

The law in the United States and the First Amendment

The First Amendment prohibits Congress from making any law that abridges freedom of speech. Adult pornography is covered by this protection, unless it is obscene according to the *Miller* standard for obscenity,

[53] At paras 127–9. At the time of the *Sharpe* judgments, there was a four-year difference between the two.

[54] At para. 229.

[55] Persky and Dixon 2001: 212.

a standard that clearly reflects underlying moral concerns.[56] In contrast, child pornography can be prohibited whether or not it is obscene. This was the judgment given in *New York* v. *Ferber*, the rationale being that the production of child pornography is intrinsically related to the sexual abuse of children.[57] The courts thus differentiate between adult and child pornography. However, as Duncan has recently argued: 'Child pornography and hard-core pornography … are close neighbours in the same lurid neighbourhood. The fact that the Court has elected to treat them as separable doctrinal categories should not obscure the fact that employing children in pornography remains a particularly sickening subgenre of an already diseased field.'[58] Indeed, as I will discuss, Congress has referred back to obscenity laws to prohibit material that cannot be caught by child pornography provisions without falling prey to constitutional challenge.[59]

The specific offences relating to child pornography, including employing, using, persuading, inducing, enticing or coercing 'any minor to engage in … any sexually explicit conduct for the purpose of producing any visual depiction of such conduct'[60] and knowingly receiving, distributing, reproducing and possessing such material[61] are laid out in Chapter 110 of the US Code.[62] A minor is defined as being under the age of eighteen in this chapter.[63] It defines child pornography as a visual depiction where the production of a visual depiction 'involves the use of a minor engaging in sexually explicit conduct',[64] 'such visual depiction is, a digital image, computer image, or computer-generated image that is, or is indistinguishable from, that of a minor engaging in sexually explicit conduct'[65] and 'such a visual depiction has been created, adapted, or modified to appear that an identifiable minor is engaging in sexually explicit conduct'.[66] Thus, this definition encompasses images featuring real children and morphed pseudo-images. Also, as will be discussed, the

[56] *Miller* v. *California* 413 US 15 (1973). Consider, e.g. the following parts of the standard: the need to apply 'contemporary community standards' to ascertain whether the material 'appeals to the prurient interest' and whether the work depicts sexual conduct 'in a patently offensive way' (at 39).

[57] 458 US 747 (1982) at 759 and 764. Particularly, the Supreme Court emphasized the further harm suffered to children through there being a permanent record of their abuse, the market reduction argument and the lack of serious literary, scientific or educational value of child pornography (at 759–60 and 763). See also Adler 2001a: 932.

[58] Duncan 2007: 684. [59] Ibid. [60] 18 USC S. 2251(a). [61] S. 2252A.

[62] The first piece of legislation to insert child pornography provisions into the US Code was the Protection of Children Against Sexual Exploitation Act 1977.

[63] S. 2256(1). The age of sexual consent in the US differs from state to state.

[64] S. 2256(8)(A). [65] S. 2256(8)(B). [66] S. 2256(8)(C).

definition of child pornography under the Code extends to pseudo-images which do not involve the manipulation of a real child's image. Sexually explicit conduct is defined as actual or simulated sexual intercourse, including genital-genital, oral-genital, anal-genital or oral-anal, bestiality, masturbation, sadistic or masochistic abuse or the lascivious exhibition of the genitals or pubic area of a minor.[67] It is the latter example of sexually explicit conduct which has posed the most difficulties in terms of judicial interpretation, as I will discuss shortly. Moreover, it is significant to note that the phrase used to describe such sexually explicit conduct, particularly the term 'lascivious', has clear moral undertones, evidencing that a morality discourse bears some influence upon the definition of child pornography under US law. In *US* v. *Knox*, the Court of Appeals for the Third Circuit referred to the definition of lascivious as being: '[t]ending to excite lust; lewd; indecent; obscene; sexual impurity; tending to deprave morals in respect to sexual relations; licentious'.[68] Finally, with regard to the definition of child pornography, unlike Canadian law, written material that describes sexual activities with a child does not fall under the legal definition of child pornography under US federal law. In fact, provided such material does not meet the obscenity test, it is protected by the First Amendment.

Congress has struggled to create legislation that tackles the problem of pseudo-images, or virtual child pornography, without in some way violating the First Amendment. In *Free Speech Coalition* v. *Reno*, the Court of Appeals for the Ninth Circuit held that provisions under the Child Pornography Prevention Act 1996, which prohibited computer-generated pseudo-photographs and the pandering of material described as depicting children in sexually explicit acts, were unconstitutionally vague and overbroad. They violated the right to receive ideas and freedom of speech under the First Amendment. The first provision prohibited 'any visual depiction, including any photograph, film, video, picture, or computer or computer-generated image or picture' that 'is, or appears to be, of a minor engaging in sexually explicit conduct'.[69] The second prohibited 'a sexually explicit image that is 'advertised, promoted, presented, described or distributed in such a manner that conveys the impression' of depicting 'a minor engaging in sexually explicit conduct'.[70] In giving

[67] S. 2256(2)(A).

[68] 32 F.3d 733 (1994), at 745 (*per* Cowan J). Cowan J was referring to the definition provided in *Black's Law Dictionary*. 1990. 6th edn.: 882.

[69] S. 2256(8)(B) in its pre-revised form, as inserted by the Child Pornography Prevention Act 1996.

[70] S. 2256(8)(D) as it existed under the 1996 Act.

judgment, Molloy J stated that the wording within the provisions, such as 'appears to be' and 'conveys the impression', were highly subjective, causing difficulty in identifying whether a crime had actually been committed.[71] Furthermore, the Court held that, as actual children were not involved in the production of such images, their creation did not cause harm to children.[72]

Subsequently, in *Ashcroft* v. *Free Speech Coalition*, the Supreme Court affirmed the Court of Appeals for the Ninth Circuit's decision, judging that the provisions under the Act were over-broad and unconstitutional. Delivering the opinion of the Court, Kennedy J held that there were no victims of pseudo-photographs and no crime underpinning such images, because they did not bear an intrinsic relationship to the sexual abuse of real children, as did the materials in *Ferber*.[73] One of the government's justifications for criminalizing virtual child pornography was that such material encourages paedophiles to commit crimes against children. The Court rejected this argument, holding that the possibility that speech can encourage unlawful acts was not a sufficient ground for prohibiting it. Further, the government had only demonstrated a remote connection between virtual child pornography and resulting child sexual abuse.[74] The government additionally argued that such material should be banned because it can be used to groom and seduce children,[75] yet Kennedy J challenged such a rationale for the provision. He stated that paedophiles may use 'innocent' material for the same purpose, but it would not be appropriate to ban such material because of this misuse.[76] The Court also held that the government's argument that such images could facilitate crimes against children did not justify the provision, since: 'The evil in question depends upon the actor's unlawful conduct defined as criminal quite apart from any link to the speech in question.'[77] The pandering provision was judged to be substantially overbroad since it was concerned with the way in which sexually explicit material was presented, rather than its actual content. Kennedy J demonstrated the over-breadth of this provision as follows: 'Once a work has been described as child pornography, the taint remains on the speech

[71] At 1095. [72] At 1096.

[73] Ibid.: 250. For a challenge to the view that *Ferber* only recognized the harm of images of real child pornography, see Liu 2007. Cf. Lodato 1998: 1347.

[74] At 253. [75] At 241.

[76] Ibid.: 251. See also the judgment reached by the Court of Appeals for the Ninth Circuit, at 1094.

[77] Ibid.: at 251–2.

in the hands of subsequent possessors, making possession unlawful even though the content otherwise would not be objectionable.'[78]

In light of this judgment, Congress claimed that due to technological advances since *Ferber*, there was now a loophole in the law. Defendants were able to argue that images in their cases were not of real children and the government was required to establish beyond reasonable doubt that they were not computer-generated.[79] Congress thus sought to enact legislation that prohibited virtual child pornography, but remedied the over-breadth of the provisions under the 1996 Act which were in violation of the First Amendment. Consequently, the Prosecutorial Remedies and Other Tools to End the Exploitation of Children Today Act 2003 (PROTECT Act) was passed, revising the federal law provisions on pseudo images. As noted above, S. 2256(8)(B) now prohibits a digital image, computer image or computer-generated image 'that is, or is *indistinguishable from*, that of a minor engaging in sexually explicit conduct'.[80] The term 'indistinguishable' is explained as meaning 'virtually indistinguishable, in that the depiction is such that an ordinary person viewing the depiction would conclude that the depiction is of an actual minor engaged in sexually explicit conduct'.[81] Moreover, the definition 'does not apply to depictions that are drawings, cartoons, sculptures, or paintings depicting minors or adults'.[82] However, despite the justifications given for the need for the federal legislation to encompass pseudo-images, Akdeniz has argued that cases arriving before the courts after *Ashcroft* did not suggest that the ability to prosecute had been adversely affected.[83] Furthermore, the arguments to be found in the majority decision in *Ashcroft* regarding the lack of a proven connection between pseudo-images and harm remain.

The Supreme Court's decision in *Ashcroft* evidences that the inclusion of drawings, cartoons and other non-photographic visual representations depicting children in explicit sexual conduct within the child pornography provisions would not withstand constitutional

78 At 243.

79 PROTECT Act, Title V, S. 501: Findings, paras. 9–10. This was a concern highlighted by O'Connnor J who partially concurred with the majority decision in the Supreme Court in *Ashcroft* (at 264).

80 My emphasis. 81 S. 2256(11).

82 Ibid. The PROTECT Act also created an affirmative defence to charges of distributing or possessing child pornography if the defendant can establish that the image was not produced using an actual minor, although this does not apply to morphed pseudo-images under S. 2256(8)(C). The affirmative defence exists under S. 2252A(C).

83 Akdeniz 2008: 118–19 and 136–9.

challenge. In order to catch the most graphic of such visual representations, Congress included a provision within the PROTECT Act that added a new obscenity offence to the US Code. This provision criminalizes obscene visual representations of the sexual abuse of children which depict minors engaged in sexually explicit conduct.[84] It also prohibits a visual representation that 'depicts an image that is, or appears to be, of a minor engaging in graphic bestiality, sadistic or masochistic abuse, or sexual intercourse, including genital-genital, oral-genital, anal-genital, or oral-anal, whether between persons of the same or opposite sex' and 'lacks serious literary, artistic, political, or scientific value'.[85] This part of the provision is aimed at prohibiting 'a narrow category of "hardcore" pornography involving real or apparent minors'.[86] The images caught under this provision can be visual depictions of any kind, including drawings, cartoons, sculptures or paintings. Therefore, the government has been able to fall back on obscenity provisions to achieve what it would have failed to do through the federal law on child pornography.[87]

Until 2008, the 'pandering provision' under the PROTECT Act (which now exists under S. 2252A) had been held to fall foul of the First Amendment. This provision targets individuals who advertise, distribute, offer or solicit material presented as child pornography. In *US* v. *Williams*,[88] the Court of Appeals for the Eleventh Circuit held that the pandering provision was unconstitutionally over-broad and vague, that it 'wrongly punishes individuals for the non-inciteful expression of their thoughts and beliefs'.[89] As the provision covers material that is presented, or purports to be child pornography, the court concluded that it criminalizes pandering speech 'even when the touted materials are clean or non-existent', and 'deluded' pandering.[90] However, in May 2008, the Supreme Court reversed the Eleventh Circuit's judgment,[91] ruling that the provision was not over-broad or vague. In delivering the majority judgment, Scalia J held that offers to engage in illegal transactions are

[84] S. 1466A(a)(1). [85] S. 1466A(a)(2).

[86] (House Commentary) HR Rep. No. 108–66 (2003), at 62.

[87] The provision withstood constitutional challenge under the First and Fifth Amendments in *US* v. *Whorley* 2005 US Dist LEXIS 19606.

[88] 444 F.3d 1286 (11th Cir. 2006).

[89] See www.ca11.uscourts.gov/opinions/ops/200415128.pdf, at 30.

[90] Ibid.: 26 and 27. Note also that whilst it is a defence under the PROTECT Act if it can be established that the material in question in fact depicts actual adults and no actual minors were involved in the production of the material (S. 2252A(c)), this defence does not apply to the 'pandering' provision under S. 2252A.

[91] *US* v. *Williams* 553 US (2008). See www.supremecourtus.gov/opinions/07pdf/06–694.pdf.

categorically excluded from First Amendment protection. What is more, just because 'close' cases could be envisioned, this did not make the provision vague and the provision contained no indeterminacy as to the fact that must be proved.[92]

In addition to the federal law on child pornography, legislation which criminalizes child pornography has been enacted in many states and such laws have also been subject to constitutional challenges.[93] In *Osbourne* v. *Ohio*, the Supreme Court held that a state statute prohibiting the possession of child pornography was constitutional, notwithstanding the individual right to receive information in the privacy of one's home, because of the strength of the state's interest in protecting children.[94] The state presented the same justification for criminalizing possession as that given in this jurisdiction: 'it is now difficult, if not impossible, to solve the child pornography problem by only attacking production and distribution'.[95] It was emphasized that the prohibition on the possession of child pornography protected the victims of child pornography, reduced the market for the exploitative use of children and encouraged the destruction of child pornography. Furthermore, the majority judgment served to indicate that the judges accepted evidence put before the court which suggested that child sexual abusers use child pornography as part of their grooming process, as a seductive method prior to committing child sexual abuse.[96]

The definition of child pornography under US law: protecting or sexualizing children?

> Child pornography law has changed the way we look at children … The law requires us to study pictures of children to uncover their potential sexual meanings, and in doing so, it explicitly exhorts us to take on the perspective of the pedophile.[97]

Whilst the English legislation remains silent on what amounts to an indecent image of a child, leaving this for the jury and judicial interpretation, as we have seen, the federal legislation in the United States provides a list of what amounts to sexually explicit conduct for the purposes

[92] Ibid.: 20.

[93] By way of example, see *People* v. *Geever* 122 Ill. 2d 313 (1988); and *State* v. *Foster* 838 S.W.2d 60 (Mp. Ct. App. E.D. 1992).

[94] In contrast to the legal position upon the possession of obscene materials and the right to privacy, on which, see *Stanley* v. *Georgia* 394 US 557 (1969).

[95] At 110. Note Brennan J's dissenting view upon this, at 145.

[96] At 111. For a critique of the decision in this case, see Quigley 1991.

[97] Adler 2001b: 256.

of the child pornography law. The first four types of such conduct bear some resemblance to levels two to five of the Sentencing Advisory Panel's league table, which assists the English judiciary in deciding on the appropriate sentence to pass for offences relating to indecent images of children.[98] However, the final category of such conduct under the federal legislation, the lascivious exhibition of the genitals or pubic area of a minor, has no English parallel. In contrast to the other categories listed, it is much more a matter of interpretation as to the nature of the image. It bears similarities to the Canadian legislative provision that requires the judge to assess whether a sexual organ or the anal region of a person under the age of eighteen years is being depicted for a sexual purpose, an approach which I have already critiqued.

In *US* v. *Dost*,[99] a multi-factor list was articulated which can assist in the decision as to whether an image consitutes the lascivious exhibition of a minor's genitals or pubic area:

1. whether the focal point of the visual depiction is on the child's genitalia or pubic area;
2. whether the setting of the visual depiction is sexually suggestive, i.e. in a place or pose generally associated with sexual activity;
3. whether the child is depicted in an unnatural pose, or in inappropriate attire, considering the age of a child;
4. whether the child is fully or partially clothed, or nude;
5. whether the visual depiction suggests sexual coyness or a willingness to engage in sexual activity; and,
6. whether the visual depiction is intended or designed to elicit a sexual response in the viewer.

This multi-factor test has become known as the '*Dost* test'. It is not necessary that the image displays all of these factors and other factors may be relevant. The *Dost* test has since been applied in numerous cases, one of which was *US* v. *Knox*. Here, the materials in question were video tapes featuring girls between the age of ten and seventeen dancing and striking provocative poses, wearing bathing costumes, leotards and underwear. Whilst there was no nudity depicted in the videos, for extended periods of time the camera zoomed in on the girls' genital areas. The Court of Appeals for the Third Circuit was required to interpret the lascivious exhibition provision to ascertain whether such material could fall under the definition of child pornography. The Court found that, in ordinary

[98] See Chapter 2, at 58. [99] F.Supp. 828 (S.D.Cal.1986).

legal usage, the term 'exhibit' meant to show or put on display. Having explicated the meaning of 'lascivious' as noted earlier, the Court held that 'lascivious exhibition' thus meant 'a depiction which displays or brings forth to view in order to attract notice to the genitals or pubic area of children, in order to excite lustfulness or sexual stimulation in the viewer'.[100] It was concluded that the genital area did not need to be nude or partially nude to be shown or displayed, and there was no nudity requirement in the *Dost* test. Provided the photographer unnaturally focused on a child's clothed genital area with the obvious intent of producing an image sexually arousing to paedophiles, then the harm Congress was attempting to eradicate was present.[101]

There are serious difficulties with this interpretation of the provision. Focusing on the viewer's interpretation of and reaction to the image is problematic, given research findings that indicate that individuals with a sexual interest in children are stimulated by non-pornographic imagery of children.[102] When this is combined with the fact that there is no requirement that the depicted child be nude, the range of material that could potentially fall under the definition of child pornography becomes worryingly expansive. This was not a concern for the Court in *Knox*. In fact, Cowen J stated that: 'Only a miniscule fraction' of images of children would be 'sufficiently sexually suggestive and unnaturally focussed on the genitalia' and thus capable of amounting to a lascivious exhibition of a minor's genitals.[103] However, the way in which the Court interpreted 'lascivious exhibition' to make the intention of the photographer and, most importantly, the reaction of the viewer so central to the matter, does not provide reassurance that this is the case. Take, for instance, a photograph of a child in a swimsuit on the beach which has been surreptitiously taken. The photographer has centred in on the child's genital area and intends to distribute this image to others whom he knows will be sexually excited by it. According to the decision in *Knox*, this could be interpreted as an image that constitutes the lascivious exhibition of a minor's genitals. Surely this evidences the over-breadth of this provision, as interpreted in *Knox*, and brings into question the crucial matter of the harm caused to the child, the harm Congress was attempting to eradicate?

Both Danay and Adler are especially critical of the effects of this provision under the federal legislation and its judicial interpretation. Their

[100] At 745 (*per* Cowen J). [101] At 744 and 750. [102] See Chapter 4, at 185–6.
[103] At 752.

concern is that whether the image is a 'lascivious exhibition' becomes a subjective matter of what the viewer perceives and, that following *Knox*, even the child's shrouded body can be construed as sexual. For Danay:

> The Court in *Knox* required judges in future cases to carefully, explicitly and publicly scrutinize the genital and pubic regions of clothed minors in an effort to reveal the images' sexually stimulating nature … Through such analyses, police, judges, lawyers, and, ultimately, members of the public are forced to closely inspect increasingly innocuous images of children (and children generally) to determine whether the depicted children might be acting in a sexual manner.[104]

Such legislative endeavours and judicial interpretations may have extended the remit of the law and, no doubt, Congress would argue, have enabled more of those individuals who pose a threat to children to be caught. However, as is the case with the social discourses surrounding the exposure of children's naked bodies in public, it is the negative impact that this presentation of children's bodies has on children themselves that I am concerned about. In *Knox*, Cowan J considered the effects on the child of an image which constitutes a lascivious exhibition of their genital area, asserting that: 'The child is treated as a sexual object and the permanent record of this embarrassing and humiliating experience produces … detrimental effects to the mental health of the child'.[105] However, this could well be the potential effect of the legal response to photographs of the child's body, such as the example I give above of a child on the beach. Whilst those who are sexually stimulated by such a photograph are treating the child as a sexual object, is this not also the consequence of the court's dissection and scrutiny of the image? Furthermore, the written judgment of the court would amount to 'the permanent record' of the 'embarrassing and humiliating experience' of this dissection. Similar concerns would seem to trouble Higonnet. In analyzing US law, she comments: 'Recent child pornography law casts shame on the child's body. When every photograph of a child's body becomes criminally suspect, how are we going to avoid children feeling guilt about any image of their bodies?'[106] Again, as with social discourses on the display of children's naked bodies in public, this is a clear example of a powerful and dangerous discourse which frames children's bodies as sexual.[107]

[104] Danay 2005: 155–6; and Adler 2001a: 955–6. [105] At 750.
[106] Higonnet 1998: 180. [107] Adler 2001b: 270; and Danay 2005: 153.

THE CRIMINALIZATION OF GROOMING THROUGH COMMUNICATION SYSTEMS IN CANADA AND THE UNITED STATES

The legislature in this jurisdiction is not unique in choosing to target grooming that occurs online. Canadian and US laws criminalize grooming which occurs via communication systems, and I shall briefly examine how both countries have responded to this particular method of forming a relationship with a child in order to facilitate sexual abuse.

Section 172.1 of the Canadian Criminal Code[108] criminalizes 'luring a child', which involves the communication with a child by means of a computer system for the purpose of facilitating the commission of one of the listed (primarily) sexual offences against that child.[109] The penalty is a maximum of five years' imprisonment. Importantly, in contrast to English law, Canadian law criminalizes the communication itself without a requirement of actually meeting or travelling with the intention to meet the child.[110] This thus casts the net much wider, imposing liability at a stage earlier in the online grooming process.

There is a further indication of the broad nature of the offence. Under s. 172.1, although almost all of the offences that the individual must intend to facilitate are sexual, two relate to the abduction of a child and one to corrupting morals.[111] In *R.* v. *Brown*,[112] the defendant pleaded guilty to the s. 172.1 offence for the purposes of committing the offence of abducting a person under sixteen under s. 280. Although there was evidence that he was romantically involved with M, the thirteen-year-old girl he communicated with online and subsequently met, there was no evidence of any sexual activity or discussion of such activity at any point during the relationship that developed between them. M had told the defendant that she had an unhappy home life and he was concerned for her safety and wellbeing. The defendant and M arranged for her and her friend to leave their homes and stay with him. Whalen J accepted that there was no evidence of sexual intent, commenting that:

108 Introduced by the Criminal Amendment Act 2001.

109 Three subsections deal with children under eighteen years of age, under sixteen and under fourteen respectively, as different sexual offences exist in relation to these different age groups.

110 Although see 'Alberta judge acquits man in internet luring case', CTV News report, 1 April 2006, www.ctv.ca/servlet/ArticleNews/story/CTVNews/20060401/alberta_luring_cp_060401?s_name=&no_ads=.

111 Under ss. 280, 281 and 163.1 respectively.

112 [2006] OJ 1523. For other examples of cases involving the s. 172.1 offence, see *R.* v. *Deck* 2006 ABCA 92; and *R.* v. *Harvey* [2004] OJ 1389.

> Virtually all of the reported sentencing cases deal with situations where the perpetrator had a clear sexual purpose, and to that end used the computer to lure the child into participating in some sexual act, or sexual materials were communicated to the child … I agree with the defence that this is not the typical Internet luring case involving identifiable sexual grooming or other direct acts of sexualisation.[113]

Nonetheless, the judge concluded that it still amounted to a very serious offence that warranted a term of one year's imprisonment. The judgment evidences that the s. 172.1 offence can thus be committed 'without there being an underlying sexual purpose'.[114] In contrast, whilst the offence of abducting a girl under eighteen[115] is one that the individual can intend to commit for the purposes of the English offence of meeting a child following sexual grooming, this is the only listed offence that is not sexual and the crime is framed around *sexual* grooming.

Turning to the United States, under federal law it is an offence to use the mail or any facility or means of interstate or foreign commerce to knowingly persuade, induce, entice or coerce any individual under eighteen years of age to engage in any unlawful sexual activity, or to attempt to do so. The maximum sentence that can be passed upon conviction for this offence is substantial: thirty years' imprisonment.[116] In *US* v. *Kaye*,[117] the appellant unsuccessfully argued that the offence unconstitutionally criminalized speech. The Court of Appeals for the Fourth Circuit held that: 'The First Amendment does not protect attempts to coerce and entice a minor to engage in illegal sex … Speech attempting to arrange the sexual abuse of children is no more constitutionally protected than speech attempting to arrange any other crime.'[118] It is clear that the offence of attempt is still committed even if the actual commission of an act of unlawful sexual activity is impossible. In *US* v. *Davies*,[119] the defendant engaged in explicit sexual conversations in an internet chatroom with an undercover officer posing as a female child. There was no defence to the charge of attempt because the non-existence of this female child made the completion of the actual offence a factual impossibility. The court also held that the offence of attempting to coerce and entice a minor to engage in sexual activity was not unconstitutionally over-broad.

In addition to this federal offence, there are also numerous state laws which prohibit similar conduct. For example, Georgia's Computer or

113 At para. 103. 114 At para. 118.

115 Under s. 7 of the Criminal Law Amendment Act 1885.

116 18 USC S. 2422(b). 117 2007 WL 1109934 (4th Cir. 2 April 2007). 118 At 15–16.

119 2006 WL 226038 (C.A.10 (Utah)).

Electronic Pornography and Child Exploitation Prevention Act of 2007[120] criminalizes the intentional or wilful utilization of 'a computer on-line service or Internet service … to seduce, solicit, lure, or entice, or attempt to seduce, solicit, lure, or entice a child or another person believed by such person to be a child to commit any [specified sex offence]'.[121] Furthermore, the Act also makes it an offence to engage in 'obscene Internet contact with a child'.[122] Such contact is described as involving 'any matter containing explicit verbal descriptions or narrative accounts of sexually explicit nudity, sexual conduct, sexual excitement, or sadomasochistic abuse that is intended to arouse or satisfy the sexual desire of either the child or the person'. As another example of state legislation, the CyberCrimes Against Children Act came into force in October 2007 in Florida. This legislation makes it an offence to contact a child online and then attempt to meet that child for the specific purpose of sexually abusing her.[123]

Thus, it is apparent that Canadian and US legislators have busied themselves with criminalizing grooming through modern communications. As with this jurisdiction, this is clearly the form of grooming that has been prioritized in these societies, with the offence being broader in Canada and the maximum sentence being substantially higher in the United States.

RIGHTS AND CONCERNS WITHIN THE ENGLISH LAW CONTEXT

The particular individual rights of privacy and free speech have formed the backbone of challenges to child pornography laws in Canada and the United States and, to a lesser extent, the laws on online enticement in the United States. Whilst I will consider those rights here in the context of English law, I am also going to focus on the right to a fair trial and, more broadly, the impact on those suspected of child pornography and grooming offences and the issue of fair labelling.

The impact upon those suspected and convicted of child pornography and grooming offences

I have already noted the social stigma attached to any behaviour related to child sexual abuse. The impact of being suspected of committing

[120] Ga. Code Ann. s.16–12–100.2. [121] Ibid.:(1). [122] Ibid.:(1).

[123] See further http://myfloridalegal.com/pages.nsf/Main/DF75DF6F54BDA68E8525727B00645478 and flhouse.gov/sections/HouseNews/preview.aspx?PressReleaseId=85. Various other offences relating to grooming through communication systems exist in other states. For the law in Virginia, see *Brooker* v. *Commonwealth of Virginia* 41 Va. App. 609, 587 S.E.2d 732 (2003).

offences related to child pornography or grooming (and then in some cases, arrested, charged and convicted), is especially significant and grievous.[124] There are numerous media reports detailing the negative effects on individuals' careers, family lives and mental health.[125]

As discussed in Chapter 1, the United Kingdom's Operation Ore was one part of the international investigation of internet-based child pornography code-named Operation Avalanche. Akdeniz has highlighted concerns about the reliability of the evidence passed by the FBI to British police.[126] The impact on innocent individuals of being investigated as suspects by Operation Ore is made abundantly clear by the case of a doctor whose credit card was fraudulently used. He lost his job because he was a suspect. At trial, his name was cleared when his electronic diary revealed that he could not have visited the child pornography site at the time stated on the database used by Operation Avalanche. Yet, despite his innocence being proven, he was not reinstated.[127] Another suspect in the Operation Ore investigation was a Scottish man who was never charged, although he was suspended by his employers for fourteen months during the investigation and his marriage ended. A naval officer was suspended from the Royal Navy when he was investigated for downloading child pornography as part of Operation Ore, even though the Navy was aware that there was insufficient evidence to press charges. He was found dead at his home shortly after his suspension.[128] Luckily for another suspect, Brian Cooper, he was able to prove that he had been a victim of credit card fraud and thus clear his name, although his home was first searched and he was taken away by police officers in front of his family.[129] It has been argued that numerous suspects were the innocent victims of wholesale credit card fraud.[130] According to one newspaper report, thirty-three individuals have committed suicide following investigation as part of Operation Ore.[131] The Canadian investigation resulting from Operation Avalanche also led to at least one suspect committing suicide after he lost his job, reputation and friends, despite the charges against him being withdrawn.[132] Moreover, there is a significant

124 See also Gillespie 2005: 30.

125 See the Introduction: n. 85.

126 Akdeniz 2008: 26–7 and 275. See also 'Child porn accused tell of ordeal', BBC News report, 5 October 2007, http://news.bbc.co.uk/go/pr/fr/-/1/hi/uk/6642465.stm; and 'Is Operation Ore the UK's worst-ever policing scandal?', *The Guardian*, 26 April 2007.

127 See 'Global child porn probe led to false accusations', CBC News, 14 March 2006.

128 See 'No evidence against man in child porn inquiry who "killed himself"', *The Independent*, 1 October 2005.

129 Ibid.

130 See 'Child porn accused tell of ordeal', above, n. 126.

131 Above, n. 128.

132 Above, n. 127.

negative impact on the families of those who are suspected of committing offences relating to child pornography and child sexual abuse.[133]

In light of these examples, there is surely a strong case for arguing that the anonymity of those arrested and charged for offences relating to child pornography and grooming and, indeed, other child sexual offences, should be preserved unless and until they are proven guilty.[134] The anonymity of victims can be provided for in cases involving sexual offences against children through two legislative provisions.[135] In some cases, it may be possible to prevent the identification of the defendant being released, if this could lead to the identification of the child.[136] However, the argument that the defendant's anonymity should be provided for his own protection rather than the victim's is more controversial. It could face challenges on the basis of the public interest in evidence in criminal cases being communicated to the public,[137] and on the grounds that naming defendants deters others from committing offences.[138] Further, it could be contended that allowing anonymity in child sexual offence cases is unfair, as defendants will receive different treatment depending on the offence they are charged with.[139] However, given the particularly

[133] See 'The real truth about paedophiles and us', *The Guardian*, 9 January 1998; and Critcher 2006: 139.

[134] An amendment was introduced during the House of Lords' debates upon the Sexual Offences Bill which would have allowed for the anonymity of suspects and defendants alleged to have committed a sexual offence until charged. The amendment was defeated. See Hansard HL Deb. 18 November 2003: column 1911. Currently, there is a system of guidance from the Association of Chief Police Officers that the media should not release details of an allegation relating to a sex offence until a defendant is charged. See Hansard HC Deb. 6 June 2006: column 230.

[135] Children and Young Persons Act 1933, s. 39 (under which a judge can make an order to restrict publicity of a case in order to avoid the identification of any child involved in the proceedings). There is an amendment pending to this provision which will cause it to apply in proceedings other than criminal proceedings. See also the Sexual Offences (Amendment) Act 1992, s. 1 (which automatically provides for the lifetime anonymity of victims of numerous sexual offences, including the offences related to child pornography and grooming under the SOA 2003 – see s. 2 of the 1992 Act).

[136] As a result of a practical application of the Children and Young Persons Act 1933, s. 39(a), although 'section 39 does not as a matter of law empower a court to order in terms that the names of the defendants be not published'. See *Ex parte Godwin and Others* [1992] QB 190, 196; and *R. (Gazette Media Co Ltd)* v. *Teeside Crown Court* [2005] EWCA Crim. 1983.

[137] See Gillespie and Bettinson 2007: 116; and *Attorney-General* v. *Leveller Magazine Ltd* [1979] AC 440: 'As a general rule the English system of administering justice does require that it be done in public … as respects proceedings in the court itself [this] requires that they should be held in open court to which the press and public are admitted and that, in criminal cases at any rate, all evidence communicated to the court is communicated publicly.' *Per* Lord Diplock, 449–50.

[138] See *Ex parte Godwin*, 195.

[139] See, for instance, Hansard HC Deb. 6 June 2006: column 230.

severe stigma attached to anyone suspected of committing child sexual abuse, and the potential grave repercussions for their families, I would argue that an exception to the norm is defensible in such cases. In addition, the courts have recognized that the general rule that justice be seen to be done in public can be departed from if this is considered 'necessary in order to serve the ends of justice'.[140] The above cases are just some examples to indicate that the lack of anonymity for those arrested and charged with child sex offences works against the interests of justice.

The right to privacy and freedom of expression

The presence of the Human Rights Act 1998 (HRA)[141] and the United Kingdom's obligations under the European Convention on Human Rights (ECHR) have led to individual rights concerns infiltrating cases involving child pornography.[142] It is the rights to privacy and freedom of expression that are the most pertinent. Under Art. 8: 'Everyone has the right to respect for his private and family life, his home and his correspondence.' The right to freedom of expression under Art. 10 includes 'freedom to hold opinions and to receive and impart information and ideas without interference by public authority and regardless of frontiers'. However, neither right is absolute. Both can be justifiably violated for the protection of the rights and freedoms of others (especially significant in light of the United Kingdom's obligations under the UN Convention on the Rights of the Child), or if this is necessary to protect morals.[143] Unsurprisingly, continued legislative and judicial acceptance of the argument that children are harmed by any activity involving child pornography, and the strength of moral attitudes towards such behaviour, means that the pendulum has swung resolutely away from safeguarding rights to privacy and freedom of expression. In *R.* v. *Smethurst*, for instance, protecting children from exploitation was stated to be a legitimate reason for infringing either of the rights under Arts. 8 and 10.[144] As Johnson observes: 'Child pornography pushes the furthest boundaries of the principle of freedom of expression, as such content tends to fall

[140] *Attorney-General* v. *Leveller Magazine Ltd*, 450, *per* Lord Diplock. See also O'Donnell and Milner's empirical research regarding the views of district court and circuit court judges in Ireland on this point. 2008: 139.

[141] See HRA, Sch. 1, Pt. 1. Statutory provisions must be interpreted in a manner that is compatible with the rights under the HRA (see HRA, s. 3).

[142] See, for instance, *R.* v. *Smethurst*; *O'Carroll* v. *UK*; and Chapter 2, at 57.

[143] See Art. 8(2) and Art. 10(2). Also note the Court of Appeal's judgment in *R.* v. *Chief Constable of North Wales, ex parte Thorpe* [1998] 3 WLR 57.

[144] At para. 24.

outside almost any argument for the value of protecting what individuals wish to write, say, or draw.'[145]

In Chapter 3, I assessed the way in which the making, distributing and possessing child pornography offences and the offence relating to grooming can be legitimated on the basis of harm and harmful exploitation. However, there is one specific area of the child pornography law, that regarding completely fabricated pseudo-images, that is much harder to defend on this basis and should therefore be more vulnerable to challenge under Arts. 8 and 10. Since the creation, distribution and possession of these images do not cause direct harm to children, it is much harder to make a persuasive argument that their criminalization is a justifiable violation of Arts. 8 and 10. There is simply a question of possible harm if the market argument holds true, and seeking out pseudo-images encourages the creators of child pornography to abuse real children. Whilst a privacy argument could be challenged by the claim that such images might be used as part of the grooming process, as Akdeniz notes, criminal offences such as the SOA offence relating to grooming and other sexual offences may well be applicable.[146] All that remains, therefore, is to cite the moral repugnance society feels towards images which depict child sexual abuse, even if fabricated, and to argue that breaching the rights to privacy and freedom of expression is justified to protect morals. However, reliance on the morality discourse surrounding child pornography to violate vital individual rights should not suffice to satisfy the demands of a liberal society. Statutory provisions that would be a more legitimate violation of privacy and freedom of expression rights would be ones which only criminalize child pornography where a real child has been harmfully exploited by the creation of the image.[147]

The right to a fair trial and previous convictions

Under Art. 6 of the ECHR: 'In the determination of … any criminal charge against him, everyone is entitled to a fair and public hearing within a reasonable time by an independent and impartial tribunal established by law.' Further, under Art. 6(2): 'Everyone charged with a criminal offence shall be presumed innocent until proved guilty according to law.' I will argue here that statutory rules governing the admissibility of previous convictions may potentially have an impact on the right to a

[145] Johnson 2006: 377. [146] Akdeniz 2008: 92.

[147] As my analysis in Chapter 3 should demonstrate, this would include morphed pseudo-images.

fair trial possessed by an individual accused of an offence related to child pornography or grooming, or an individual who is subsequently accused of another non-related offence.

The Criminal Justice Act 2003 (CJA 2003) has allowed for the increased admissibility of the defendant's previous convictions. Under the CJA 2003, bad character evidence is admissible through one of seven 'gateways' under s. 101. The most significant of these for my purposes is s. 101(1)(d), which states that the evidence is admissible if 'it is relevant to an important matter in issue between the defendant and the prosecution'. Whether the defendant has a propensity to commit offences of the kind with which he has been charged is stated to be an important matter in issue between the defendant and the prosecution under s. 103. It is possible to establish this propensity through evidence that the defendant has been convicted of an offence of the same description as the one with which he is currently charged.[148] These provisions have led Dennis to conclude that the once-prohibited chain of reasoning at common law – because a defendant previously committed an offence of the same type as that of which he is now accused, he is more likely to be guilty – is now 'positively encouraged'.[149] According to two different research studies, mock jurors were more likely to reach a guilty verdict if told a defendant had a recent previous conviction for a similar offence.[150] I submit that this is especially problematic for the defendant who has previously committed an offence relating to child pornography and grooming, because of the moral abhorrence attached to such behaviour. Upon hearing that the defendant has a prior conviction for the same offence, the clear risk is that the jury becomes prejudiced towards him. Indeed, 'the nature of the misconduct may so poison their minds against [him] as to cause them to convict in circumstances when the other evidence would not have persuaded them to do so'.[151] According to Lloyd-Bostock, research indicates that, in the context of charges involving child sex abuse, many potential jurors feel that they would be unable to be fair to the defendant purely because of their reaction to the nature of the charge.[152]

[148] S. 103(2)(a). See *R.* v. *Hanson* [2005] EWCA Crim. 824 for further clarification upon the circumstances when previous convictions establish a propensity to commit offences of the kind charged. On the defendant's application, the judge can exercise his or her discretion to exclude evidence admissible through s. 101(1)(d) if it would have such an adverse effect on the fairness of the proceedings that it should not be admitted (s.101(3)).

[149] Dennis 2007: 805.

[150] Law Commission 1996: para. 7.7. See also Lloyd-Bostock 2000: 737.

[151] Law Commission, ibid.: para. 5.18.

[152] Lloyd-Bostock 2000: 738.

It can also be possible for the prosecution to adduce evidence that shows a 'disposition towards misconduct'.[153] Take, for example, a defendant on trial for the possession of child pornography. If he makes an assertion that he does not have a sexual interest in children, for example, the prosecution may be permitted to admit evidence that he had previously stated such an interest under s. 101(1)(f) of the CJA 2003, in order to correct the false impression given by the defendant. Again, the strong public revulsion towards such behaviour could cause the jury to become morally prejudiced,[154] and lead them to convict the defendant even if the evidence against him lacks probative force.[155] In such circumstances, there is a definite risk that the defendant's right to a fair trial is compromised.

The fact that a defendant has a previous conviction for an offence relating to child pornography or grooming could also have a bearing on whether he subsequently receives a fair trial, even if he is charged with a completely different offence. For instance, an individual is charged with robbery and, in court, the defence adduces evidence relating to the defendant's lack of previous convictions. The prosecution is then permitted to refer to a past conviction, which is for the possession of child pornography.[156] The jury may consequently be more likely to convict the individual of robbery on the basis that anyone who possesses child pornography is a monster and must be a criminal.[157] The disclosure of this previously imposed conviction for reprehensible conduct causes the sanction imposed for possessing child pornography to effectively be carried over, and to taint the individual's subsequent behaviour.

It seems, therefore, that where previous convictions can now be introduced, there is a real risk that a defendant who has been convicted for an offence regarding child pornography or grooming could suffer an infringement of his right to a fair trial. In cases where the defendant's trial is not prejudiced by the matter of previous convictions, he may still be branded with an unfair and inappropriate label, as I will now discuss.

153 See CJA 2003 s. 98.

154 Law Commission 1996: para. 7.10.

155 See Law Commission 2001: para. 8.18; and Dennis 2007: 758.

156 Again, such evidence could be admissible under gateway s. 101(1)(f).

157 I am grateful to Peter Rowe for suggesting this scenario. According to the findings of the Oxford research study referred to by the Law Commission, if mock jurors were told that the defendant had a previous conviction for indecent assault upon a child, they were more likely to consider him untruthful and deserving of punishment. Law Commission 1996: para. 7.11; and Lloyd-Bostock 2000: 748.

The matter of fair labelling

In critiquing Canadian law's treatment of 'the possession of harmless sexual representations' under the same statutory provision as offences that cause direct harm to children, Danay comments that 'the producers and consumers of materials that did not involve any harm to children in their production are falsely branded as "child pornographers," "Sex offenders," and "pedophiles"'.[158] His criticism can be applied more broadly to legal and societal labels attached to offences involving child pornography in this jurisdiction. According to Ashworth; 'Fairness demands that offenders be labelled and punished in proportion to their wrongdoing'.[159] The issue of fair labelling would seem to be of particular pertinence in the context of individuals convicted for offences relating to pseudo-images, especially completely fabricated pseudo-images. For, in order to reflect the degree of wrongdoing, there should be a clear demarcation between the labels attached to producers of material which causes children to suffer harm, and those who create completely computer-generated material that does not exploit real children. It is thus imperative that the Court of Appeal's statement in *R.* v. *Oliver* that it 'will usually be desirable' for each count on an indictment to specify whether the image in question is a real or pseudo-image, is always followed in all such cases.[160]

Fair labelling is also an issue for those individuals who download child pornography and are convicted for the making offence. I have already noted the blurring of the distinction between the making and possession offences through judicial interpretation. The consequence of this is that, although downloading images equates with possession in terms of wrongdoing, the making offence can be the actual charge in such cases. Thus, for example, in *R.* v. *Breeze*,[161] the Court of Appeal judgment records the twenty counts of making indecent photographs or pseudo photographs that the appellant was convicted for. All of these counts in fact relate to the downloading of child pornography.[162] This could be especially problematic if the individual applies for a job and the prospective employer requests a Criminal Records Bureau disclosure check. If this disclosure only reveals what the individual was convicted for, further enquiries may not be made by the potential employer, who could take the disclosure at face value and automatically assume he has sexually

158 Danay 2005: 185. 159 Ashworth 2006: 88–9.

160 At para. 15. See also *R.* v. *Thompson* [2004] 2 Cr. App. R. 16, para. 11.

161 [2007] EWCA Crim. 3442. 162 See also *R.* v. *Bloomfield* [2007] EWCA Crim. 3394.

abused a child in order to make child pornography. The individual's criminal record would thus give a false impression of the extent of his wrongdoing and unfairly stigmatize him.[163] The appropriateness of the label of 'sex offender' could also be questioned for those who download and possess child pornography and who create a fabricated pseudo-image.[164] Despite the fact that these individuals have not caused direct, primary harm to children,[165] the sex offender label implies that the individual has committed a sexual contact offence. A final issue here with regards to fair labelling is that media reports on child pornography cases can also misrepresent an individual's wrongdoing, given the tendency to sensationalize and to make use of abbreviated non-legal terms.[166]

The discourse of rights is applicable to both parties involved in child pornography and grooming – the defendant and the child victim, although, in the case of the child, rights are directed more towards protection. In the remainder of this chapter, I examine the protection that the international community provides to children in this context.

THE INTERNATIONAL COMMUNITY'S PRIORITIZATION OF CHILDREN'S RIGHTS AND PROTECTION

Child pornography and grooming are not confined within legal borders, and have increasingly come to be seen as worldwide problems. As a consequence, and especially in light of the increased worldwide availability of the internet as a means of facilitating behaviour related to both phenomena and other forms of child exploitation, international protection for children has increased in recent years.

The biggest challenge for those bodies that have sought to provide children with international protection from exploitation is achieving harmonization between different national laws. Whilst worldwide unanimity of agreement upon the importance of protecting children from the harms of exploitation may be realizable, when it comes to the intricacies

[163] See Chalmers and Leverick 2008: 225–6 and 234.

[164] The details of any individual convicted, cautioned or released from prison for a sexual offence against children or adults since September 1997 are contained on the register. Individuals convicted under s. 1 of the PCA and s. 160 of the CJA must register (although in some cases, this is only if they have been sentenced to at least twelve months' imprisonment). See Sch. 3, (13) and (15) of the SOA.

[165] Although note my argument that knowledge of distribution and possession could cause the child who features in the image to suffer further primary harm. See Chapter 3, at 118–20.

[166] See Chalmers and Leverick 2008: 228.

of how this should be ensured at the legal level, difficulties emerge because of cultural and political variances. According to Archard, as far as the international promotion of children's welfare and rights is concerned: 'any agreement across very different political, religious, moral and cultural identities and traditions about how, even at a minimum, children should be treated has been secured only by deliberate ambiguity of language or resort to the lowest common denominator'.[167]

As will become apparent, international agreements pertaining to children's rights to protection from behaviour related to sexual abuse all adopt a very similar approach, focusing on exploitation, which I have emphasized as the harm of child pornography and grooming. It is arguable, therefore, that protecting children from exploitation is the crucial starting point or, to employ Archard's terminology, the 'lowest common denominator'. Thus, it is vital that jurisdictions such as England, Denmark and Hungary cast aside legal standards like indecency and obscenity, which revolve around the wrong conception of harm, to ensure that exploitation can truly become the accepted international presentation of harm. More problematically, the international agreements I will discuss consistently present the exploitation as sexual. Whilst this is understandable, given their focus, I have called for a more universalized conception of exploitation that does not place an emphasis on the sexual. As I have argued, there is a real risk of over-prioritizing sexual exploitation above other forms of exploitation, and it is a potentially damaging morality discourse that highlights the sexual in the context of children's bodies.[168]

There is one other matter which I wish to raise before discussing various endeavours of the United Nations, the Council of Europe and the European Union to protect children from sexual exploitation.[169] All of these endeavours are framed around protection, even the UN Convention on the Rights of the Child, which promotes a rights discourse. This is unsurprising, since emphasizing the protectionist stance towards children is most likely to generate international agreement. However, as I have shown regarding this jurisdiction, prioritizing children's rights to protection means that other significant rights, particularly the right to autonomy, are left by the wayside. As Wendy and

[167] Archard 1999: 85. See also Boyden 1997: 203; and James and James 2004: 91.

[168] See Chapter 3, at 139–40; and Chapter 4, at 189–91.

[169] An in-depth examination of all relevant efforts to combat child pornography at European and UN levels is undertaken by Akdeniz 2008: Pt. 2. For the purposes of this work, I have chosen to focus on the main, most directly relevant Conventions and decisions.

Rex Stainton Rogers note: 'Efforts to protect children from sexual abuse and exploitation have led to policies and practice which can deny children quite fundamental human and citizenship rights.'[170] Moreover, the international children's rights discourse that does exist is more likely to be reflective of European and North American cultural ideologies.[171]

The United Nations Convention on the Rights of the Child and the Optional Protocol on the Sale of Children, Child Prostitution and Child Pornography

The Convention on the Rights of the Child was adopted by the United Nations in 1989 and came into force on 2 September 1990.[172] It has since been ratified by all but two countries in the world: Somalia and the United States.[173] Member States are publicly and internationally accountable for their commitment to the Convention and their protection of children's rights.[174] A child is defined as being below eighteen years of age.[175] Children's rights to autonomy are promoted in Art. 12 of the Convention, which I have already discussed in Chapter 2. The Article emphasizes that children should have the right to freely express their views in all matters affecting them, and that due weight should be given to their views. In light of my analysis of the failure of our laws regarding child pornography to respect older teenagers' autonomy and sexual liberty, it is significant that the Committee on the Rights of the Child has criticized the United Kingdom for its record in failing to comply with Art. 12.[176] Based on progress reports submitted by the government to the Committee in 1994 and 1999 regarding its implementation of the Convention's provisions, the Committee emphasized the government's under-prioritization of children's rights and noted that 'most children are not aware of their rights included in the Convention'.[177] The most

170 Stainton Rogers and Stainton Rogers 1999: 184. 171 See Boyden 1997: 203.

172 20 November 1989, Resolution 44/25. For the full text of the Convention, see the United Nations' web page: www.unhchr.ch/html/menu3/b/k2crc.htm.

173 As of June 2008. Somalia and the US are both signatories to the Convention. The UK ratified the Convention in December 1991.

174 For a critical assessment of whether the UK is complying with the Convention, see Rendel 2000.

175 Art. 1. 176 James and James 2004: 86.

177 Committee on the Rights of the Child. 4 October 2002. *Concluding Observations of the Committee on the Rights of the Child: United Kingdom of Great Britain & Northern Ireland*, CRC/C/15/Add.188, para. 20; Committee on the Rights of the Child. 15 February 1995. *Concluding Observations of the Committee on the Rights of the Child: United Kingdom of Great Britain & Northern Ireland*, CRC/C/15/Add.34. See also ibid.: 86 and 89.

recent report on progress was produced by the government in 2007 and examined by the Committee in 2008.[178]

Article 34 requires all states that have ratified the Convention to 'undertake to protect the child from all forms of sexual exploitation and sexual abuse'. This includes the taking of all appropriate measures to prevent the 'inducement or coercion of a child to engage in any unlawful sexual activity' and 'the exploitative use of children in pornographic performances and materials'. Despite the fact that Art. 34 emphasizes the exploitative use of children in child pornography, in 1997 the Special Rapporteur encouraged the UN Committee on the Rights of the Child that, as a matter of interpretation, Art. 34 should be interpreted to 'include an absolute prohibition on "pseudo-child pornography"'.[179] Whilst this interpretation catches morphed pseudo-images, images that have involved the manipulation of a real child's image and therefore exploitation, it also captures non-morphed, completely fabricated pseudo-images.

Notwithstanding the existence of Art. 34, the UN's Commission on Human Rights was keen to extend the measures Member States were required to undertake to protect children from being sold, from prostitution and child pornography. All of these phenomena were identified as increasing in magnitude internationally.[180] As a consequence, the Optional Protocol on the Sale of Children, Child Prostitution and Child Pornography was drafted and introduced in 2000. Any party to the Convention was invited to sign it.[181] The definition of child pornography under the Optional Protocol encompasses 'any representation, by whatever means, of a child engaged in real or simulated explicit sexual activities or any representation of the sexual parts of a child for primarily sexual purposes'.[182] In important ways, this is a similar definition to that under Canadian law, which I have critiqued as being too wide because it includes more than visual representations, and requires consideration of whether images of children that show their genital areas possess sexual elements. In fact, under the Optional Protocol, it is not even necessary

[178] Committee on the Rights of the Child. 20 October 2008. *Concluding Observations: United Kingdom of Great Britain and Northen Ireland*. CRC/C//gbr/Co/4. The Committee noted that the level of knowledge of the Convention amongst children in the UK continues to be low (at 20).

[179] Special Rapporteur. 16 October 1997. *Report on the sale of children, child prostitution and child pornography*, A/52/482: 12, para. 53.

[180] As noted at the start of the *Optional Protocol to the Convention on the Rights of the Child on the Sale of Children, Child Prostitution and Child Pornography*. 25 May 2000. A/RES/54/263. Available at www.unhchr.ch/html/menu2/6/crc/treaties/opsc.htm.

[181] Ibid.: Art. 13. [182] Art. 2(c).

to establish that this is the dominant characteristic of such an image, as under Canadian law. The crucial matter is whether the image is primarily for sexual purposes. However, surely this would mean that an innocuously taken image of a child which shows her genital area could constitute child pornography, if it is subsequently viewed by an individual whose purpose is primarily sexual?

At a minimum, state parties should criminalize producing, distributing, disseminating, importing, exporting, offering, selling or possessing child pornography for these purposes, whether this occurs at the domestic or transnational level, and make these extraditable offences in any treaty existing between themselves.[183] Notably, then, the Optional Protocol does not demand that state parties criminalize possession in itself without any connection to the purpose of distribution, for instance. State parties are also required to 'take all necessary steps to strengthen international cooperation by multilateral, regional and bilateral arrangements' for preventing, detecting and prosecuting individuals for the offences.[184] In addition, parties to the Protocol must promote international cooperation to address root causes that contribute to children's vulnerability to prostitution, child pornography and child sex tourism, such as poverty and underdevelopment.[185] This is significant, given my concern that sexual exploitation is currently emphasized over and above other ways in which children are harmed. However, it appears that the harms caused by poverty and underdevelopment are only stressed because of their connection to the forms of sexual exploitation to which the Protocol relates.

A total of 128 of the 192 UN Member States are now party to the Optional Protocol and 115 are signatories.[186] Parties to the Protocol are required to submit a report to the Committee on the Rights of the Child explaining the measures they have taken to implement the Protocol's provisions within two years of the Protocol being in force for their particular state.[187] In a 2004 report on child pornography on the internet, the Special Rapporteur on the sale of children, child prostitution and child pornography stated that 'many countries' still did not have child pornography laws and urged the ratification of the Optional Protocol to address this 'legal vacuum'.[188] He recommended that legislation apply to children

[183] Arts. 3.1(c) and 5.1. [184] Art. 10.1. [185] Art. 10.3.

[186] See www2.ohchr.org/english/bodies/ratification/11_c.htm, last updated 29 July 2008. The UK is a signatory to the Protocol, but has not yet ratified it.

[187] Art. 12.1.

[188] Special Rapporteur on the sale of children, child prostitution and child pornography. 2005 *Thematic Report* (child pornography on the Internet) E/CN.4/2005/78: 2.

under the age of eighteen even if the age of sexual consent was lower, since 'a child under 18 should not be considered as able to consent to engagement in pornography'.[189] The Special Rapporteur gives no consideration to the autonomy and sexual liberty rights of children over the age of sexual consent here. Finally, although the Optional Protocol does not cover grooming, the Special Rapporteur also highlighted the use of chat rooms by child sexual abusers to groom children and recommended that countries enact legislation 'creating the offence of "Internet grooming or luring"'.[190]

The Council of Europe's Conventions on Cybercrime and on the Protection of Children against Sexual Exploitation and Sexual Abuse

In 1991, the Council recommended that Member States harmonize laws on the sexual exploitation of children and emphasized the significance of international cooperation. The Council also recommended that states should consider the advisability of criminalizing the possession of child pornography.[191] Then, 2001 saw the introduction of the Council's Convention on Cybercrime.[192] The Convention came into force in 2004 and requires signatory states to cooperate with other countries in the investigation of cybercrime. The use of computer systems to produce, make available, distribute, procure and possess child pornography is one of the Convention's targets, covered under Art. 9, and Member States are required to ensure that such behaviour is criminalized.[193]

As with the definitions under US and Canadian law, the Framework Decision defines child pornography according to the specific nature of its content, namely, 'sexually explicit conduct'.[194] Pseudo-images are included in this definition, although Member States have discretion as to whether to criminalize such images.[195] According to the Explanatory Report to the Convention, sexually explicit conduct includes 'the lascivious exhibiton of the genitals or the pubic area of a minor'.[196] The

[189] At 8, para. 123. [190] Ibid.: 23, para. 123 and 8, para. 26.

[191] Council of Europe 1991. *Recommendation No. R (91) 11 concerning sexual exploitation, pornography and prostitution of, and trafficking in, children and young adults*. Available at www.legislationline.org/documents/action/popup/id/8354.

[192] Council of Europe 2001. Convention on Cybercrime ETS No. 185. Available at http://conventions.coe.int/Treaty/EN/Treaties/Html/185.htm.

[193] Art. 9(1). Although they reserve the right not to criminalize making available or possessing child pornography in a computer system (Art. 9(4)).

[194] Art. 9(2). [195] Art. 9(2)(c) and (4).

[196] Council of Europe, *Explanatory Report to the Convention on Cybercrime* 2001 ETS No. 185, available at http://conventions.coe.int/Treaty/EN/Reports/Html/185.htm.

definition thus reproduces this problematic aspect of the definition under US law. Therefore, in the case of visual depictions of children that do not involve sexually explicit conduct, such as images of naked children, the Council recommends a definiton which demands scrutiny of such images to ascertain whether they contain a sexual element, an approach which I have criticized under US law.

Member States and external supporters were invited to sign the Convention from when it was introduced in 2001. Although forty-four Member States and external supporters have signed the Convention, only twenty-three have ratified it,[197] leading Akdeniz to describe the process as 'extremely slow'.[198] There are now few Member States which do not have child pornography laws in place.[199] Whilst the Convention may thus go some way in harmonizing national responses to child pornography, some divergence may remain since, as Akdeniz observes, Member States have the discretion not to criminalize certain offences, most notably the offence of possession.[200]

More specific to child pornography and other acts involving sexual abuse or exploitation is the Council's recently introduced Convention on the Protection of Children against Sexual Exploitation and Sexual Abuse.[201] As of June 2008, twenty-eight Member States have signed this Convention.[202] It is directed to 'promoting national and international co-operation against sexual exploitation and sexual abuse of children'[203] and defines a child as being under eighteen years of age.[204] Member States and external supporters who sign the Convention are required to criminalize essentially the same child pornography offences as under Art. 9 of the Convention on Cybercrime, but these offences are not limited to those occurring through the use of a computer system.[205] Parties

[197] As of June 2008. The list of signatures and ratifications of the Convention is available at http://conventions.coe.int/Treaty/Commun/ChercheSig.asp?NT=185&CM=8&DF=&CL=ENG. The UK is one of the Member States yet to ratify the Convention.

[198] Akdeniz 2008: 199. [199] Ibid. [200] Ibid.: 203.

[201] Council of Europe. 2007. *Convention on the Protection of Children against Sexual Exploitation and Sexual Abuse* CETS No.201. Available at http://conventions.coe.int/Treaty/EN/treaties/Html/201.htm.

[202] A list of signatures and ratifications is available at conventions.coe.int/Treaty/Commun/ChercheSig.asp?NT=201&CM=7&DF=6/26/2008&CL=ENG.

[203] Art. 38 requires international cooperation to combat the sexual exploitation and abuse of children, and for the purpose of connected investigations or proceedings, between parties to the Convention.

[204] Art. 1.

[205] Art. 20. The definition of child pornography is that given under the Optional Protocol to the United Nations Convention. An additional offence under Art. 20(f) is 'knowingly obtaining

to the Convention can decide not to criminalize behaviour involving child pornography where the material consists 'exclusively of simulated representations or realistic images of a non-existent child' or where the children in the images have reached the age of sexual consent, and the 'images are produced and possessed by them with their consent and solely for their own private use'.[206] This is an important area in which to allow Member States discretion since, as I have already argued, blanket criminalization of images featuring children aged over the age of sexual consent infringes on older children's autonomy and sexual liberty rights.[207]

As with the UN Convention, the 2007 Convention promotes the child's voice and autonomy. Article 9 recommends 'the participation of children, according to their evolving capacity, in the development and the implementation of state policies, programmes or others initiatives concerning the fight against sexual exploitation and sexual abuse of children'. The ethos behind this Article should be supported, as such participation is vital if children are to have more of a say in shaping legal and societal responses to their exploitation.

Under Art. 18, Member States should ensure that they have criminal law provisions which prohibit intentionally engaging in sexual activities with a child under the age of sexual consent. Engaging in sexual activities with a child (regardless of whether they are over the age of sexual consent) must also be prohibited where coercion or threats have been used, there has been an abuse of a position of trust, 'including within the family', or the child is in a particularly vulnerable situation. In the Explanatory Report on the Convention, the Council emphasizes that child sexual abuse can frequently occur in the family and that such abuse in this context can be especially psychologically damaging and have long-lasting consequences for the victim.[208] The Convention's reflection of the reality of the situation in which child sexual abuse so commonly occurs is particularly important.

Finally, Art. 23 covers a certain type of grooming behaviour. Once again, the focus is on the use of the internet and other communication

access, through information and communication technologies, to child pornography'. Art. 20 also requires Member States who sign the Convention to criminalize other behaviour related to the participation of a child in pornographic performances, such as causing a child to take part in such performances.

206 Art. 20(3). 207 See Chapter 2, at 62–7.

208 Council of Europe 2007. *Explanatory Report to the Convention on the Protection of Children against Sexual Exploitation and Sexual Abuse*. CETS No. 201: para. 125. Available at http://conventions.coe.int/Treaty/EN/Reports/Html/201.htm.

technologies. The Article requires Member States to criminalize 'the intentional proposal, through information and communication technologies, of an adult to meet a child [below the age of sexual consent], for the purpose of [engaging in sexual activities with a child or producing child pornography] against him or her, where this proposal has been followed by material acts leading to such a meeting'.

The European Council Framework Decision on Combating the Sexual Exploitation of Children and Child Pornography

Since the late 1990s, there have been numerous EU initiatives that have related to child sexual exploitation and child pornography,[209] the most significant of which is the Council Framework Decision. Prior to this, the European Council Decision to Combat Child Pornography on the Internet,[210] adopted in 2000, was concerned with preventing and combating 'the production, processing, distribution and possession of child pornography material through the Internet' and required Member States to cooperate in the investigation and prosecution of such offences.[211] In 2001, although the European Commission welcomed this decision, it concluded that further action was required and urged the Council to produce a Framework Decision to ensure a harmonized approach in Member States to the sexual exploitation of children and child pornography.[212]

The Council's Framework Decision[213] came into force in January 2004 and all Member States were required to ensure compliance with it by January 2006. There is thus an important difference to highlight between this decision and initiatives at UN and Council of Europe levels. Whilst it is easy for states to show that they recognize the importance of combating child pornography and the other forms of sexual exploitation by signing up to the Council of Europe Conventions and the UN Protocol, they

[209] Between 1999 and 2008, the European Commission has worked on an Action Plan promoting safer use of the internet by combating illegal and harmful content, including child pornography. The plan will be further taken forward in 2009 to 2013 to encompass other communications services 'such as social networking', and to fight 'harmful conduct' such as grooming. See http://ec.europa.eu/information_society/activities/sip/index_en.htm for further details.

[210] 9 June 2000. 2000/375/JHA L138, OJ 1–4.

[211] Ibid.: Art. 2.

[212] European Commission 26 January 2001. Communication to the Council and the European Parliament, *Creating a Safer Information Society by Improving the Security of Information Infrastructures and Combating Computer-related Crime*, COM (2000) 890.

[213] 20 January 2004. 2004/68/JHA [2004] OJ L13 44–8. Available at http://eur-lex.europa.eu/LexUriServ/LexUriServ.do?uri=CELEX:32004F0068:EN:HTML.

only have to pay 'lip service' to these treaties until they ratify them.[214] In contrast, the Council Framework Decision was binding on Member States as soon as it came into force. It highlights child sexual exploitation and pornography as 'serious violations of human rights and of the fundamental right of a child to a harmonious upbringing and development',[215] and warns that child pornography is a growing phenomenon that is becoming more prolific through the internet.[216] As the decision is designed to ensure a commonality of approach in the legal response to child sexual exploitation and pornography, it includes a definition of child pornography and states the offences that Member States should introduce if they have not done so already.[217] A child is defined as being below eighteen years of age and the definition of child pornography is as follows:

> pornographic material that visually depicts or represents:
>
> (i) a real child involved or engaged in sexually explicit conduct, including lascivious exhibition of the genitals or the pubic area of a child; or
> (ii) a real person appearing to be a child involved or engaged in the conduct mentioned in (i); or
> (iii) realistic images of a non-existent child involved or engaged in the conduct mentioned in (i).[218]

There are two matters to note here. First, the Framework Decision defines child pornography similarly to the Council of Europe's Convention on Cybercrime. Thus, when it comes to visual representations of children that do not involve sexually explicit conduct, the decision advocates a definition which encourages viewing children's bodies through a sexual lens. Secondly, the definition captures non-morphed pseudo-images, the creation of which has not involved the exploitation of any real child.

The child pornography offences listed are producing, distributing, supplying and acquisition or possession.[219] Member States may exclude criminal liability in certain contexts. I have already discussed the exception

[214] Although if public interest is lacking then, even after ratification, governments may do little to ensure implementation unless there are effective ways of ensuring enforcement. See James and James 2004: 97.

[215] At (4). [216] At (5).

[217] The decision also requires Member States to criminalize the instigation, aiding, abetting and attempt of the offences it lays out (Art. 4), and to set 'effective, proportionate and dissuasive' criminal sanctions (Art. 7).

[218] Art. 1(b). [219] Art. 3.1.

where children over the age of sexual consent agree to the taking of the image and keep it for their private use,[220] and criticized English law for a much more restricted exception which requires the parties to be married or in an 'enduring relationship'.[221] Another context in which Member States can exclude criminal liability is where non-morphed pseudo-images are produced and possessed by the producer solely for his or her own private use, as long as this does not involve a risk of the images being disseminated.[222] The laws in Member States that exclude criminal liability in these circumstances will better reflect the fact that the creation of such images involves no harm to a real child.

Article 2 provides a list of 'Offences concerning sexual exploitation of children' that Member States should criminalize, which includes:

> engaging in sexual activities with a child, where
>
> (i) use is made of coercion, force or threats;
> (ii) money or other forms of remuneration or consideration is given as payment in exchange for the child engaging in sexual activities; or
> (iii) abuse is made of a recognized position of trust, authority or influence over the child.[223]

This could cover grooming, but only if it results in sexual activity with the child; the act of grooming *per se* is not behaviour that Art. 2 requires to be criminalized. Also, the Article makes no reference to sexual activity with a child that follows the giving of gifts as part of the grooming process, rather than as recompense for the child engaging in sexual activity. It seems, however, that grooming is to be one of the next targets for EU initiatives. The Vice-President of the European Commission stated in November 2007 that 'we are considering the possibility of strengthening the EU legislative framework especially concerning offences committed through the Internet, in particular the criminalisation of "grooming"'.[224]

As Akdeniz notes, although the Framework Decision is unlikely to make any real impact on policy and law-making in this country, given that our laws are compatible with it, it will have an effect on policy and laws elsewhere in newer EU Member States.[225] A recent European

[220] Art. 3.2(b). [221] See Chapter 2, at 63–4. [222] Art. 3.2(c). [223] Article 2.(c).

[224] EU, Press Release 20 November 2007. 'Member States implement EU legislation to combat the sexual exploitation of children and child pornography. But Member States can still do more' IP/07/1730. Available at http://europa.eu/rapid/pressReleasesAction.do?reference=IP/07/1730.

[225] Akdeniz 2008: 191.

Commission report revealed that most Member States have met the key requirements of the Framework Decision.[226] There is much to be gained from ensuring that the legal approaches to child pornography and other forms of child exploitation in the EU are harmonized and I generally support the Framework Decision's approach to child pornography. However, to avoid the sexualization of children's naked bodies, when it comes to images without any explicit sexual content, the 'lascivious exhibition' part of the definition should have been rejected in favour of an approach that considers instead whether the child was exploited in order to create the image.

Is there a need for an international law to protect children from acts related to child sexual abuse?

The International Centre for Missing and Exploited Children (ICMEC) has urged that model legislation on child pornography be enacted worldwide.[227] This raises the question of whether international laws relating to child pornography and grooming and other acts related to child sexual abuse would offer better protection to children alongside the national laws that currently exist. It is certainly difficult for individual jurisdictional laws to deal successfully with these forms of child exploitation beyond national borders. For instance, despite the commonality of approach urged by the international treaties I have examined, there remain varying definitions of child pornography. What constitutes an offence in one country may not be prohibited by the criminal law in another. However, whilst this suggests the need for an international law, it also makes the advent of such a law very unlikely, given national variations and the difficulty of reaching universal agreement.[228] It would also be a difficult task to achieve consensus on enforcement and sanctions. Commitment to international treaties may, therefore, be the most that can realistically be achieved. However, international police investigations into child pornography reveal that international collaboration can effectively lead to the tracking down and prosecution of individuals who make, distribute and possess child pornography and groom children. If such collaboration continues and countries adhere to the same international agreements, this may well be the best way forward to protect children's rights to be free from exploitation, regardless of where in the world they live.

[226] See above, n. 224. [227] ICMEC 2007. [228] Ibid.: iii–iv.

CHAPTER SIX

CONCLUSIONS AND IMPLICATIONS

> Once the real as opposed to the surface legitimations of the societal reaction are exposed, there is a possibility of undermining them and devising policies that are both more effective and more humane.[1]

In this concluding chapter, I stress the critical tensions and problematic constructions that my analysis has addressed, and present what I see as the reality of the societal and legal response to child pornography and sexual grooming for children. I consider how the current legal and societal reaction is likely to progress. Finally, I urge the introduction of a new approach to child pornography and grooming and, more broadly, to the way in which society and law view children.

THE REPERCUSSIONS OF THE CURRENT SOCIETAL AND LEGAL RESPONSE FOR CHILDREN

The current legal and social responses examined by this work are the result of thirty years of prioritizing the reduction of harm caused to children by child pornography and sexual abuse, and preventing harm and potential risks of harm before they occur. Thus, the intentions behind increased criminalization and the protectionist movement were laudable. However, perhaps inevitably, the way in which we perceive and respond to the problems of child pornography and grooming is influenced by a morality discourse involving juxtaposing constructions that can blur reality. Such moral narratives of disparity can only encourage a moral panic reaction and demand conformity with the symbolic universe surrounding children, child pornography and grooming that we have created. Given the nature of the wrongs and harm of these phenomena, it would be next to impossible for us to leave behind the discourse of morality. The morally loaded words used by the legislature and judiciary when describing behaviour related to child pornography and grooming, for instance, are clear evidence that we all exist within a social reality in which the dominantly communicated moral norm is that child pornographers and groomers are evil corrupters of children's innocence. What

[1] Cohen 2007: 172.

I am advocating is a move away from the more damaging aspects of this morality discourse.

We need to step back and truly see the way in which we socially construct children and portray the harm that child pornography and grooming represent, if we really wish to offer children the greatest protection from harm. Children are indeed vulnerable, but this vulnerability is as much socially constructed as natural. In our desire to protect this vulnerability, in our fixation upon the notion of innocence and preventing the corruption of their perceived innocence, we could well be increasing their vulnerability to child pornography and grooming. What is more, we are presenting a damaging ideal of what children should and should not be. Whilst childhood innocence has been accentuated in order to support calls for greater protection for children, through this construction we are exploiting, objectifying and oppressing children and moulding them into what adults see as the ideal representation of childhood. We have reached a stage where any image of a naked child can be treated with suspicion. Legal tests such as that in America which require consideration of whether an image is a lascivious exhibition of a minor's genitals or pubic area invite the viewer to find an element of sexuality about the image. These attitudes towards images of children's bodies, and the media and advertising, sexualize children's naked bodies and make them more attractive to the very individuals from whom we seek to protect them. Our determination to ensure that the law reflects a broad protectionist stance, and to preserve innocence regardless of whether it in fact exists, means that we are failing to recognize the autonomy rights of adolescents, of older 'knowing' children.

What impact is this having on children? More than one author has emphasized the way in which children engage in the symbolic universe around them. Holland argues that 'children live in a world of meanings and of visual spectacle. They too respond to imagery that surrounds us all, and make use of it to define themselves and account for their experiences'.[2] Children's engagement with the imagery, ideology and constructions of childhood that exist around them must, at the very least, produce a state of confusion about what an 'appropriate' childhood is. If their lived experience of childhood is different from that which they are taught to experience, they have a choice of either wearing the straightjacket of innocence and vulnerability or stepping free from this constraint and being seen as the 'other', as non-children. Any real power to challenge dominant adult constructions only comes when the child

[2] Holland 2006: 205. See also James and Prout 1997: 8.

becomes an adult and, by then, her lived experience of being a child has passed; childhood, and the opportunity to live this childhood differently, have both gone. As I will argue shortly, we would need to undertake a radical revision of the way in which we respond to children in order for this to change. Kitzinger has highlighted the need for 'the deconstruction and reconstruction of childhood … [This] means dealing openly with children about power and thinking in terms of "oppression" rather than "vulnerability", "liberation" rather than "protection".'[3]

The child's right to be heard currently remains a theoretical concept. Indeed, society and law pay 'lip service' to all rights claims other than a right to protection when it comes to children. This is especially apparent in the blanket criminalization approach to child pornography that fails to recognize older teenagers' autonomy and sexual liberty rights. The SOA provisions were brought into being without any convincing attempts to obtain the views of teenagers and children, those upon whom it would have such a significant impact.[4] This is undoubtedly because the right to protection reflects the preferred adult construct of children as vulnerable and reliant on adults for safety. In contrast, respecting autonomy and sexual liberty rights would require acceptance of the fact that children are not the innocent and vulnerable beings we wish them to be.

When it comes to children who are the victims of grooming and sexual abuse, our notions of the innocent child can lead to the harm suffered by children who do not meet societal expectations of the ideal child and victim being overlooked or underplayed.[5] Current legal and social responses could also be perceived to be failing children because they are so focused on preventing harm and future risks to children, and on apprehending and prosecuting offenders, that the very real harm suffered by pre-existing victims of child pornography is in danger of being overlooked. Taylor and Quayle note that:

> A substantive criticism of the criminal justice system's response to child pornography is that it has over-focused on offender issues, at the expense of victim issues. At its worst, the child victim becomes an object around which adults (offenders, police and social services) devote resources to

[3] Kitzinger 1997: 184.

[4] A point also made by Spencer 2004: 360; and see Home Office 2000: para. 3.3.9.

[5] See the later discussion at 244. Two of the police officers in my study expressed concern that some young teenagers who are groomed may be perceived to have encouraged the groomer (Interviews RX2 and RX5).

> sustain their own construction of events, and their own vested interests, rather than those of the child.[6]

In 2004, the United Nations' Special Rapporteur on the sale of children, child prostitution and child pornography stated that Member States should undertake more efforts to identify the victims of child pornography.[7] However, this is a highly sensitive matter that requires serious consideration before any such efforts are undertaken. Taylor and Quayle draw attention to the fact that victims of older child pornography may now have families of their own and thus they and their families may suffer additional negative consequences if their identification is dealt with insensitively.[8] It might also be the case that the victim has chosen to bury the memory of her involvement in child pornography, and any uncovering of this involvement and attempts to help might cause more harm than good. Therefore, whilst this is perhaps a valid criticism of the current social and legal responses, I support moves to increase efforts to identify child pornography victims with caution.

WHERE A CONTINUATION OF THE CURRENT RESPONSE WILL TAKE US

The analysis throughout this book should have revealed that a rational assessment of the harms of child pornography and grooming has been consistently absent. Thus, the next stage of intensity for what I have argued seems to be a moral panic surrounding child pornography and grooming is likely to involve calls for the criminalization of other behaviour that may potentially cause indirect harm. In fact, following a Home Office consultation in 2007,[9] government proposals have already emerged to prohibit drawings and computer-generated images depicting child sexual abuse.[10] Significantly, these proposals have not been made as a consequence of any research that demonstrates such non-photographic visual depictions are harmful. It is stated in the consultation paper that:

> We are unaware of any specific research into whether there is a link between accessing these fantasy images of child sexual abuse and the

[6] Taylor and Quayle 2003: 206. See also O'Donnell and Milner 2007: 71–3.

[7] See previous chapter, n. 188, at para. 125. See also Akdeniz 2008: 278–9.

[8] Taylor and Quayle 2003: 19. [9] Home Office 2007a.

[10] 'New proposals will make all obscene images of children illegal', Ministry of Justice Press Release, 28 May 2008, www.justice.gov.uk/news/newsrelease280508a.htm.

> commission of offences against children, but it is felt by police and children's welfare organisations that the possession and circulation of these images serves to legitimize and reinforce highly inappropriate views about children.[11]

The two primary arguments provided to support criminalization are that such images may be used to groom children and could 'fuel abuse of real children by reinforcing potential abusers' inappropriate feelings towards children'.[12] As we have seen before when other legislative reforms have been on the cards regarding child pornography and grooming, these arguments are accompanied by a warning of the consequences of failing to act. The outlined consequence here is 'an increased market for such images in the future'.[13] A child protection group has reinforced the proposals by merging the possible, unproven, indirect harm of such images with the harm of real child pornography. According to a spokesperson for the Children's Charity NCH, the move 'makes a clear statement that drawings or computer-generated images of child abuse are as unacceptable as a photograph'.[14] This statement also reveals more about what the primary objection to these images is: that, in the absence of any proven harm, non-photographic images depicting child sexual abuse should still be prohibited because they threaten the moral values of our symbolic universe. I predict that, if these proposals do become law, they will soon be followed by calls for a legal response that would take us even nearer to the Canadian approach, along the lines that written, fictitious material should also be criminalized because it might incite child sexual abuse. Such a continued escalation is unlikely to offer any better protection to children, and is remote from the harm-based rationale of criminalizing images of real child pornography.[15]

Turning to grooming, social constructions of stranger danger encourage a climate of fear in which people are increasingly becoming afraid to engage in any interaction with a child they do not know for fear their behaviour will be misconstrued. Furedi and Bristow comment that: 'Adults today would probably not dream of offering sweets to strange children – they even think twice about comforting a distressed toddler, or helping a child in trouble, in case their actions are misconstrued.'[16] In a 2007 survey conducted in Scotland, 48 per cent of the adults who

[11] Home Office 2007a: 1. [12] Ibid.: 5. [13] Ibid.: 7.

[14] 'Computer generated abuse "banned"', BBC News report, 28 May 2008, http:\\news.bbc.co.uk/1/hi/uk/7422595.stm.

[15] See also Akdeniz 2008: 270–1 on this point. [16] Furedi and Bristow 2008: 52.

participated stated that they would not engage in contact with children or young people, due to a fear that they would be falsely accused of causing harm. For men in particular, this was because they were afraid of being falsely accused of being a paedophile.[17] If stranger danger constructions continue to prevail, this can only further breed a culture of suspicion and mistrust in which relationships between adults and children become increasingly tense and estranged.

ADVOCATING A NEW APPROACH

A re-assessment of the harm(s) of child pornography and grooming and a reframing of the child pornography legislation

Shortly after Trenholm's explanation of the way in which communication is vital in maintaining social structures and constructions, as quoted in the introduction to this book, she continues: 'Through communication we can act on and change the very structures that create us.'[18] In my view, it is the responsibility of society and law to communicate different narratives and constructions that offer children a better symbolic universe in which to live. We must provide a new ideological framework that does not revolve around social and legal moral constructions of indecency and the corruption of innocence, for example, but remains directed towards exploitation, the main harm of child pornography and grooming.

A more careful and lucid assessment of the real empirical harms of child pornography and grooming needs to be undertaken by the government, to provide a stronger and more rational justification for the large amount of criminalization in these areas. Special attention should be paid to the prevailing rationalization of prohibiting the possession of child pornography on the basis of the market reduction argument. I have contended that the more persuasive justification for criminalizing possession is that the possessor underwrites and benefits from the primary harm caused by the producer. The legal responses to child pornography and grooming provide rich examples of the criminalization of prospective and remote harms and crimes of ulterior intent. What these responses also reveal is a failure to demarcate the point at which the line should be drawn when it comes to such criminalization. A liberal

[17] 'Adults "too afraid" of youth work', BBC News report, 16 October 2007, http://news.bbc.co.uk/1/hi/scotland/7045544.stm; and Furedi and Bristow 2008: 16–17.

[18] Trenholm 1991: 9.

society should demand that this crucial matter must be addressed, not least because of the damaging effect that charges and convictions have on individuals and because of the violation of older teenage children's autonomy rights.

I have argued that both child pornography and grooming should be presented in legal and social discourses as forms of exploitation. Feinberg's explication of the concepts of exploitation and harm has provided valuable guidance as to when it is appropriate to criminalize behaviour related to child pornography, as I hope my analysis has demonstrated. I have concluded that it is behaviour that harmfully exploits a child that should be criminalized. This legitimates the criminalization of grooming and real child pornography. However, it is much harder to justify the criminalization of completely fabricated pseudo-images on the basis of an undistorted harm principle. My analysis also leads to the conclusion that the creation of images of naked children should only be criminalized if the context in which the image was taken is exploitative and harmful. So what are the practical consequences of my analysis and advocated approach for the child pornography laws?

It is my conclusion that we must remove the legal construct of indecency from child pornography laws and replace it with a framework of exploitation. The legislation should thus refer to *exploitative photographs of child pornography*. This is not dissimilar to Art. 34 of the UN Convention on the Rights of the Child's reference to the 'exploitative use of children in pornographic performances and materials'. Given that the UK has ratified this Convention, it is apposite that legislative measures should mirror its framing of child pornography. Exploitative images of child pornography would include real images of child pornography and morphed pseudo-images. Rather than the jury considering whether the image in question is indecent, the Sentencing Advisory Panel's league table could be utilized to help them decide whether the material amounts to child pornography. Images at level one of the table – depicting nudity with no sexual activity – would only amount to images of abuse if the jury concludes that they were taken in an exploitative context. Since no child is exploited to create completely computer-generated images, these images would also not be criminalized.[19]

[19] As discussed in Chapter 3, in cases where it cannot be ascertained whether the image is real, morphed or completely computer-generated, a defence would exist if the defendant can establish that the image falls into the latter category.

Grooming is not presented in legal discourses within a framework of moral harm. As a consequence, I am not calling for revision to the legal framework here, although I am arguing that the legal constructions of grooming require revision. The legislature's contemporary focus has been on stranger and online grooming and this is not a distinctive feature of the approach in this jurisdiction; Canadian and US law-makers have also prioritized the criminalization of such grooming. Whilst offences exists under the SOA that can tackle grooming in situations where the s. 15 offence may not be made out – notably, s. 14 – our legislature can be charged with over-prioritizing stranger grooming and therefore presenting a distorting construction of grooming and the threat that it poses. The legal discourses surrounding grooming do not reflect the common reality of the contexts in which grooming most often occurs. It is thus vital that public education and prevention programmes emphasize grooming in different contexts other than the internet, to avoid the encouragement of inaccurate perceptions that children are in greatest danger from online predators, as I will discuss below.[20] The media must also play a role in this. As long ago as 1991, the Council of Europe recommended that Member States invite the media to contribute to public awareness of child sexual exploitation and, crucially, 'to adopt appropriate rules of conduct'.[21] An essential rule of conduct must be to ensure that the media's presentation of child pornography and grooming is accurate and not sensationalized.

It is imperative to ensure that the correct balance is struck between safeguarding children and their rights and the rights of those accused of offences relating to child pornography and grooming. The forfeiture of individual rights is in evidence not just in this jurisdiction, but elsewhere, by the erosion of First Amendment protection in the United States and the inclusion of written material within the Canadian definition of child pornography, for example. Although there may have been much attention paid to particular offender issues, such as the level of risk posed by offenders, it is much harder to argue that the rights of those suspected and convicted of offences related to child pornography and grooming have been seriously considered. In this jurisdiction in particular, legal constructions of pseudo-images and of the downloading of child pornography are violating the principle of fair labelling. The prejudicial

[20] Wolak *et al.* 2008.

[21] *Recommendation No. R (91) 11 concerning sexual exploitation, pornography and prostitution of, and trafficking in, children and young adults* (1991), A.a(5).

impact of the increased admissibility of evidence of previous convictions is threatening the right to a fair trial. Moreover, the gravely damaging impact on those suspected of child pornography and grooming offences warrants serious consideration of whether anonymity should be granted until individuals are proven guilty.

The incorporation of situational crime prevention techniques as an alternative strategy to ever-increasing criminalization

Whilst protecting children from harm and the risk of harm remains the main endeavour, strategies of situational crime prevention may offer a better way forward than increased criminalization, by reducing the opportunity for individuals to produce child pornography or to groom a child. For whilst criminalization targets the offending behaviour and focuses on the offender, it does not tackle the situation surrounding and facilitating the offender's behaviour. The rationale of situational crime prevention (SCP) theory is to concentrate on understanding the environmental factors that enable crime, developing techniques and strategies directed towards preventing its occurrence by making it harder or more risky for offenders to engage in such behaviour.[22] Wortley and Smallbone have recently highlighted the need for attention to be paid to the 'design and organization of physical and social environments so that the potential for ... offenses to occur might be minimized' in order to better tackle and prevent child sexual abuse.[23] One strategy suggested by the authors is 'target hardening', making the intended target of would-be offenders' crime more unobtainable. Their research leads them to argue that one of the most effective methods of making a child less susceptible to grooming is to develop child-focused prevention programmes which promote children's assertiveness and confidence and thereby make it easier for them to resist a groomer's advances. Part of such an education programme aimed at adolescents could focus on recognizing and evading sexual victimization.[24] In 1991, the Council of Europe advised Member

[22] See, e.g. Clarke 1997; Wortley and Smallbone 2006: 8–10; Beauregard and LeClerc 2007: 118; and von Hirsch *et al.* 2000: preface. Although, again, I do not wish to over-emphasize the prevalence of stranger internet grooming, one SCP method that may reduce the opportunity for online grooming is the use of covert sting operations. Knowledge of such operations on the part of would-be offenders could bring an 'element of uncertainty into their online grooming activities' that might act as a deterrence. See Gardner 2003: 7; Select Committee on Home Affairs 2003: App. 7, para. 5 (Childnet International's memorandum); and Taylor and Quayle 2006: 187–90.

[23] Wortley and Smallbone 2006: 2. See also Simon and Zgoba 2006: 69–72.

[24] See Wolak *et al.* 2008: 122.

States to provide education programmes to primary and secondary school children on 'the dangers of sexual exploitation and abuse' that they might be exposed to and how they might defend themselves.[25]

There are already teaching resources available on how to use the internet safely.[26] However, more needs to be done to educate children about other situations in which they are at risk from grooming. For instance, the *Awaken Project* currently being run in Blackpool by Lancashire Constabulary provides bespoke education packages, giving talks to high school children to inform them about the situations in which they could be groomed.[27] A number of the police officers I interviewed emphasized the need to educate young people about the dangers of risk-taking behaviour as a priority. In the words of one: 'The only way we can win this battle is by ensuring our children are given the means and the tools to say no … Take away the victims and there is nobody left to exploit.'[28] Another officer highlighted the situation in which, I would argue, education is most vital:

> the majority of people are groomed and abused by people who are known to them … people who are introduced by the parents and we go to an awful lot of trouble and have done over years [to say] 'Don't go with strangers, don't take sweets'. However what we don't say is 'Don't do what the babysitter tells you when they tell you to go and do this'. 'Don't do what your uncle says when he tells you to do this'. What we tell them is 'Do everything the babysitter tells you to do'. 'Be good for your uncle' … All the preventative work is around that small percentage of people who abuse outside the home.[29]

I recognize that when children are victims of child pornography or grooming in the home by someone they love and trust, 'target hardening' may be a lot harder to achieve.[30] However, the key here seems to be educating parents as well as children. Wortley and Smallbone advocate the

[25] *Recommendation No. R (91) 11*, 1991: A.a(3). See also Art. 6 of the Council of Europe's *Convention on the Protection of Children against Sexual Exploitation and Sexual Abuse* 2007; and Akdeniz 2008: 280.

[26] See the *Thinkuknow* website, www.thinkuknow.co.uk/teachers/. Another teaching resource for helping young adolescents understand the dangers of online communications with individuals they do not know, *Jenny's Story*, was launched in January 2005. See www.childnet-int.org/jenny/index.html. One of the police officers I interviewed used *Jenny's Story* as a case study with pupils at nineteen schools in Lancashire (Interview RX2).

[27] Interview RX4.

[28] Ibid. Similar views were expressed by the officer in Interview RX5.

[29] Interview RX3. A similar view on the need to educate the public regarding the contexts in which grooming commonly occurs was shared by other officers (Interviews RX7 and RX8).

[30] See also Kaufman *et al.* 2006: 118; and Marshall *et al.* 2006: 43–4.

adoption of a number of other strategies, including public education programmes, that will make parents better able to spot 'danger signals' in the behaviour of friends, neighbours and relatives.[31] Implementing such programmes is all the more imperative in light of the over-attention paid to stranger, online grooming by the legislature. Simon and Zgoba express concern that the focus on stranger molestation means that parents do not understand that their children are at most risk during unsupervised contact with acquaintances.[32] In light of their findings that only 16 per cent of child sex abuse victims are abused by strangers when a much larger number, 49 per cent, are abused by acquaintances,[33] Simon and Zgoba propose SCP strategies of controlling acquaintances' access to children and extended parental and family guardianship so that children's time with acquaintances is supervised. In their opinion, adopting such strategies could prevent nearly one-half of sex crimes against children.[34] It is thus hoped that the Home Office's plan to pilot a community awareness scheme to promote greater risk awareness and understanding among parents, which was highlighted in a recent review, is put into practice effectively.[35] I acknowledge that this will be difficult to achieve without the current suspicion directed towards strangers who show an interest in children being transferred to individuals known and previously trusted by parents. It is thus important to recognize the need for caution when deciding how best to convey the information through such schemes to avoid creating a climate of fear and distrust.[36] Moreover, educational programmes must ensure that children who have been subject to a successful grooming process are not made to feel that they are in the wrong. Lanning argues that:

> societal attitudes and prevention programmes that focus only on 'unwanted' sexual activity and tell potential child victims to avoid sexual abuse by saying no, yelling and telling ... might work better with the stranger lurking behind a tree, but children who are seduced and actively participate in their victimization ... often feel guilty and blame themselves because they did not do what they were 'supposed' to do.[37]

The introduction of public education programmes addressing the various contexts in which grooming can occur should also be supported, since

[31] Wortley and Smallbone 2006: 23–6. See also Craven *et al.* 2006: 297.
[32] Simon and Zgoba 2006: 87. [33] According to the data in their study. See Chapter 1, n. 10.
[34] Simon and Zgoba 2006: 83–4. See also McAlinden 2006: 354–6.
[35] Home Office 2007b. [36] See also Marshall *et al.* 2006: 56.
[37] Lanning 2005: 50. See also Lanning 2004: 561–2.

this should encourage society to assess how much children's vulnerability is constructed, and to move away from its current protectionist (suffocating) stance. Furthermore, children's education programmes should foster an approach that promotes children's autonomy, enabling them to take control of their situation and defend themselves, rather than making them reliant on adult protection. Without the implementation of additional strategies, such as the SCP methods and education programmes I have discussed, the social and legal responses to child pornography and grooming do not go far enough to reduce the exploitation of children.

A move away from 'the sexual' and our fixation with childhood innocence

In contemporary Western society, child sexual abuse is perceived as being one of the most serious forms of abuse that governments must respond to and seek to eliminate. This is undoubtedly the reason why the international treaties I have discussed prioritize child sexual exploitation. However, children are exploited in many other ways, and as much social and political attention needs to be paid to the harm caused to children by such social phenomena as poverty, neglect and commercialization.[38] It is unsurprising that such matters, lacking the sensationalist value of sex, are of less interest to the media. However, as Ennew rightly observes: 'If moral debate is reduced to sexual matters, then all other inequalities are bound to be obscured by insistent screams of shock and horror – by exaggeration and distortion.'[39] Given worldwide levels of child poverty,[40] for instance, there is clearly a need for a re-evaluation of the disproportionate emphasis upon harms caused through sexual abuse in social and legal national and international responses.

Even in the more specific contexts of child pornography and grooming, it is my view that we should remove the emphasis from *sexual* exploitation. The concentration on the sexual aspects of behaviour relating to these phenomena encourages a distortive moral reaction. Furthermore, such an emphasis might be hampering social and legal efforts to understand and tackle such behaviour. In the words of Taylor and Quayle, 'perhaps our understanding of these kinds of offences and offenders may be improved if we turn attention away from the sexual qualities of these

[38] See Danay 2005: 169–71; Hacking 1999: 133; Kincaid 1998: 290; and O'Donnell and Milner 2008: 226.

[39] Ennew 1986: 147.

[40] See 'British children: poorer, at greater risk and more insecure', *The Guardian*, 14 February 2007.

offences, and focus more on the processes whereby offending takes place and the particular behaviors involved'.[41]

We must also abandon innocence as the dominant construct of childhood and turn the focus away from vulnerability to empowering children, especially older children. We need to listen to children's voices and let them tell adults how childhood should be understood and perceived.[42] The focus should thus be on children's participation as much as their protection. Greater account must be taken of their autonomy and of the sexual liberty rights of teenagers over the age of sexual consent, and public support for such a social and legal approach is vital.[43] In essence, then, I am arguing that children should be able to shape their own constructed universe as adults do theirs.

CONCLUDING THOUGHTS

To revisit the quotation from D. H. Lawrence's *The White Peacock* with which this book began, it is, of course, the child pornographers, groomers and child sex abusers who ravish children in the most literal sense. Whilst society's and law's ravishment is more metaphorical in nature, it is no less real. We have fashioned a symbolic universe in which children are in real danger of becoming like the snowdrops in Lawrence's vividly depicted symbolic landscape. Children are defined, confined, moralized and exploited by adults in this social and legal world. They are constrained and made vulnerable by an unrealistic, dangerous ideal of purity and innocence and sexualized by the taboo we have placed upon their naked bodies. We frame the laws surrounding child pornography around the wrong harm and commonly present the risks of grooming in an inaccurate, misleading light. We do not pay adequate regard to children's autonomy rights; we over-protect them and safeguard them from strangers, but not from those who are more likely to cause them to suffer harm. In this symbolic universe we have constructed for them, children's meaning is in as much danger of being lost to them, as it has been lost to us.

It is time to create a new symbolic universe, one in which we tackle head on the exploitation of children that continues to exist and be

41 Taylor and Quayle 2006: 183.

42 'To negotiate with a less powerful person … is not merely a liberal action of recognizing their humanity, it is to involve them in the very core of the human endeavour – the construction, deconstruction and reconstruction of the social world.' Stainton Rogers 1989: 29.

43 See generally James and James 2004: 97.

exacerbated in the universe they currently live within. I hope that, in the context of child pornography and grooming, this book has gone some way to expose a number of taken-for-granted assumptions, constructions and critical tensions that must be confronted in order for society and law to take a step closer to presenting children with this new, safer, more rational and respecting universe.

APPENDIX A: DETAILS OF DATES OF INTERVIEWS WITH POLICE OFFICERS

RX1: 30 April 2008
RX2: 2 May 2008
RX3: 10 June 2008
RX4: 1 July 2008
RX5: 7 July 2008
RX6: 10 July 2008
RX7: 22 July 2008
RX8: 31 July 2008

BIBLIOGRAPHY

Adelman, Ronald W. 1996. 'The Constitutionality of Congressional Efforts to Ban Computer-Generated Child Pornography', *John Marshall Journal of Computer and Information Law* 14(3): 483–92.

Adler, Amy 2001a. 'Inverting the First Amendment', *University of Pennsylvania Law Review* 149(4): 921–1002.

Adler, Amy 2001b. 'The Perverse Law of Child Pornography', *Columbia Law Review* 101(2): 209–73.

Akdeniz, Yaman 1996. 'Computer Pornography: a Comparative Study of the US and UK Obscenity Laws in Relation to the Internet', *International Review of Law, Computers and Technology* 10(2): 235–61.

Akdeniz, Yaman 1997a. 'Governance of Pornography and Child Pornography on the Global Internet: A Multi-Layered Approach' in Edwards, Lilian and Waelde, Charlotte (eds.), *Law and the Internet: Regulating Cyberspace*. Oxford: Hart, pp. 223–41.

Akdeniz, Yaman 1997b. 'The Regulation of Pornography and Child Pornography on the Internet', *Journal of Information, Law and Technology* 1.

Akdeniz, Yaman 2008. *Internet Child Pornography and the Law: National and International Responses*. Aldershot: Ashgate.

Alexy, Eileen M., Burgess, Ann W. and Baker, Timothy 2005. 'Internet Offenders: Traders, Travelers and Combination Traders-Travelers', *Journal of Interpersonal Violence* 20(7): 804–12.

American Psychiatric Association 1994. *Diagnostic and Statistical Manual of Mental Disorders*. 4th edn. Washington, DC: American Psychiatric Association.

American Psychological Association 2007. *Report of the APA Task Force on the Sexualization of Girls*. Washington, DC: American Psychological Association.

Araji, Sharon and Finkelhor, David 1986. 'Abusers: A Review of Research' in Finkelhor, David (ed.), *A Sourcebook on Child Sexual Abuse*. Newbury Park: Sage, pp. 89–118.

Archard, David 1993. *Children: Rights and Childhood*. London: Routledge.

Archard, David 1999. 'Can Child Abuse be Defined?' in King (ed.), pp. 74–89.

Aries, Philippe 1962. *Centuries of Childhood*. New York: Vintage Books.

Ashworth, Andrew 2006. *Principles of Criminal Law*. 5th edn. Oxford University Press.

Baker, Dennis J. 2007. 'The Moral Limits of Criminalizing Remote Harms', *New Criminal Law Review* 10: 370–91.

Beauregard, Eric and Leclerc, Benoit 2007. 'An Application of the Rational Choice Approach to the Offending Process of Sex Offenders: A Closer Look at the Decision-Making', *Sexual Abuse: A Journal of Research and Treatment* 19: 115–33.

Beck, Ulrich 1992. *Risk Society*. London: Sage.

Becker, Gary S. 1976. *The Economic Approach to Human Behavior*. University of Chicago Press.

Beech, Anthony R., Elliott, Ian A., Birgden, Astrid and Findlater, Donald 2008. 'The Internet and Child Sexual Offending', *Aggression and Violent Behaviour* 13(3): 216–28.

Bell, Vikki 2002. 'The Vigilant(e) Parent and the Paedophile: The News of the World Campaign 2000 and the Contemporary Governmentality of Child Sexual Abuse' *Feminist Theory* 3(1): 83–102.

Berger, Peter L. and Luckmann, Thomas 1967. *The Social Construction of Reality*. New York: Anchor Books.

Bergmann, Jörg R. 1998. 'Introduction: Morality in Discourse' *Research on Language and Social Interaction* 31: 279–94.

Best, Joel 1990. *Threatened Children*. University of Chicago Press.

Bowling, Ann 1997. *Research Methods in Health: Investigating Health and Health Services*. Buckingham: Open University Press.

Boyden, Jo 1997. 'Childhood and the Policy Makers: A Comparative Perspective on the Globalization of Childhood' in James and Prout (eds.) 1997, pp. 190–229.

Brazier, Margaret and Bridge, Caroline 1996. 'Coercion or Caring: Analysing Adolescent Autonomy', *Legal Studies* 15: 84–109.

Burke, Debra 1997. 'The Criminalization of Virtual Child Pornography: A Constitutional Question', *Harvard Journal on Legislation* 34: 439–72.

Carol, Avedon and Pollard, Nettie 1993. 'Changing Perceptions in the Feminist Debate' in Assiter, Alison and Carol, Avedon (eds.), *Bad Girls and Dirty Pictures: The Challenge to Reclaim Feminism*. London: Pluto Press, pp. 44–56.

Carr, John 2003. *Child Abuse, Child Pornography and the Internet*. London: NCH.

Cavanagh, Allison 2007. 'Taxonomies of Anxiety: Risks, Panics, Paedophilia and the Internet', *Electronic Journal of Sociology*. Available at www.sociology.org/content/2007/.

Chalmers, James and Leverick, Fiona 2008. 'Fair Labelling in Criminal Law', *Modern Law Review* 71(2): 217–46.

Childs, Mary 1991. 'Outraging Public Decency: The Offence of Offensiveness', *Public Law* Spring 20–9.

Christiansen, John R. and Blake, Reed H. 1990. 'The Grooming Process in Father-Daughter Incest' in Horton, Anne L., Johnson, Barry L., Roundy,

Lynn M. and Williams, Doran (eds.), *The Incest Perpetrator*. London: Sage, pp. 88–98.

Clarke, Ronald V. (ed.) 1997. *Situational Crime Prevention: Successful Case Studies*. 5th edn. New York: Harrow and Heston.

Clegg, Christine, Lebeau, Vicky and Myerscough, Paul 2001. 'The Ruins of Childhood: Editorial', *New Formations* 42: 5–12.

Cohen, Stanley 1972. *Folk Devils and Moral Panics: The Creation of the Mods and Rockers*. London: MacGibbon and Kee.

Cohen, Stanley 2007. *Folk Devils and Moral Panics*. 3rd edn. London: Routledge.

Committee on Homosexual Offences and Prostitution 1957. *Report of the Committee on Homosexual Offences and Prostitution*. Cmnd 247. London: Stationery Office.

Committee on Obscenity and Film Censorship 1979. *Report of the Home Office Committee on Obscenity and Film Censorship*. Cmnd 7772. London: Stationery Office.

Conservative Party 2002. *Protecting Children: Strengthening the Laws on Paedophiles*. London: Conservative Party.

Conte, Jon R. and Berliner, Lucy 1981. 'Sexual Abuse of Children: Implications for Practice', *Social Casework* 62: 601–6.

Conte, Jon R., Wolf, Steven and Smith, Tim 1989. 'What Sexual Offenders Tell Us about Prevention Strategies', *Child Abuse and Neglect* 13: 293–301.

Cooper, Sharon W., Estes, Richard J., Giardino, Angelo P., Kellogg, Nancy D. and Vieth, Victor I. (eds.) 2004. *Medical, Legal and Social Science Aspects of Child Sexual Exploitation*, vols. 1 and 2. Louis MO: GW Medical Publishing.

Corsaro, William 1997. *The Sociology of Childhood*. Thousand Oaks, California: Pine Forge Press.

Cowburn, Malcolm and Dominelli, Lena 2001. 'Masking Hegemonic Masculinity: Reconstructing the Paedophile as the Dangerous Stranger', *British Journal of Social Work* 31: 399–415.

Cox, Roger 1996. *Shaping Childhood*. London: Routledge.

Craissati, Jackie and McClurg, Grace 1996. 'The Challenge Project: Perpetrators of Child Sexual Abuse in South East London', *Child Abuse and Neglect* 20(11): 1067–77.

Craven, Samantha, Brown, Sarah and Gilchrist, Elizabeth 2006. 'Sexual Grooming of Children: Review of Literature and Theoretical Considerations', *Journal of Sexual Aggression* 12(3): 287–99.

Craven, Samantha, Brown, Sarah and Gilchrist, Elizabeth 2007. 'Current Responses to Sexual Grooming: Implications for Prevention', *Howard Journal of Criminal Justice* 46(1): 60–71.

Critcher, Chas 2002. 'Media, Government and Moral Panic: The Politics of Paedophilia in Britain 2000–1', *Journalism Studies* 3(4): 521–35.

Critcher, Chas 2003. *Moral Panics and the Media*. Buckingham: Open University Press.

Critcher, Chas (ed.) 2006. *Critical Readings: Moral Panics and the Media*. Maidenhead: Open University Press.

Danay, Robert J. 2005. 'The Danger of Fighting Monsters: Addressing the Hidden Harms of Child Pornography Law', *Review of Constitutional Studies* 11(1): 151–91.

Dan-Cohen, Meir 2002. *Harmful Thoughts: Essays on Law, Self and Morality*. Princeton University Press.

Demaré, Dano, Lips, Hilary M. and Biere, John 1993. 'Sexually Violent Pornography, Anti-Women Attitudes and Sexual Aggression: A Structural Equation Model', *Journal of Research in Personality* 27: 285–300.

Dennis, Ian 2007. *The Law of Evidence*. 3rd edn. London: Sweet & Maxwell.

Densen-Gerber, Judianne 1977 (August). 'What Pornographers Are Doing to Children: A Shocking Report', *Redbook* 86.

Densen-Gerber, Judianne and Hutchinson, Stephen F. 1978. 'Medical-Legal and Societal Problems Involving Children – Child Prostitution, Child Pornography and Drug-Related Abuse', in Smith, Selwyn M. (ed.), *The Maltreatment of Children*. Baltimore: University Park Press, pp. 317–50.

Devlin, Patrick 1968. *The Enforcement of Morals*. London: Oxford University Press.

Diduck, Alison 1999. 'Justice and Childhood' in King (ed.), pp. 120–37.

Dubber, Markus D. 2005. 'The Possession Paradigm: The Special Part and the Police Power Model of the Criminal Process', in Duff, R. Anthony and Green, Stuart P. (eds.) *Defining Crimes: Essays on the Criminal Law's Special Part*. Oxford University Press, pp. 91–118.

Duff, R. Anthony 2007. *Answering for Crime*. Oxford: Hart.

Duncan, Kyle 2007. 'Child Pornography and First Amendment Standards' *Mississippi Law Journal* 76: 677–703.

Durkin, K. F. 1997. 'Misuse of the Internet by Paedophiles: Implications for Law Empowerment', *Federal Probation* 61: 14–18.

Edge, Sarah and Baylis, Gail 2004. 'Photographing Children: The Works of Tierney Gearon and Sally Mann', *Visual Culture in Britain* 5(1): 75–90.

Edwards, Susan H. 1994. 'Pretty Babies: Art, Erotica or Kiddie Porn?' *History of Photography* 18(1): 38–46.

Edwards, Susan S. M. 1996. *Sex and Gender in the Legal Process*. London: Blackstone.

Edwards, Susan S. M. 2000. 'Prosecuting "Child Pornography": Possession and Taking of Indecent Photographs', *Journal of Social Welfare and Family Law* 22(1): 1–21.

Edwards, Susan S. M. 2003. 'Discourses of Denial and Moral Panics: The Pornographisation of the Child in Art, the Written Word, Film and Photograph' in Rowbotham and Stevenson (eds.), pp. 177–92.

Elliott, Michelle, Browne, Kevin and Kilcoyne, Jennifer 1995. 'Child Sexual Abuse Prevention: What Offenders tell Us', *Child Abuse and Neglect* 19(5): 579–94.

Ennew, Judith 1986. *The Sexual Exploitation of Children*. Cambridge: Polity Press.

Feinberg, Joel 1984. *The Moral Limits of the Criminal Law: Harm to Others*. Oxford University Press.

Feinberg, Joel 1985. *The Moral Limits of the Criminal Law: Offense to Others*. Oxford University Press.

Feinberg, Joel 1988. *The Moral Limits of the Criminal Law: Harmless Wrongdoing*. Oxford University Press.

Finkelhor, David 1984. *Child Sexual Abuse: New Theory and Research*. New York: Free Press.

Finkelhor, David and Araji, Sharon 1986. 'Explanations of Pedophilia: A Four Factor Model', *The Journal of Sex Research* 22(2): 145–61.

Finkelhor, David, Mitchell, Kimberly J. and Wolak, Janis 2000. *Online Victimization: A Report on the Nation's Youth*. National Center for Missing and Exploited Children.

Fischer, Donald G. and McDonald, Wendy L. 1998. 'Characteristics of Intrafamilial and Extrafamilial Child Sexual Abuse', *Child Abuse and Neglect* 22(9): 915–29.

Foucault, Michel 1972. *The Archaeology of Knowledge* (Sheridan Smith, A. M. trans.) London: Tavistock.

Foucault, Michel 1986. *The History of Sexuality: An Introduction*, vol. 1. London: Penguin Books.

Foucault, Michel 1990. *Politics, Philosophy, Culture: Interviews and Other Writings 1977–1984*. Kritzman, L. (ed.). London: Routledge.

Friel, Samantha L. 1997. 'Porn By Any Other Name? A Constitutional Alternative to Regulating "Victimless" Computer-Generated Child Pornography', *Valparaiso University Law Review* 32: 208–67.

Furedi, Frank and Bristow, Jenny 2008. *Licensed to Hug*. London: Civitas.

Gallagher, Bernard, Christmann, Kris, Fraser, Claire and Hodgson, Beth 2003. 'International and Internet Child Sexual Abuse and Exploitation', *Child and Family Law Quarterly* 15: 353–70.

Gardner, Will 2003. 'The Sexual Offences Bill: Progress and the Future'. Keynote Speech. Available at www.childnet-int.org/downloads/online-grooming2.pdf.

Gergen, Kenneth 1999. *Invitation to Social Construction*. London: Sage.

Gibbons, Tom 1995. 'Computer Generated Pornography', *International Yearbook of Law, Computers and Technology* 9: 83–95.

Gillespie, Alisdair A. 2002. 'Child Protection on the Internet – Challenges For Criminal Law', *Child and Family Law Quarterly* 14: 411–28.

Gillespie, Alisdair A. 2004. 'The Sexual Offences Act 2003 (3) Tinkering With "Child Pornography"' *Criminal Law Review* 361–8.

Gillespie, Alisdair A. 2005. 'Child Pornography: Balancing Substantive and Evidential Law to Safeguard Children Effectively from Abuse', *International Journal of Evidence and Proof* 9: 29–49.

Gillespie, Alisdair A. 2006. 'Indecent Images, Grooming and the Law', *Criminal Law Review* 412–21.

Gillespie, Alisdair A. and Bettinson, Vanessa 2006. 'European Court of Human Rights: "Indecent" Images: European Convention on Human Rights, Article 7', *Journal of Criminal Law* 70(2): 127–30.

Gillespie, Alisdair A. and Bettinson, Vanessa 2007. 'Preventing Secondary Victimisation Through Anonymity', *Modern Law Review* 70(1): 114–27.

Gittins, Diana 1998. *The Child in Question*. London: Macmillan Press.

Glasser, M, 1990. 'Paedophilia' in Walker, Nigel, Bluglass, Robert and Bowden, Paul (eds.), *Principles and Practice of Forensic Psychiatry*. Edinburgh: Churchill Livingstone, pp. 739–48.

Goode, Erich and Ben-Yehuda, Nachman 1994. *Moral Panics: The Social Construction of Deviance*. Oxford: Blackwell.

Goodin, Robert E. 1985. *Protecting the Vulnerable: A Reanalysis of Our Social Responsibilities*. University of Chicago Press.

Goodin, Robert E. 1987. 'Exploiting a Situation and Exploiting a Person' in Reeve, Andrew (ed.), *Modern Theories of Exploitation*. London: Sage, pp. 166–200.

Gorham, Deborah 1978. 'The "Maiden Tribute of Modern Babylon" Re-examined', *Victorian Studies* 21(3): 353–79.

Gottfredson, Michael and Hirschi, Travis 1990. *A General Theory of Crime*. Stanford University Press.

Grasz, L. Steven and Pfaltzgraff, Patrick J. 1998. 'Child Pornography and Child Nudity: Why and How States may Constitutionally Regulate the Production, Possession and Distribution of Nude Visual Depictions of Children', *Temple Law Review* 71: 609–35.

Grosz, Candace A., Kempe, Ruth S. and Kelly, Michele 2000. 'ExtraFamilial Sexual Abuse: Treatment for Child Victims and their Families', *Child Abuse and Neglect* 24(1): 9–23.

Hacking, Ian 1999, *The Social Construction of What?* Cambridge, Mass: Harvard University Press.

Hall, Stuart, Critcher, Charles, Jefferson, Tony, Clarke, John and Roberts, Brian 1978. *Policing the Crisis: Mugging, the State and Law and Order*. London: Macmillan.

Harcourt, Bernard E. 1999. 'The Collapse of the Harm Principle', *The Journal of Criminal Law and Criminology* 90(1): 109–94.

Hart, Herbert L. A. 1982. *Law, Liberty and Morality*. Oxford University Press.

Heinze, Eric (ed.) 2000. *On Innocence and Autonomy: Children, Sex and Human Rights*. Aldershot: Ashgate.

Hendrick, Harry 1997. 'Constructions and Reconstructions of British Childhood: An Interpretative Survey, 1800 to the Present' in James and Prout (eds.) 1997, pp. 34–62.

Hendrick, Harry 1994. *Child Welfare, England 1872–1989.* London: Routledge.

Higonnet, Anne 1998. *Pictures of Innocence: The History and Crisis of Ideal Childhood.* London: Thames and Hudson.

Hirschi, Travis 1969. *Causes of Delinquency.* Berkeley: University of California Press.

Holland, Patricia 2006. *Picturing Childhood: The Myth of the Child in Popular Imagery.* London: Tauris.

Home Affairs Committee 1994. First Report, *Computer Pornography.* 126. London: Stationery Office.

Home Office 2000. *Setting the Boundaries: Reforming the Law on Sex Offences.* London: Stationery Office.

Home Office 2002. *Protecting the Public.* Cmnd 5668. London: Stationery Office.

Home Office 2007a. *Consultation on the Possession of Non-photographic Visual Depictions of Child Sexual Abuse.* London: Home Office.

Home Office 2007b. *Review of the Protection of Children from Sex Offenders.* London: Home Office.

Horder, Jeremy 1996. 'Crimes of Ulterior Intent' in Simester and Smith (eds.), pp. 153–72.

Howitt, Dennis 1995a. *Paedophiles and Sexual Offences Against Children.* New York: Wiley & Sons.

Howitt, Dennis 1995b. 'Pornography and the Paedophile: Is it Criminogenic?' *British Journal of Medical Psychology* 69: 15–27.

Husak, Douglas 2008. *Overcriminalization: The Limits of the Criminal Law.* Oxford University Press.

International Centre for Missing and Exploited Children 2007. Child Pornography: Model Legislation and Global Review, 3rd edn. Available at www.icmec.org/en_X1/English__3rd_Edition_.pdf.

Jackson, Stevi 1982. *Childhood and Sexuality.* Blackwell: Oxford.

Jackson, Stevi and Scott, Sue 1999. 'Risk Anxiety and the Social Construction of Childhood' in Lupton, Deborah (ed.), *Risk and Sociocultural Theory.* Cambridge University Press, pp. 86–107.

Jacobson, Michael and Mazur, Laurie 1995. 'Sexism and Sexuality in Advertising' in Jacobson, Michael and Mazur, Laurie (eds.), *Marketing Madness: A Survival Guide for a Consumer Society.* Boulder: Westview Press, pp. 74–87.

James, Allison and James, Adrian L. 2004. *Constructing Childhood.* Basingstoke: Palgrave Macmillan.

James, Allison, Jenks, Chris and Prout, Alan 1998. *Theorizing Childhood.* Cambridge: Polity Press.

James, Allison and Prout, Alan (eds.) 1990. *Constructing and Reconstructing Childhood.* London: Falmer Press.

James, Allison and Prout, Alan (eds.) 1997. *Constructing and Reconstructing Childhood*. 2nd edn. London: Falmer Press.

James, Allison and Prout, Alan 1997. 'Re-presenting Childhood: Time and Transition in the Study of Childhood', in James and Prout (eds.) 1997, pp. 230–50.

Jenkins, Philip 1992. *Intimate Enemies: Moral Panics in Contemporary Great Britain*. New York: Aldine de Gruyter.

Jenkins, Philip 1998. *Moral Panic: Changing Concepts of the Child Molester in Modern America*. New Haven: Yale University Press.

Jenkins, Philip 2001. *Beyond Tolerance: Child Pornography on the Internet*. New York University Press.

Jenks, Chris 1996. *Childhood*. London: Routledge.

Johnson, Travis 2006. 'Child Pornography in Canada and the United States: The Myth of Right Answers', *Dalhousie Law Journal* 29: 375–411.

Kappeler, Susanne 1986. *The Pornography of Representation*. Minneapolis: University of Minnesota Press.

Kaufman, Keith L., Mosher, Megan, Carter, Heather and Estes, Laura 2006. 'An Empirically Based Situational Prevention Model for Child Sexual Abuse' in Wortley and Smallbone (eds.), pp. 101–44.

Kenney, Cortelyou 2006. 'Questioning the Image: The Constitutionality of Child Pornography', *Dartmouth Law Journal* 4: 30–55.

Kincaid, James R. 1998. *Erotic Innocence*. London: Duke University Press.

King, Michael (ed.) 1999. *Moral Agendas for Children's Welfare*. London: Routledge.

King, Michael and Piper, Christine 1995. *How the Law Thinks About Children*. Aldershot: Arena.

Kitzinger, Jenny 1997. 'Who Are You Kidding? Children, Power and the Struggle Against Sexual Abuse' in James and Prout (eds.) 1997, pp. 165–89.

Kitzinger, Jenny 1998. 'Defending Innocence: Ideologies of Childhood', *Feminist Review* 28: 77–87.

Kitzinger, Jenny 2004. *Framing Abuse: Media Influence and Public Understandings of Sexual Violence Against Children*. London: Pluto.

Kleinhans, Martha-Marie 2002. 'Criminal Justice Approaches to Paedophilic Sex Offenders', *Social and Legal Studies* 11: 233–55.

Knight, Robert A., Carter, Daniel L. and Prentky, Robert A. 1989. 'A System for the Classification of Child Molesters: Reliability and Application', *Journal of Interpersonal Violence* 4: 3–23.

Knudson, Dean D. 1988. 'Child Sexual Abuse and Pornography: Is There a Relationship?', *Journal of Family Violence* 3(4): 254–67.

Kuran, Timur, and Sunstein, Cass R. 1999. 'Availability Cascades and Risk Regulation', *Stanford Law Review* 51: 683–768.

Labour Party 2001. *Ambitions for Britain*. London: Labour Party.

Lanning, Kenneth V. 1984. 'Collectors' in Burgess, Ann W. (ed.), *Child Pornography and Sex Rings*. Massachusetts: Lexington Books, pp. 83–92.

Lanning, Kenneth V. 2004. 'Acquaintance Child Molesters: A Behavioural Analysis' in Cooper et al. (eds.), vol. 2, pp. 529–94.

Lanning, Kenneth V. 2005. 'Compliant Child Victims: Confronting an Uncomfortable Reality' in Quayle and Taylor (eds.), pp. 49–60.

Lansdown, Gerison 1994. 'Children's Rights' in Mayall (ed.), pp. 33–44.

Law Commission 1996. *Evidence in Criminal Proceedings*. CP 141. London: Stationery Office.

Law Commission 2001. *Evidence of Bad Character in Criminal Proceedings* Com. no. 273. Cmnd 5257. London: Stationery Office.

Leclerc, Benoit, Carpentier, Julie and Proulx, Jean 2006. 'Strategies Adopted by Sexual Offenders to Involve Children in Sexual Activity' in Wortley and Smallbone (eds.), pp. 251–70.

Liu, Shephard 2007. 'Ashcroft, Virtual Child Pornography and First Amendment Jurisprudence', *UC Davis Journal of Juvenile Law and Policy* 11(1): 1–54.

Lloyd-Bostock, Sally 2000. 'The Effects on Juries of Hearing About the Defendant's Previous Criminal Record: A Simulation Study', *Criminal Law Review* 734–55.

Lodato, Vincent 1998. 'Computer-Generated Child Pornography: Exposing Prejudice in Our First Amendment Jurisprudence?', *Seton Hall Law Review* 28: 1328–64.

Loizidou, Elena 2000. 'Lolita at the Interface of Obscenity: Children and the Right to Free Expression' in Heinze (ed.), pp. 124–39.

Looman, Jan, Gauthier, Claudine and Boer, Douglas 2001. 'Replication of The Massachusetts Treatment Center Child Molester Typology in a Canadian Sample', *Journal of Interpersonal Violence* 16: 753–67.

Mackinnon, Catharine A. 1991. *Toward A Feminist Theory of The State*. Cambridge, Mass: Harvard University Press.

Mann, Patricia, S. 1997. 'Glancing at Pornography' in Meyers, Diana T. (ed.), *Feminist Social Thought: A Reader*. London: Routledge, pp. 417–39.

Marshall, William L. 1988. 'The Use of Sexually Explicit Stimuli by Rapists, Child Molestors, and Nonoffenders', *The Journal of Sex Research* 25(2): 267–88.

Marshall, William L., Serran, Geris A. and Marshall, Liam E. 2006. 'Situational and Dispositional Factors in Child Sexual Molestation' in Wortley and Smallbone (eds.), pp. 37–63.

Mayall, Berry (ed.) 1994. *Children's Childhoods: Observed and Experienced*. London: Falmer Press.

McAlinden, Anne-Marie 2006. '"Setting 'Em Up": Personal, Familial and Institutional Grooming in the Sexual Abuse of Children', *Social and Legal Studies* 15(3): 339–62.

McCarthy, M. A. and Moodie, R. A. 1981. 'Parliament and Pornography: The 1978 Child Protection Act', *Parliamentary Affairs* xxxiv(1): 47–62.

McElroy, Wendy 1995. *A Woman's Right to Pornography*. New York: StMartin's Press.

McRobbie, Angela 1994. *Postmodernism and Popular Culture*. London: Routledge.

Meyer, Anneke, 2007. *The Child at Risk: Paedophiles, Media Responses and Public Opinion*. Manchester University Press.

Middleton, David, Beech, Anthony R. and Mandeville-Norden, Rebecca 2005. 'What Sort of Person Could Do That? Psychological Profiles of Internet Pornography Users' in Quayle and Taylor (eds.), pp. 99–107.

Middleton, David, Elliott, Ian A., Mandeville-Norden, Rebecca and Beech, Anthony R. 2006. 'An Investigation into the Applicability of the Ward and Siegert Pathways Model of Child Sexual Abuse with Internet Offenders', *Psychology, Crime and Law*, 12(6): 589–603.

Mill, John Stuart 1993. *On Liberty* in Mill, John Stuart, *Utilitarianism, On Liberty, Considerations on Representative Government*. London: Orion, pp. 69–185.

Mitchell, Sebastian 2001. "'But Cast Their Eyes on These Little Wretched Beings': The Innocence and Experience of Children in the Late Eighteenth Century', *New Formations* 42: 115–30.

Najafi, Sina 2002. 'Picturing Innocence: An Interview with Anne Higonnet', Cabinet Magazine 9. Available at www.cabinetmagazine.org/issues/9/picturing_innocence.php.

National Viewers' and Listeners' Association Archives, Albert Sloman Library, University of Essex.

Nicholas, Stan, Kershaw, Chris and Walker, Alison 2007. *Crime in England and Wales 2006/7*, Home Office Statistical Bulletin 12/06. Home Office: London.

Nielsen, Kai and Ware, Robert (eds.) 1997. *Exploitation*. New Jersey: Humanities Press.

O'Brien, Mark 2006. 'The Witchfinder-General and the Will-o'-the Wisp: The Myth and Reality of Internet Control', *Information and Communications Technology Law* 15(3): 259–73.

O'Connell, Rachel 2000. 'Child Sex Iconography. Iconic Narratives of Child Sex Myths' in Von Feilitzen, Cecilia and Carlsson, Ulla (eds.), *Children in the New Media Landscape. Games Pornography Perceptions*. Gothenburg: Nordicom, pp. 211–32.

O'Connell, Rachel 2003. A Typology of Child Cybersexploitation and Online Grooming Practices. Available at http://image.guardian.co.uk/sys-files/Society/documents/2003/07/24/Netpaedoreport.pdf.

O'Donnell, Ian and Milner, Claire 2007. *Child Pornography: Crime, Computers and Society*. Cullompton: Willan.

Ogus, Anthony 2006. *Costs and Cautionary Tales: Economic Insights for the Law*. Oxford: Hart.

O'Riordan, Maurice 2008 (July). 'Editorial: To Dream a Child', *Art Monthly* 211.

Ormerod, David 2001. 'Indecent Photographs of Children: Making an Indecent Photograph of a Child Whether Breach of European Convention on Human Rights, Articles 8 and 10', *Criminal Law Review* 657–9.

Ormerod, David 2002. 'Indecent of Children', *Criminal Law Review* 659–63.

Ormerod, David 2007. 'Sexual Offences: Sexual Offences Act 2003 – Sexual Gratification', *Criminal Law Review* 184–6.

Ost, Suzanne 2002. 'Children at Risk: Legal and Societal Perceptions of the Potential Threat that the Possession of Child Pornography Poses to Society', *Journal of Law and Society* 29: 436–60.

Ost, Suzanne 2004. 'Getting to Grips with Sexual Grooming? The New Offence Under the Sexual Offences Act 2003', *Journal of Social Welfare and Family Law* 26: 147–59.

Oswell, David 2006. 'When Images Matter: Internet Child Pornography, Forms of Observation and an Ethics of the Virtual', *Information, Communication and Society* 9: 244–65.

Parker, David 1989. 'Original Sin: A Study In Evangelical Theory', *Evangelical Quarterly* 61(1): 51–69.

Persak, Nina 2007. *Criminalising Harmful Conduct*. New York: Springer-Verlag.

Persky, Stan and Dixon, John 2001. *On Kiddie Porn: Sexual Representation, Free Speech and the Robin Sharpe Case*. Vancouver: New Start Books.

Peysakhovich, Sofya 2004. 'Virtual Child Pornography: Why American and British Laws Are at Odds With Each Other', *Albany Law Journal of Science and Technology*, 14: 799–823.

Piper, Christine 1999. 'Moral Campaigns for Children's Welfare in the Nineteenth Century' in King (ed.), pp. 33–52.

Piper, Christine 2000. 'Historical Constructions of Childhood Innocence: Removing Sexuality' in Heinze (ed.), pp. 26–45.

Prentky, Robert A., Knight, Raymond A. and Lee, Austin F. S. 1997. *Child Sexual Molestation: Research Issues*. Washington: National Institute of Justice.

Proulx, Jean and Ouimet, Marc 1995. 'Criminologie de l'Acte et pédophile? *Revue Internationale de Criminologie et de Police Technique* 48: 294–310.

Quayle, Ethel, Erooga, Marcus, Wright, Louise, Taylor, Max and Harbinson, Dawn 2006. *Only Pictures? Therapeutic Work with Internet Sex Offenders*. Dorset: Russell House Publishing.

Quayle, Ethel and Taylor, Max (eds.) 2005. *Viewing Child Pornography on the Internet*. Dorset: Russell House Publishing.

Quigley, John 1991. 'Child Pornography and the Right to Privacy', *Florida Law Review* 43: 347–404.

Radin, Margaret J. 2000. 'Humans, Computers and Binding Commitment', *Indiana Law Journal* 75: 1125–62.

Rendel, M. 2000. 'The Convention on the Rights of the Child and British Legislation' in Heinze (ed.), pp. 64–76.

Renvoize, Jean 1993. *Innocence Destroyed: A Study of Child Sexual Abuse*. London: Routledge.

Robins, Sydney 2000. *Protecting Our Students: A Review to Identify and Prevent Sexual Misconduct in Ontario Schools*. Ontario: Queen's Printer.

Robinson, Paul H. and Darley, John M. 2004. 'Does Criminal Law Deter? A Behavioural Science Investigation', *Oxford Journal of Legal Studies* 24: 173–205.

Rodgerson, Gillian and Wilson, Elizabeth 1991. *Pornography and Feminism*. London: Lawrence & Wishart.

Rousseau, Jean-Jacques 1979 (1762). *Émile or On Education*. (Bloom, Allan trans.) New York: Basic Books.

Rowbotham, Judith and Stevenson, Kim (eds.) 2003. *Behaving Badly: Social Panic and Moral Outrage – Victorian and Modern Parallels*. Aldershot: Ashgate.

Russell, Diana E. H. 1984. *Sexual Exploitation: Rape, Child Sexual Abuse and Workplace Harassment*. London: Sage.

Ryder, Bruce 2003. 'The Harms of Child Pornography Law', *University of British Columbia Law Review* 36: 101–35.

Saatchi Gallery 2001. *I Am A Camera: The Saatchi Gallery*. London: Booth-Clibborn Editions.

Sachsenmaier, Susan J. 1998. 'Investigating Child Sexual Abuse Allegations: Do Experts Agree on Anything?', The American Academy of Experts in Traumatic Stress, Inc. Available at www.aaets.org/article50.htm.

Salter, Anna 2004. *Predators: Pedophiles, Rapists, and Other Sex Offenders*. New York: Basic Books.

Schonsheck, Jonathan 1994. *On Criminalization*. Dordrecht: Kluwer.

Schuijer, Jan and Rossen, Benjamin 1992. 'The Trade in Child Pornography', *Issues in Child Abuse Accusations* 4(2): 55–107.

Searle, John, R. 1995. *The Construction of Social Reality*. London: Penguin.

Select Committee on Home Affairs 2003. *Fifth Report – Sexual Offences Bill*, HC 639. London: Stationery Office.

Sentencing Advisory Panel 2002. Offences Involving Child Pornography. Available at www.sentencing-guidelines.gov.uk/docs/advice_child_porn.pdf.

Sentencing Advisory Panel 2004. 'The Sexual Offences Act 2003 – The Exploitation Offences: A Consultation', *Justice of the Peace and Local Government Law* 168(17): 308–23.

Seto, Michael C., Cantor, James M. and Blanchard, Ray 2006. 'Child Pornography Offenses are a Valid Diagnostic Indicator of Pedophilia', *Journal of Abnormal Psychology* 115(3): 610–15.

Seto, Michael C. and Eke, Angela W. 2005. 'The Criminal Histories and Later Offending of Child Pornography Offenders', *Sexual Abuse: A Journal of Research and Treatment* 17(2): 201–10.

Sexual Offences Act: Explanatory Notes 2004. London: Stationery Office.

Shute, Stephen 2004. 'The Sexual Offences Act 2003: (4) New Civil Preventative Orders – Sexual Offences Prevention Orders; Foreign Travel Orders; Risk of Sexual Harm Orders', *Criminal Law Review* 417–40.

Silverman, Jon and Wilson, David 2002. *Innocence Betrayed: Paedophilia, the Media and Society*. Cambridge: Polity Press.

Simester, A. P. and Smith, A. T. H. (eds.) 1996. *Harm and Culpability*. Oxford: Clarendon Press.

Simon, Leonore 2000. 'An Examination of the Assumptions of Specialization, Mental Disorder, and Dangerousness of Sex Offenders', *Behavioural Sciences and the Law* 18: 275–308.

Simon, Leonore, Sales, Bruce, Kaszniak, Alfred and Khan, Marvin 1992. 'Characteristics of Child Molesters: Implications for the Fixated-Regressed Dichotomy', *Journal of Interpersonal Violence* 7(2): 211–25.

Simon, Leonore and Zgoba, Kristen 2006. 'Sex Crimes against Children: Legislation, Prevention and Investigation' in Wortley and Smallbone (eds.), pp. 65–100.

Smallbone, Stephen and Wortley, Richard 2000. *Child Sexual Abuse in Queensland: Offender Characteristics and Modus Operandi*. Brisbane: Queensland Crime Commission.

Smallbone, Stephen and Wortley, Richard 2001. 'Child Sexual Abuse: Offender Characteristics and Modus Operandi', *Australian Institute of Criminology Trends and Issues in Crime and Criminal Justice #193*. Canberra: Australian Institute of Criminology.

Smallbone, Stephen and Wortley, Richard 2004. 'Criminal Diversity and Paraphilic Interests Among Adult Males Convicted of Sexual Offenses Against Children', *International Journal of Offender Therapy and Comparative Criminology* 48: 175–88.

Smart, Carol 1989 *Feminism and the Power of Law*. London: Routledge.

Spencer, John R. 2004. 'The Sexual Offences Act 2003: (2) Child and Family Offences', *Criminal Law Review* 347–60.

Stainton Rogers, Rex 1989. 'The Social Construction of Childhood' in Stainton Rogers, Wendy, Hevey, Denise and Ash, Elizabeth (eds.), *Child Abuse and Neglect*. London: Open University, pp. 23–9.

Stainton Rogers, Wendy and Stainton Rogers, Rex 1999. 'What is Good and Bad Sex for Children?' in King (ed.), pp. 179–97.

Sullivan, Joe and Beech, Anthony R. 2002. 'Professional Perpetrators', *Child Abuse Review* 11: 153–67.

Summit, Roland 1990. 'The Specific Vulnerability of Children' in Oates, R. Kim (ed.), *Understanding and Managing Child Sexual Abuse*. Sydney: Harcourt Brace Jovanovich, pp. 59–74.

Summit, Roland and Kryso, JoAnn 1978. 'Sexual Abuse of Children: A Clinical Spectrum', *American Journal of Orthopsychiatry* 48(2): 237–51.

Surette, Ray and Otto, Charles 2001. 'The Media's Role in the Definition of Crime' in Henry, Stuart and Lanier, Mark M. (eds.), *What is Crime?* Lanham: Rowman and Littlefield, pp. 139–54.

Sutter, Gavin 2003. 'Penny Dreadfuls and Perverse Domains: Victorian and Modern Moral Panics' in Rowbotham and Stevenson (eds.), pp. 159–75.

Tate, Tim 1990. *Child Pornography: An Investigation*. London: Methuen.

Taylor, Max, Holland, Gemma and Quayle, Ethel 2001. 'Typology of Paedophile Picture Collections', *Police Journal* 74: 97–107.

Taylor, Max and Quayle, Ethel 2003. *Child Pornography: An Internet Crime*. Hove: Brunner-Routledge.

Taylor, Max and Quayle, Ethel 2006. 'The Internet and Abuse Images of Children: Search, Pre-Criminal Situations and Opportunity' in Wortley and Smallbone (eds.), pp. 169–95.

Thompson, Kenneth 1998. *Moral Panics*. London: Routledge.

Tien, Lee 1994. 'Children's Sexuality and the New Information Technology: A Foucaultian Approach', *Social and Legal Studies* 3: 121–47.

Townsend, Cyril 1979. 'Protecting Our Children', *Contemporary Review* 234(1356): 1–7.

Trenholm, Sarah 1991. *Human Communication Theory*. 2nd edn. Englewood, NJ: Prentice Hall.

Uniacke, Suzanne 2004. 'Harming and Wronging: The Importance of Normative Context' in Oderberg, David, S. and Chappell, Timothy (eds.), *Human Values: New Essays on Ethics and Natural Law*. Basingstoke: Palgrave Macmillan, pp. 166–83.

van Dam, Carla 2001. *Identifying Child Molesters: Preventing Child Sexual Abuse by Recognizing the Patterns of the Offenders*. New York: Haworth Press.

Victor, Jeffrey S. 1998. 'Moral Panics and the Social Construction of Deviant Behaviour: A Theory and Application to the Case of Ritual Child Abuse', *Sociological Perspectives* 41(3): 541–65.

von Hirsch, Andrew. 1996. 'Extending the Harm Principle: "Remote" Harms and Fair Imputation' in Simester and Smith (eds.), pp. 259–76.

von Hirsch, Andrew, Bottoms, Anthony E., Burney, Elizabeth and Wikström, P-O. 2000. *Criminal Deterrence and Sentence Severity*. Oxford: Hart.

Waddington, P. A. J. 1986. 'Mugging as a Moral Panic: A Question of Proportion', *British Journal of Sociology* 37(2): 245–59.

Waites, Matthew 2005. *The Age of Consent: Young People, Sexuality and Citizenship*. Basingstoke: Palgrave Macmillan.

Walkowitz, Judith, R. 1992. *City of Dreadful Delight: Narratives of Sexual Danger in Late-Victorian London*. University of Chicago Press.

Ward, Tony and Keenan, Thomas 1999. 'Child Molesters' Implicit Theories', *Journal of Interpersonal Violence* 14: 821–38.

Ward, Tony, Louden, Kirsten, Hudson, Stephen M. and Marshall, William L. 1995. 'A Descriptive Model of the Offense Chain for Child Molesters', *Journal of Interpersonal Violence* 10: 452–72.

Ward, Tony and Siegert, Richard J. 2002. 'Toward a Comprehensive Theory of Child Sexual Abuse: A Theory Knitting Perspective', *Psychology, Crime and Law* 8: 319–51.

Wasserman, Adam J. 1998. 'Virtual.Child.Porn.Com: Defending the Constitutionality of Computer Generated Child Pornography by the Child Pornography Prevention Act of 1996', *Harvard Journal on Legislation* 35: 245–82.

Watney, Simon 1993. *Policing Desire: Pornography, AIDS and the Media*. 2nd edn. Minneapolis: University of Minnesota Press.

Watson, Bruce and Lefever, Shyla R. 2004. 'Understanding the Impact of Pornography on Adults and Children' in Cooper, Estes, Giardino, Kellogg and Vieth (eds.), pp. 193–202.

Wertheimer, Alan 1996. *Exploitation*. Princeton University Press.

Williams, Glanville 1961. *Criminal Law: The General Part*. 2nd edn. London: Stevens & Sons.

Williams, Katherine S. 2003. 'Controlling Internet Child Pornography and Protecting the Child', *Information and Communication Technology Law* 12(1): 3–24.

Williams, Katherine S. 2004. 'Child Pornography Law: Does it Protect Children?', *Journal of Social Welfare and Family Law* 26(3): 245–61.

Wolak, Janis, Finkehor, David and Mitchell, Kimberly J. 2005. 'The Varieties of Child Pornography Production' in Quayle and Taylor (eds.), pp. 31–48.

Wolak, Janis, Finkelhor, David, Mitchell, Kimberly J. and Ybarra, Michele L. 2008. 'Online "Predators" and Their Victims', *American Psychologist* 63(2): 111–28.

Wolak, Janis, Mitchell, Kimberly J. and Finkelhor, David 2006. *Online Victimization of Youth: Five Years Later*. National Center for Missing and Exploited Children.

Wolff, Jonathan 1999. 'Marx and Exploitation', *The Journal of Ethics* 3: 105–20.

Wood, Allen W. 1997. 'Exploitation' in Nielsen and Ware (eds.), pp. 2–26.

Wortley, Richard and Smallbone, Stephen 2006. 'Applying Situational Principles to Sexual Offenses against Children' in Wortley and Smallbone (eds.), pp. 7–35.

Wortley, Richard and Smallbone, Stephen (eds.) 2006. *Situational Prevention of Child Sexual Abuse: Crime Prevention Studies 19*. Cullompton: Willan.

Young, Alison 1996. *Imagining Crime: Textual Outlaws and Criminal Conversations*. London: Sage.

Young, Jock 1971. 'The Role of the Police As Amplifiers of Deviance, Negotiators of Drug Control As Seen in Notting Hill' in Cohen, Stanley (ed.), *Images of Deviance*. London: Penguin, pp. 27–61.

INDEX

Note: legislative measures are UK unless otherwise stated.